JOURNAL FOR THE STUDY OF THE OLD TESTAMENT
SUPPLEMENT SERIES
403

Editors
Claudia V. Camp, Texas Christian University
and
Andrew Mein, Westcott House, Cambridge

Founding Editors
David J.A. Clines,
Philip R. Davies
and
David M. Gunn

Editorial Board
Richard J. Coggins, Alan Cooper, John Goldingay,
Robert P. Gordon, Norman K. Gottwald, John Jarick,
Andrew D.H. Mayes, Carol Meyers, Patrick D. Miller

Retelling the Torah

The Deuteronomistic Historian's Use of Tetrateuchal Narratives

John E. Harvey

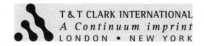

T & T CLARK INTERNATIONAL
A Continuum imprint
LONDON • NEW YORK

Copyright © 2004 T&T Clark International
A Continuum imprint

Published by T&T Clark International
The Tower Building, 11 York Road, London SE1 7NX
15 East 26th Street, Suite 1703, New York, NY 10010

www.tandtclark.com

BWHEBB [Hebrew] and BWGRKL [Greek] PostScript© Type 1 and TrueType™
fonts Copyright© 1994–2002 BibleWorks, LLC. All rights reserved. These Biblical
Greek and Hebrew fonts are used with permission and are from BibleWorks,
software for Biblical exegesis and research.

British Library Cataloguing-in-Publication Data
A catalogue record for this book is available from the British Library

Library of Congress Cataloging-in-Publication Data
A catalogue record for this book is available from the Library of Congress

Typeset by ISB Typesetting, Sheffield
Printed on acid-free paper in Great Britain by MPG Books Ltd, Bodmin, Cornwall

ISBN 0-567-0809-51 (hardback)

CONTENTS

PREFACE

On more than one occasion my wife Suzanne has jokingly referred to this work as 'the other woman'. Rightly so, for I have spent several years and more than one sleepless night pondering and shaping it. As endearing as it has been, the one perplexing aspect of this work has been its unavoidable breadth. Genesis to Kings covers a wide swath of early Israel's literature and thought, and a veritable plethora of modern research accompanies it. Since the dissertation stage, I have sought to make this work more interdisciplinary – for, among other things, my contention that Dtr patterned a host of his stories after Tetrateuchal accounts touches on Dtr's particular historiography and worldview. I have many to thank. I thank Professor Brian Peckham for being a wonderful thesis adviser. I also thank Professors J. Glen Taylor and Baruch Halpern who carefully interacted with earlier drafts of this work (*Retelling the Tetrateuch: The Deuteronomistic Historian's Use of Tetrateuchal Narratives* [unpublished dissertation; Toronto, ON: University of St Michael's College, 1997]). Suzanne carefully edited the writing style of the final draft. Thank you, Professors Peckham, Halpern and Taylor for your many insights and recommendations. And thank you Suzanne for lovingly seeing me through the whole process. It is to you that I dedicate this work.

ABBREVIATIONS

AB	Anchor Bible
AnBib	Analecta Biblica
BEATAJ	Beiträge zur Erforschung des Alten Testaments und des antiken Judentum
BETL	Bibliotheca ephemeridum theologicarum lovaniensium
BJS	Brown Judaica Studies
BTB	*Biblical Theology Bulletin*
BZAW	Beihefte zur Zeitschrift für die alttestamentliche Wissenschaft
Bib	*Biblica*
CBQ	*Catholic Biblical Quarterly*
ETL	*Ephemerides theologicae lovanienses*
FB	Forschung zur Bibel
FOTL	Forms of Old Testament Literature
HAR	*Hebrew Annual Review*
HSM	Harvard Semitic Monographs
HUCA	*Hebrew Union College Annual*
ICC	International Critical Commentary
IDB	*Interpreter's Dictionary of the Bible*
Int	*Interpretation*
JBL	*Journal of Biblical Literature*
JSOT	*Journal for the Study of the Old Testament*
JSOTSup	Journal for the Study of the Old Testament Supplemental Series
NCBC	New Century Bible Commentary
NEB	*New English Bible*
NJPS	*Tanakh. The Holy Scriptures. The New JPS Translation According to the Traditional Hebrew Text.*
OBO	Orbis biblicus et orientalis
OTL	Old Testament Library
OTS	*Oudtestamentische Studiën*
SBLDS	Society of Biblical Literature Dissertation Series
SBT	Studies in Biblical Theology
SEÅ	*Svensk Exegetisk Årsbok*
ST	*Studia theologica*
TB	Tyndale Bulletin
TDNT	Gerhard Kittel and Gerhard Friedrich (eds.), *Theological Dictionary of the New Testament* (trans. Geoffrey W. Bromiley; 10 vols.; Grand Rapids: Eerdmans, 1964–)
USQR	*Union Seminary Quarterly Review*
VT	*Vetus Testamentum*
VTSup	*Vetus Testamentum*, Supplements
WBC	Word Biblical Commentary
ZAW	*Zeitschrift für die alttestamentliche Wissenschaft*

The abbreviations of the biblical books are those of *JBL*. See the *Society of Biblical Literature Membership Directory and Handbook* (Decatur: Society of Biblical Literature, 1994): 223–40.

INTRODUCTION

Living in a storied world is integral to the human condition. Our interpretations of the past, our understandings of the present, and our anticipations of the future are all profoundly defined by stories – be they folk tales, scripture, or the meta-narratives that we assume. Storied worlds captivate individuals and nations, they determine how stories are interpreted, and they themselves are the product of earlier stories that have organized and defined a myriad of data.[1] Exilic Israel's storied world was made up in part by its Torah. The antecedents of this world lay in early monarchic times when the traditions of the nation were rehearsed at cultic sites, recited by bards, taught in the home, and indelibly impressed upon the mind. Not later than the seventh century, and prior to the emergence of a Pentateuch, a corpus that approximated the Tetrateuch became an authoritative outline of Israel's sacred traditions. In this work I contend that the Deuteronomistic Historian's storied world was shaped by this Tetrateuch, such that he patterned many of his stories after Tetrateuchal accounts.[2]

I begin with a set of parallel stories to whet our appetites. In his account of Jeroboam, Dtr used Moses (the first deliverer of Israel) and Aaron (the first apostate of Israel) as models. The parallels between these figures are striking and serve to accentuate Jeroboam's sin. Both Moses and Jeroboam lived under oppressive kings who forced the people to build or rebuild cities: Moses' people built Pithom and Ramses under Pharaoh, and Jeroboam rebuilt Jerusalem under Solomon (Exod. 1.11; 1 Kgs 11.27-28). Both figures nevertheless enjoyed positions of grandeur – Moses in Pharaoh's court and Jeroboam in the court of Solomon (Exod. 2.10-11; 1 Kgs 11.28).[3] As Moses then fled from Pharaoh to Midian, so Jeroboam fled from Solomon to King Shishak of Egypt (Exod. 2.15; 1 Kgs 11.40). Like Moses, Jeroboam returned to his land after the death of his enemy (Exod. 4.19-20; 1 Kgs 11.40; 12.1-3). Both Pharaoh and Jeroboam were thereafter confronted by miracles, stubbornly refused to obey the LORD, but nevertheless sought divine healing: Moses confronted Pharaoh with ten miracles, and while Pharaoh was initially defiant, he

---

1. See the essays and bibliography in Hinchman and Hinchman (1997).

2. Martin Noth (1981) argued that Deuteronomy–2 Kings, the Deuteronomistic History (= DtrH), is the work of an exilic author/redactor, the Deuteronomistic Historian (= Dtr), who assembled various sources and supplemented them with his own work to explain why Judah was in exile. For an overview of Noth's seminal thesis and subsequent reactions see Campbell 1994: 31–62.

3. The parallel between Moses and Jeroboam in 1 Kgs 11.28 is furthered by the use of the root סבל, 'to burden': reminiscent of the pharaohs' burdening of the Hebrews with forced labour (Exod. 1.11; 2.11; 5.4-5; 6.6-7) is Solomon's placement of Jeroboam to burden the people with labour (1 Kgs 11.28).

nevertheless pled for mercy (Exodus 7–12); a man of God similarly confronted Jeroboam by miraculously destroying the altar, and although Jeroboam was initially recalcitrant, he too pled for mercy (1 Kgs 13.1-6).

The story of Jeroboam parallels that of Moses, but only up to the beginning stages of Israel's deliverance under Moses.[4] At this point Jeroboam ceased to resemble the deliverer Moses only to share parallels with Aaron. The literary contexts of the sins of Aaron parallel those of Jeroboam. Aaron's offence follows the climax of the Tetrateuch – the covenant and guidelines for the construction of the tabernacle (Exodus 19–31). Jeroboam's apostasy similarly follows the cultic pinnacle of the DtrH – Solomon's construction of the temple and worship in Jerusalem (1 Kings 6–8). More specifically, just as Aaron made the molten calf from gold in response to the request of the people, so Jeroboam's decision to make the two golden calves was initiated by his counselors (Exod. 32.1; 1 Kgs 12.28). The subsequent declarations of Aaron's people and Jeroboam are almost identical: 'These are your gods, O Israel, who brought you up from the land of Egypt' (Exod. 32.4, 8); 'Behold your gods, O Israel, who brought you up from the land of Egypt' (1 Kgs 12.28). After the construction of the calf/calves both Aaron and Jeroboam celebrated a festival, for which Aaron built an altar and Jeroboam ascended an altar (Exod. 32.5-6; 1 Kgs 12.32-33). Just as Moses then ordered the Levites to slay the transgressors who worshiped the calf, so a man of God prophesied that Josiah would slaughter the priests who sacrificed at the calf of Bethel (Exod. 32.26-28; 1 Kgs 13.2).[5] Finally, both Aaron and Jeroboam had two sons who share similarities.[6] First, their names parallel one another: Aaron's sons were Nadab and Abihu and Jeroboam's sons were Nadab and Abijah.[7] Second, both pairs of sons died for cultic infractions: Aaron's sons died because they offered 'strange fire' while Jeroboam's sons died because he set up the golden calves (Lev. 10.1-2; 1 Kgs 14.6-14; 15.25-30). Third, there was no possibility that either pair of sons could have descendants: Aaron's sons died childless and Jeroboam's line was annihilated (Num. 3.4; 1 Kgs 14.10-11; 15.29).

The story of Jeroboam thus parallels that of Moses as far as Exodus 5 (immediately before the beginning stages of Israel's deliverance), but at the very inception of his kingdom Jeroboam ceased to resemble the deliverer Moses only to become a new Aaron. Jeroboam was incomplete Moses and Aaron *redivivus*.

A third set of parallels complements such equations. To be sure, Jeroboam's Mosaic path abruptly ended with his Aaronic apostasy. But Moses nevertheless reappeared in the 'man of God'. Moses' confrontation of Aaron and Miriam was Dtr's basis for his depiction of a man of God who confronted Jeroboam (Numbers 12; 1 Kgs 13.1-6). Just as the LORD challenged Aaron and Miriam for their affront to

---

4.   For the parallels between Aaron and Jeroboam, see also Aberbach and Smolar (1967: 129–40) and Knoppers (1995: 92–104).

5.   As with the slaying of the transgressors in Kings, the transgressors slain by the Levites in Exodus were likely priests, as is evident from Exod. 32.27 where Moses commanded the Levites to slay 'brother, neighour, and kin' (cf. 32.29).

6.   I am here partially indebted to Gradwohl 1963: 288–96.

7.   The names Abihu and Abijah have the same meaning. Abihu means 'he (YHWH) is my father' while Abijah means 'YHWH is my father'.

Moses' prophetic office, so a man of God confronted Jeroboam for his defiance of centralized worship (Num. 12.4-9; 1 Kgs 13.2-4). Miriam was stricken with a skin ailment for her offence, and Jeroboam's arm became rigid for his sin; and just as Moses then pled to the LORD on Miriam's behalf and the LORD healed her, so the man of God prayed for Jeroboam and the LORD healed him (Num. 12.10-15; 1 Kgs 13.6). This reappearance of Moses as a prophet in the man of God is consistent with Dtr's concern elsewhere to base the prophetic task on the pattern given by Moses. Although Jeroboam failed to follow the Mosaic schema, Moses' voice nonetheless remained alive in the prophets.

Different questions concerning the above parallels confront us. Are such parallels due to literary dependence? If so, what is the direction of dependence, and what are the reasons for their existence? As I hope to substantiate in this work, answers to such questions can only be given in light of the approximately four dozen other parallel narratives shared by the DtrH and the Tetrateuch. To date, little effort has been made to understand the parallel narratives in this way, a lacuna that has arisen in part from the presupposition that the parallel narratives that exist between the two corpora are the product of their coterminous evolutions. Culley (1976), for instance, argued that many such parallel narratives are the product of shared oral traditions. Culley's work was pioneering insofar as it is the first (as far a I know) to discuss the parallel narratives. The essential shortcoming of Culley's treatment, however, is that he only assumed that the parallel narratives are the product of shared oral conventions. Gunn (1990: 20) similarly noted that 'much of the story from Genesis to 2 Kings' is 'richly repetitive', and he concluded that such repetition abounds in interpretational significance. Similar to Culley, Gunn assumed that the correspondences are the product of oral convention. Not unlike the conclusions of Culley and Gunn, Fields (1997) contended that many motifs in Genesis 18–19 provided later writers with grist. Fields (1997: 23-24) applied this conclusion to the story from creation to Moses:

> [The] thrust of a motif is enhanced when it occurs in a narrative which is set in the 'constitutive era', that is, in the period from creation until the settlement in Canaan…[w]hatever happens from creation to the end of Moses' life is paradigmatic, conceptually prescriptive, setting precedent and creating prototypes for all times…for whatever happens in that period is not one-time history; it determines the progress of history.

Fields is correct in his assertion that stories from creation to Moses were 'paradigmatic', 'conceptually prescriptive', and determinative for history. The evidence suggests, however, that it is only such stories *as they appeared together in a Tetrateuch* that were paradigmatic for Dtr. Damrosch (1987: 155) comes closer to the mark in his statement that the 'history of the monarchy [was] assessed and understood in conjunction with the Yahwistic stories of the foundations of society as a whole and of Hebrew history in particular in the time of the patriarchs'. Damrosch assumed that the parallels may be traced to the traditio-historical level. But the similar features shared by the parallels suggest that they are, rather, the product of common redactional activity throughout the DtrH. Damrosch also failed to provide adequate criteria for determining the direction of dependence between the parallel narratives.

Similar to this shortcoming, in his discussion of various parallels Pleins (1995: 136) suggested that parallel accounts in Genesis and the DtrH were both drawn by Deuteronomistic tradents in their attempt to 'develop the Pentateuch's final shape in the light of the themes and manner of presentation of the DtrH'. But Pleins did not consider other possibilities. Garsiel's (1985) analysis of parallels shared by 1 Samuel and passages in Genesis–Numbers is tremendously helpful. But as with other analyses, Garsiel did not discuss the given parallels in light of many others shared by the rest of the Former Prophets and the Tetrateuch.

The most exhaustive list of parallel narratives between passages in Genesis–Numbers and the Former Prophets is in Greenstein's provocative article, 'The Formation of the Biblical Narrative Corpus'. After briefly evaluating various explanations for the present form of Genesis–Kings, Greenstein (1990: 165) rightly noted that such theories fail to account for the parallel narratives between the Tetrateuch and the Former Prophets:

> The most outstanding feature of biblical narrative, from Genesis through Kings, is that between the Torah on the one side and the so-called Deuteronomistic History (or Former Prophets) on the other there is a very high incidence of repetition – of stories, motifs, characters, names of persons and places, phrases, as well as ideology and themes... Any theory of the formation of the biblical narrative corpus must account for this fact: *The narrator is all too often telling different versions of the same story* (emphasis his).

According to Greenstein, in the early monarchy various stories pertaining to kings were produced, elements of which were subsequently recombined and transformed to produce other stories, which were finally brought together in the Josianic era to comprise Genesis–Kings. Greenstein's article has not received the attention that it deserves, for it includes the most extensive list of parallel narratives shared by the Tetrateuch and the Former Prophets to date. Greenstein's article is also the first work to raise the question of the relationship between the parallel narratives and the growth of Genesis–Kings. The shortcoming of Greenstein's article is its failure to address adequately the question of the direction of dependence between the parallel narratives. Greenstein (1990: 177) contended that the Tetrateuchal narratives are derivative because he supposed that the narratives in the Former Prophets stem from the early monarchy whereas the Tetrateuchal traditions cannot be traced to earlier than the eighth century. But this argument only leans upon the conjectured early dating of the narratives in the Former Prophets and the late dating of Tetrateuchal narratives.

The burgeoning field of 'inner-biblical exegesis' also merits discussion. Michael Fishbane's masterful *Biblical Interpretation in Ancient Israel* of 1985 is representative. Fishbane demonstrated that Pentateuchal stories had a formative influence in much of the Hebrew Bible, as is clear from the multitude of instances in which Pentateuchal accounts are 'exegeted' by biblical writers. A fundamental weakness of Fishbane's work is its relative disregard for the place of consciousness in composition, for there is no appreciable step between intimate knowledge of Pentateuchal stories and the shaping influence that such stories have on the mind. Consonant with this, Fishbane's use of the word 'typology' with reference to parallels shared by Pentateuchal and extra-Pentateuchal stories has little to commend it. Although the Hebrew Bible is replete with typologies, the term typology does not do justice to the role that Tetrateuchal accounts had in shaping Dtr's mind. For Dtr, Tetrateuchal schemata were dynamic palimpsets that could convey varieties of meaning.[8] Dtr could use the same Tetrateuchal account in vastly different ways, and the parallel narratives that he drew often overlap each other. Dtr based the story of Joshua's spies (Joshua 2), for instance, on the visit of the messengers to Sodom (Genesis 19), the initial venture of the spies into Canaan (Numbers 13), and the seduction of Israel by Moab (Numbers 25). Referring to Dtr's use of Tetrateuchal accounts as 'typological' thus oversimplifies. Tetrateuchal accounts were metonyms of all history for Dtr; they had 'iterative power' as they defined all history; and they themselves were inscribed on Dtr's consciousness.[9]

The parallel narratives that Dtr drew amount to a Pandora's box for the historical critic. In terms of textual criticism, there are many places, for instance, in which parallels exist precisely where the MT differs with the LXX. Because the MT at such points is grammatically or contextually incongruous, emmendations of the MT abound. But the MT readings are typically to be preferred, for they are integral to the parallels that Dtr drew. Dtr consciously drew many such incongruities to call the reader's attention to the corresponding Tetrateuchal account. Regarding the existence of a Tetrateuch in Dtr's time, ample evidence for this view comes with the fact that homogenous accounts in the DtrH share parallels with two or more redactional layers of composite Tetrateuchal accounts. The parallel narratives similarly raise the question of the relation between P and non-P layers in the Tetrateuch, for in many instances the parallel narratives that Dtr drew include features from the P-layer. It follows that this layer, or a portion of this layer, was in place prior to the sixth century. As for the DtrH itself, the remarkably consistent use of Tetrateuchal accounts in the parallel narratives suggests that an individual, rather than unrelated redactors, drew the parallels.

Although I do address historical-critical questions, especially in the early chapters, my principal task is to outline and discuss the parallel narratives themselves. In Chapter 1 I analyze Deuteronomy 1–3. I argue that Dtr based his story on the synoptic Tetrateuchal accounts. I conclude that the given Tetrateuchal accounts were integral to Dtr's consciousness, such that I refer to them together as Dtr's Torah.[10] Moving roughly from the simplest to the most complex, in Chapters 2 to 5 I analyze the parallel narratives that the Former Prophets share with Dtr's Torah. In Chapter 2 I briefly discuss the influence that Dtr's Torah had on the Exilic community. I also there contend that Dtr rather than Tetrateuchal compilers drew

8.   For use of 'schemata' and associated terms in the fields of linguistics and psychology see Tannen 1979.

9.   I am here indebted to Allan's (1986: 200) statement that written works 'overflow the present, and by their iterative power stretch out their significance into enduring strands of order'.

10.   For my purposes, 'Torah' is often preferrable to 'Tetrateuch' as it has a life-defining rather than clinical nuance. Whereas 'Tetrateuch' simply delimits the contents of a corpus, 'Torah' is more concerned with faith and *Weltanschauung*, 'a universal meaning system *within which* one's biography can be located' (Berger 1963: 61; emphasis his).

the parallel narratives. In Chapter 3 I stress the relationship between Dtr's Torah and his consciousness. Finally, in Chapters 4 and 5 I emphasize the hermenuetical import of Dtr's use of Tetrateuchal narratives. In the conclusion I develop some of the implications that this work has for historical criticism.

Chapter 1

DTR'S USE OF HIS TORAH IN DEUTERONOMY 1–3

In this chapter I discuss Dtr's use of his Torah in Deuteronomy 1–3. This will provide an Archimedean point by which the parallel narratives shared by the Tetrateuch and the Former Prophets can be better understood, for I here contend the following: (1) Dtr based his accounts on the synoptic Tetrateuchal accounts; (2) Dtr used a unified Tetrateuch rather than isolated accounts; (3) in his recasting of the synoptic Tetrateuchal accounts Dtr principally relied on his memory of the written record rather than the written record itself; and (4) Dtr's retelling of the synoptic Tetrateuchal accounts was very creative and consistent with his concerns elsewhere in the DtrH. I first analyze those sections in Deuteronomy 1–3 that closely correspond to narratives in the Tetrateuch and then consider those sections of Deuteronomy 1–3 that are at a further remove from the corresponding accounts in the Tetrateuch.

Analysis of the Closely Corresponding Accounts

Narratives in Deuteronomy 1–3 that closely correspond to their counterparts in the Tetrateuch include the following:

- The spies and their failure: Numbers 13–14 = Deut. 1.6-8, 19-46
- The appointment of officials: Exod. 18.13-27; Num. 11.10-25 = Deut. 1.9-18
- Transjordan ventures: Num. 21.21-35 = Deut. 2.24–3.3
- The commissioning of Joshua and the death of Moses: Num. 27.12-23 = Deut. 3.21-28

Numbers 13–14 and Deuteronomy 1.6-8, 19-46
Deuteronomy 1.6-8, 19-46, which concerns the mission of the spies and the subsequent murmuring, includes 17 verbal parallels with the corresponding accounts in Numbers.[1]

---

1.   I am reliant on the lists compiled by Driver (1916) for the lists of lexical parallels between the synoptic texts of the Tetrateuch and Deuteronomy 1–3.

Num. 14.25   פנו וסעו לכם

turn and set out[2]

Deut. 1.7   פנו וסעו לכם

turn and set out

Num. 13.30   עלה נעלה וירשנו אתה

Let us by all means go up and take possession of it.

Deut. 1.21   עלה רש

Go up, take possession.

Num. 13.17   ועליתם את־ההר

And go up into the hill country.

Deut. 1.24   ויעלו ההרה

And they went up into the hill country.

Num. 13.23   ויבאו עד־נחל אשכל

And they came to the Valley of Eshcol.

Deut. 1.24   ויבאו עד־נחל אשכל

And they came to the Valley of Eshcol.

Num. 13.20   ולחקתם מפרי הארץ

And take some of the fruit of the land.

Deut. 1.25   ויחקו בידם מפרי הארץ

And they took in their hands some of the fruit of the land.

Num. 13.26   וישיבו אותם דבר

And they brought back word to them.

Deut. 1.25   וישבו אתנו דבר

And they brought back word to us.

Num. 13.28   והערים בצרות גדלת מאד וגם־ילדי הענק ראינו שם

And the cities are fortified and very large; moreover, we saw the sons of the Anakim there.

Deut. 1.28   ערים גדלת ובצורת בשמים וגם־בני ענקים ראינו שם

large fortified cities; moreover, we saw the sons of the Anakim there

Num. 14.9   ואתם אל־תיראו את־עם הארץ

And do not fear the people of the land.

Deut. 1.29   ולא־תיראון מהם

And do not fear them.

Num. 14.23-24   אם־יראו את־הארץ אשר נשבעתי לאבתם וכל־מנאצי לא יראוה
ועבדי כלב עקב היתה רוח אחרת עמו וימלא אחרי
והביאתיו אל־הארץ אשר־בא שמה וזרעו יורשנה

[None of the men] shall see the land that I promised on oath to their fathers; none of those who spurn me shall see it. But my servant Caleb, because he was imbued with a different spirit and remained loyal to me – him will I bring into the land that he entered, and his offspring shall hold it as a possession.

Deut. 1.35-36   אם־יראה איש באנשים האלה הדור הרע הזה את הארץ הטובה
אשר נשבעתי לתת לאבתיכם זולתי כלב בן־יפנה הוא יראנה
ולו־אתן את־הארץ אשר דרך־בה ולבניו יען אשר מלא אחרי יהוה

Not one of these men, this evil generation, shall see the good land that I swore to give to your fathers – none except Caleb son of Jephunneh; he shall see it, and to

---

2.   I often use translations from the *NJPS* in this work. The many exceptions include instances where a more literal translation is needed.

him and his descendants will I give the land on which he set foot, because he remained loyal to the LORD.

Num. 14.31   וטפכם אשר אמרתם לבז יהיה

And your little ones whom you said would become a prey

Deut. 1.39   וטפכם אשר אמרתם לבז יהיה

And your little ones whom you said would become a prey

Num. 14.25   מחר פנו וסעו לכם המדבר דרך ים־סוף

Turn tomorrow and set out to the wilderness by the way of the Sea of Reeds.

Deut. 1.40   ואתם פנו לכם וסעו המדברה דרך ים־סוף

Turn about and set out to the wilderness by the way of the Sea of Reeds.

Num. 14.40   ועלינו...כי חטאנו

We will go up...for we have sinned.

Deut. 1.41   חטאנו...אנחנו נעלה

We have sinned...we will go up.

Num. 14.42   אל־תעלו כי אין יהוה בקרבכם ולא תנגפו לפני איביכם

Do not go up for the LORD is not in your midst – lest you be struck down by your enemies.

Deut. 1.42   לא תעלו...כי אינני בקרבכם ולא תנגפו לפני איביכם

Do not go up...for I am not in your midst – lest you be struck down by your enemies.

Num. 14.41   למה זה אתם עברים את־פי יהוה

Why are you transgressing against the command of the LORD?

Deut. 1.43   ותמרו את־פי יהוה

And you rebelled against the command of the LORD.

Num. 14.44   ויעפלו לעלות אל־ראש ההר

And they were defiant to go up to the crest of the hill country.

Deut. 1.43   ותזדו ותעלו ההרה

And you acted presumptuously and you went up to the hill country.

Num. 14.45   וירד העמלקי והכנעני הישב בהר ההוא ויכום ויכתום עד־החרמה

And the Amalekites and the Canaanites who dwelt in that hill country came down and struck them and beat them down as far as Hormah.

Deut. 1.44   ויצא האמרי הישב בהר ההוא לקראתכם וירדפו אתכם...

ויכתו אתכם בשעיר עד־החרמה

And the Amorites who dwelt in that hill country came out to meet you and they pursued you...and they beat you down in Seir as far as Hormah.

Num. 20.1   וישב העם בקדש

And the people remained at Kadesh.

Deut. 1.46   ותשבו בקדש

And you remained at Kadesh.

In the following paragraphs I argue that because the account in Deuteronomy shares verbal parallels with each redactional layer of the synoptic account in Numbers, the account in Deuteronomy is dependent on that of Numbers. I also support the proposed direction of dependence by outlining how the account in Deuteronomy assumes knowledge of the corresponding account in Numbers, the oath to the fathers in Genesis, and the Exodus story.

The story in Deuteronomy includes verbal parallels with each redactional layer of its counterpart in Numbers. Most source critics have argued for the presence of J(E) and P in Numbers 13-14. Noth's (1968: 101-103) analysis is typical. He attributed Num. 13.17b-20, 22-24, 27-31; 14.4, 11-25, and 39-45 to J, and Num. 13.1-17a, 21, 25-26, 32-33; 14.1-3, 5-10, and 26-38 to P.[3] Following this analysis, there are 13 verbal parallels between the non-P layer of Numbers 13–14 and Deut. 1.19-46 and three verbal parallels between the P layer of Numbers 13–14 and Deut. 1.19-46.[4] Because Deuteronomy includes verbal parallels with more than one redactional layer of the account in Numbers, one may reasonably conclude that Deuteronomy is here dependent on Numbers.[5]

That Dtr assumed knowledge of the account in Numbers is evident, first, from a comparison of the report of the spies in Numbers and Deuteronomy. In Deut. 1.25 the spies exclaimed 'it is a good land that the LORD our God is giving to us', but in Deut. 1.28 the people stated '[The spies] have taken the heart out of us, saying, "We saw there a people stronger and taller than we are, large cities with walls sky-high, and even Anakites"'. Left to itself, the positive report of Deut. 1.25 is thus in tension with the negative report of Deut. 1.28. If, however, Dtr assumed knowledge of the corresponding account in Numbers then the tension is resolved – for unlike Deut. 1.25 and 28, in Num. 13.27-28 the spies' positive verdict that the land 'does indeed flow with milk and honey' is immediately modified by their description of the strength of the land's inhabitants and their cities.[6] The second instance of assumed knowledge concerns Caleb and Joshua. Without Numbers 14, Dtr's discussion concerning Caleb and Joshua would be difficult to understand. In the Numbers account both Caleb and Joshua are listed with the other spies (Num. 13.6, 8). Following this list we read that 'Moses changed the name of Hoshea son of Nun to Joshua' (Num. 13.16). After the spies expressed their fear of the inhabitants of Canaan, Caleb encouraged the people to take the land (Num. 13.27-30). The people were nevertheless swayed by the other spies and they longed for Egypt (Num. 14.1-4). Joshua and Caleb thereupon rent their clothes and exhorted the people to follow the LORD, but the people threatened to stone them (Num. 14.6-10). It is only after this point that the account in Deuteronomy shares parallels with Numbers: like Num. 14.22-24 and 30, Deut. 1.35-36 and 38 refer to the LORD's decision to keep the Exodus generation – with the exception of Caleb and Joshua – from seeing the land. Unlike the account in Numbers, nothing is said of Caleb or Joshua prior to this in Deuteronomy. It follows that if Dtr did not here assume knowledge of the story in

3.   See also the discussion in Budd 1984: 141–44, 150–55.

4.   Note also that Deut. 1.46 is parallel with Num. 20.1, which has traditionally been assigned to P. I say 'non-P layer' because there is some discussion over the identification of this layer as consisting of J(E) and D, especially in Num. 14.11-25. See the discussion in Budd 1984: 152-53.

5.   See also Boorer 1992: 393. The conclusion that Deut. 1.19-46 is based on the redactionally composite Numbers 13–14 holds even with Van Seters' (1992: 366) conclusions regarding the layers of Numbers 13–14. Van Seters attributed Num. 14.9 (= Deut. 1.29) and Num. 14.31 (= Deut. 1.39) to P. This conclusion also undermines the view of Plöger (1967: 49) that the theory of a shared oral tradition between these accounts explains their relationship just as well as the theory of literary dependence.

6.   See also Mayes 1979: 129–30.

Numbers, the references to Caleb and Joshua in Deut. 1.35-36, 38 would be strik-ingly laconic. Even the introductions to Caleb and Joshua would be obscure. The only reason given for the LORD's promise to let Caleb see the land was that 'he remained loyal to the LORD' (Deut. 1.36), but without Numbers one would not know of what such loyalty consisted. The case is more extreme for Joshua. Dtr simply introduced Joshua by having the LORD state, 'Joshua son of Nun, who attends you, he shall enter [the land]' (Deut. 1.38). Given that Dtr emphasized the point that not one individual of the Exodus generation was to see the land (Deut. 1.35; 2.14-15), it would be odd for him to state nothing about why Joshua was an exception. The best explanation for such data is that Dtr assumed knowledge of the Numbers account.

This brings me to the two instances in which Dtr assumed knowledge of other Tetrateuchal accounts. The first such instance concerns the Exodus. Exodus 13.21, which refers to the guidance of the LORD just prior to the crossing of the Sea, reads 'And the LORD was going before them' (ויהוה הלך לפניהם). Parallel to this is Deut. 1.30: 'the LORD your God who goes before you' (יהוה אלהיכם ההלך לפניכם). Exodus 13.21 and Deut. 1.32-33 are similarly parallel.

Exod. 13.21	*Deut. 1.32-33*
ויהוה הלך לפניהם יומם בעמוד ענן לנחתם הדרך ולילה בעמוד אש להאיר להם ללכת יומם ולילה	(32) ובדבר הזה אינכם מאמינם ביהוה אלהיכם (33) ההלך לפניכם בדרך לתור לכם מקום לחנתכם באש לילה לראתכם בדרך אשר תלכו בה ובענן יומם
And the LORD was going before them In a pillar of cloud by day To guide them along the way, And in a pillar of fire by night, To give them light To go day and night.	(32) Yet for all that you have no faith in the LORD your God (33) who goes before you on the way to scout the place you are to camp, in fire by night to give you light on the way that you are going and in cloud by day

These parallels occur in a context in which Dtr explicitly referred to the Exodus story: Moses quoted the people who had said, 'It is because the LORD hates us that he brought us out of the land of Egypt' (Deut. 1.27); Moses similarly exhorted the people to have no fear of the Amorites because the LORD would fight for them just as he had done for them while they were 'in Egypt' (Deut. 1.30). Because the above verbal parallels are accompanied by explicit references to the Exodus story, the best explanation is that Dtr was responsible for drawing them. This conclusion is supported by the fact that although the Exodus story is the most central event in salvation history for Dtr, knowledge of the story itself is only assumed. The central-ity of the Exodus story in Deuternom(ist)ic thinking is evident from the following: there are close to 70 references to the Exodus from Egypt in the DtrH;[7] the motiva-

---

7.　Deut. 1.27, 30; 4.20, 34, 37, 45-46; 5.6, 15; 6.12, 21-22; 7.8, 18; 8.14; 9.7, 12, 26; 11.4, 10; 13.5, 10; 16.1, 3, 6; 20.1; 23.4; 24.9, 18; 25.17; 26.8; 29.25; Josh. 2.10; 5.4-6; 9.9; 24.5-7, 17; Judg. 2.1, 12; 6.8-9, 13; 10.11; 11.13, 16; 19.30; 1 Sam. 6.6; 8.8; 10.18; 12.6, 8; 15.2, 6; 2 Sam.

tion given for obeying many of the Deuteronomic exhortations and laws was based on the LORD's grace in delivering his people from Egypt;[8] the LORD's power at the Exodus is recalled for confidence in future warfare;[9] the nations feared the power of the LORD as it was exemplified in the Exodus;[10] the central component of the so-called 'little credos' is the Exodus from Egypt;[11] and the most common time referent in the DtrH is the Exodus.[12]

   The second instance in which Dtr assumed knowledge of a Tetrateuchal account comes with the LORD's declaration, 'Not one of these men, this evil generation, shall see the good land that I swore to give to your fathers' (Deut. 1.35). That 'fathers' in this instance is Dtr's title for Abraham, Isaac and Jacob is evident from Deut. 1.8, 'Go, enter the land that the LORD swore to your fathers, Abraham, Isaac, and Jacob, to assign to them and to their offspring after them'. Such statements show that Dtr assumed knowledge of that tradition in Genesis regarding the oath that the LORD had made to the Patriarchs (Gen. 12.7; 13.15, 17; 15.18; 26.3-4; 28.13). Against this interpretation are the contentions of Van Seters (1972a; 1992: 227-45) and Römer (1990) that the names of the Patriarchs in Deuteronomy represent a post–Deuteronomistic redaction and that 'fathers' in Deuteronomy refers only to post–Patriarchal generations.[13] This view, however, does not do justice to the verbal parallel between Num. 14.22-24 and Deut. 1.35-36.

Num. 14.22-24	*Deut. 1.35-36*
(22) כל־האנשים...(23) אם־יראו את־הארץ אשר נשבעתי לאבתם... (24) ועבדי כלב עקב היתה רוח אחרת עמו וימלא אחרי והביאתיו אל־הארץ אשר־בא שמה וזרעו יורשנה	(35) אם־יראה איש באנשים ... את הארץ הטובה אשר נשבעתי לתת לאבתיכם (36) זולתי כלב בן־יפנה הוא יראנה ולו־אתן את־הארץ אשר דרך־בה ולבניו יען אשר מלא אחרי יהוה
(22) All the men…(23) will not see the land which I swore to their *fathers*…. (24) But my servant Caleb, because he had a different spirit and followed after me, will I bring to the land which he entered and his offspring will possess it.	(35) Not one of these men…shall see the good land which I swore to give to your *fathers* (36) except Caleb son of Jephunneh – he will see it. And to him I will give the land on which he has set foot and to his sons because he followed after the LORD.

7.6; 1 Kgs 6.1; 8.9, 16, 21, 51, 53; 9.9; 12.28; 2 Kgs 17.7, 36; 21.15.
   8.   Deut. 13.10; 15.14-15; 16.3, 11-12; 17.16; 24.17-18; 24.21-22.
   9.   Deut. 1.30; 20.1; cf. Judg. 6.13.
   10.   Josh. 2.10; 1 Sam. 4.8; cf. Deut. 29.24-25; 1 Kgs 9.8-9.
   11.   Deut. 6.20-25; 26.5-10; Josh. 24.2-15.
   12.   There are many texts, for example, in which Dtr implicitly taught that the birth of Israel as a nation came only with the Exodus: 'From the day that I brought Israel out of Egypt to this day…' (2 Sam. 7.6; see also Judg. 19.30; 1 Sam. 8.8; 1 Kgs 8.16; 2 Kgs 21.15). This accords with the fact that the DtrH commences with the Exodus. The 'fortieth year' of Deut. 1.3 in which Moses addressed all Israel in Moab is an allusion to the Exodus. This point is also clear from Solomon's commencement of the construction of the temple in 'the four hundred and eightieth year after the Israelites left the land of Egypt' (1 Kgs 6.1).
   13.   See the extensive criticism of Römer's argument by Lohfink (1990).

Few would dispute that Num. 14.22-23 refers to the Patriarchal promises regarding land in Genesis, and I have shown that Dtr based Deut. 1.19-46 on Numbers 13–14. It follows that Deut. 1.35-36 also refers to the Patriarchal promises in Genesis.

Exodus 18.13-27; Numbers 11.10-25; and Deuteronomy 1.9-18

Embedded within the account concerning the spies is Moses' appointment of officials (Deut. 1.9-18).[14] In many respects, this pericope parallels both Jethro's advice to Moses to appoint chiefs over the nation (Exod. 18.13-27), and Moses' appointment of 70 of Israel's elders to join him in the Tent (Num. 11.10-25). In only ten verses the account in Deuteronomy shares five verbal parallels with the corresponding accounts in Exodus 18 and Numbers 11.

Exod. 18.18   לא־תוכל עשׂהו לבדך
you are not able to do it alone

Deut. 1.9   לא־אוכל לבדי שׂאת אתכם
I am not able to bear you alone

Num. 11.14   לא־אוכל אנכי לבדי לשׂאת את־כל־העם הזה
I am not able to bear all this people alone.

Deut. 1.9   לא־אוכל לבדי שׂאת אתכם
I am not able to bear you alone.

Num. 11.17   ונשׂאו אתך במשׂא העם ולא־תשׂא אתה לבדך
And they will bear the burden of the people with you so that you do not bear it alone.

Deut. 1.12   איכה אשׂא לבדי טרחכם ומשׂאכם וריבכם
How can I bear alone your trouble and your burden and your bickering?

Exod. 18.21, 25   שׂרי אלפים שׂרי מאות שׂרי המשׁים ושׂרי עשׂרת
chiefs of thousands, chiefs of hundreds, chiefs of fifties, and chiefs of tens

Deut. 1.15   שׂרי אלפים ושׂרי מאות ושׂרי חמשׁים ושׂרי עשׂרת
chiefs of thousands, and chiefs of hundreds, and chiefs of fifties, and chiefs of tens

Exod. 18.26 (cf. 18.22)   את־הדבר הקשׁה יביאון אל־משׁה
The difficult matter they would bring to Moses.

Deut. 1.17   הדבר אשׁר יקשׁה מכם תקרבון אלי
The matter that is too difficult for you, you shall bring to me.

In the following paragraphs I argue that the account in Deuteronomy consists of a conflation and reformulation of the given Tetrateuchal accounts.

Van Seters contended that both the Exodus and Numbers accounts were patterned after the account in Deuteronomy. It is, according to Van Seters (1992: 214),

---

14.   Some have argued that Deut. 1.9-18 is an interpolation as it interrupts the divine command to leave Horeb in 1.6-8 and the departure from Horeb in 1.19 (e.g., Lohfink 1960: 107 n. 1; Plöger 1967: 31; Weinfeld 1972: 45). However, the formula בעת ההיא 'at that time', which introduces Deut. 1.9-18, occurs nine other times in Deuteronomy 1–3. Like its occurrence in Deut. 1.9, in each of these instances it concerns a parenthesis (Deut. 1.16, 18; 2.34; 3.4, 8, 12, 18, 21, 23; cf. the parenthetical passages that pertain to the histories of Moab and Ammon in Deut. 2.10-12, 20-23). It is therefore better to regard Deut. 1.9-18 as having come from Dtr (cf. Loewenstamm 1992: 42–50).

a 'serious methodological contradiction' to argue that the Tetrateuchal and Deuter-onomic narratives have markedly different histories:

> We are asked to believe that the Yahwist, faced with different oral traditions, had no choice but to produce a combination of these traditions whose awkwardness is clearly apparent to any reader. Yet the Dtr, when faced with the written traditions of J (or E), exercised complete freedom to combine the accounts, eliminate most of the details that did not suit him, and produce a homogenous narrative with scarcely any trace of such editorial activity. That is too hard for me to swallow!

Van Seters (1992: 208–19) concluded that it is more tenable to argue that the awk-ward accounts in the Tetrateuch were patterned after the polished account in Deuter-onomy. Entirely on the basis of this presupposition, Van Seters argued that various differences between the accounts in the Tetrateuch and Deuteronomy can be ex-plained by the priority of Deuteronomy. There is, however, nothing at all 'contra-dictory' about different authors or redactors treating their sources differently.[15] Moreover, all that Van Seters did is posit reasons why – on the supposition that J's work is later than that of Dtr – J's accounts differ from those of Dtr. But it is not enough simply to argue how the differences might be explained; rather, one must show how the differences are similar to either J or Dtr's particular concerns.

The fact is that a number of the differences between the accounts are demon-strably Deuteronomistic. To begin with, one must account for the more positive portrayal of Moses in Deuteronomy than the corresponding Tetrateuchal accounts. Whereas Deut. 1.9, for instance, refers to Moses' inability to bear the people by himself, in Num. 11.14 Moses' parallel statement is fraught with perturbation: he accused the LORD of dealing unfairly with him (Num. 11.11); he complained that he had not found favor in the LORD's sight (Num. 11.11); he was not responsible for the birth of the people (Num. 11.12); and he was not able to provide enough food for them (Num. 11.13; cf. 11.21-22). Such anxiety is dissimilar to the verbal parallel in Deut. 1.9 where Moses is thoroughly positive – Moses was not able to judge the people by himself because the LORD had multiplied them. Similarly, Moses' question 'how can I bear by myself your trouble and your burden?' (Deut. 1.12) parallels the LORD's statement, 'and they shall bear the burden of the people with you so that you do not bear it yourself' (Num. 11.17). Whereas the statement in Numbers is the result of Moses' frustration, there is nothing negative in Moses' statement in Deuteronomy: in Numbers Moses expressed consternation over 'all this people' (Num. 11.13), the 'six hundred thousand' whom he felt compelled to feed (Num. 11.21-22), while in Deuteronomy Moses exclaimed that Israel had become as populous as the stars of the heavens and he expressed his desire for Israel to become a thousand times more numerous than they were (Deut. 1.10-11). In the Exodus account, moreover, Moses is second to his father-in-law Jethro. Ac-cording to Jethro, Moses was sitting alone while the people were waiting for their cases to be judged (Exod. 18.14); what Moses was doing was not good (Exod. 18.17); and Jethro's command was equivalent to that of the LORD (Exod. 18.23; cf. 18.19). The idea to appoint 'chiefs of thousands, chiefs of hundreds, chiefs of

15. See also Brettler's (1995: 183 n. 31) criticism.

fifties, and chiefs of tens' (Exod. 18.21) was similarly Jethro's idea, whereas Deut. 1.15 – which is verbally parallel to Exod. 18.21 – credits Moses with the idea.[16] Compared to the portrayal of Moses in the accounts in Numbers 11 and Exodus 18, then, the presentation of Moses in Deut. 1.9-18 is more positive. In order to defend the view that the Tetrateuchal compilers were responsible for the parallels, one would have to explain why this positive portrayal of Moses was dropped – a most tenuous hypothesis given the high, even hagiographic view of Moses in exilic and postexilic literature.[17]

Another example in which there is a difference between Exodus 18, Numbers 11, and Deut. 1.9-18 concerns the emphasis on wisdom.[18] Whereas Exod. 18.21 reads 'You shall also seek out from among all the people capable men (אנשי־חיל) who fear God (יראי אלהים), trustworthy men (אנשי אמת) who spurn ill-gotten gain', Deut. 1.13 reads, 'Pick from each of your tribes wise (חכמים), discerning (נבנים), and knowledgeable (ידעים) men'. Deuteronomy 1.15 similarly reads, 'I took your tribal leaders, wise (חכמים) and knowledgeable (ידעים) men'. Weinfeld (1991: 64) rightly argued that, consonant with Dtr's emphasis on wisdom, the account in Exodus was reformulated because 'leaders and judges must possess intellectual qualities, wisdom, understanding, and knowledge, traits that characterize the leader and judge in wisdom literature'. This interpretation is consistent with Solomon's request for wisdom. Weinfeld (1991: 64–65) noted that similar to Moses before him, Solomon was overwhelmed by the population of the Israelites and so he asked for understanding to judge the people (1 Kgs 3.8-9). The LORD was pleased with Solomon's request and gave him 'a heart of wisdom and understanding' (לב חכם ונבון; 1 Kgs 3.11-12). Deuteronomy 16.18-20, the other passage in Deuteronomy that concerns the appointment of judges, is similarly directed. Whereas Exod. 23.8 reads, 'You shall not take bribes, for bribes blind the clear-sighted (יעור פקחים)', Deut. 16.19 reads, 'You shall not take bribes, for bribes blind the eyes of the wise (יעור עיני חכמים)'.[19] The fact that a difference between the two Tetrateuchal texts and Deut. 1.9-18 is Deuteronomistic again shows that the Tetrateuchal accounts are primary. If Exod. 18.13-27 and Num. 11.10-25 were based on Deut. 1.9-18, one would have to explain why the Tetrateuchal accounts omitted the wisdom element. Given the emphasis on wisdom in exilic and postexilic literature, such an omission would be odd.[20] A more tenable explanation is that Deut. 1.9-18 is a conflation of Exod. 18.13-27 and Num. 11.10–25.[21]

In addition to relying on Exod. 18.13-27 and Num. 11.10-25, Dtr also alluded to the promise to the Patriarchs. The divine promise of blessing and progeny to

16. Similarly, whereas in Numbers it was the LORD who told Moses to choose the men (11.15–16), in Deuteronomy Moses chose the men without having received the idea from the LORD (1.13).

17. See Jermias 1967 and Dijkstra 2003.

18. Weinfeld 1972: 244–81; 1991: 62–65. See also Frymer-Kensky 1990: 280–85 and McCarter 1990: 289–93.

19. Weinfeld 1972: 245 (cf. Fishbane 1985: 244–45; Levinson 1991: 425–30).

20. In his critique of Van Seters' view Levinson (1991: 426 n. 92) similarly queried, '[w]ere Exodus 18 indeed dependent upon Deuteronomy 1, why would the wisdom motif be deleted?'

21. The Deuteronomist(s) similarly blended unrelated Tetrateuchal accounts concerning Passover and Unleavened Bread in Deuteronomy 16 (see Levinson 1997: 53–97).

Abraham in Gen. 22.17 shares parallels with Moses' statement concerning the population of the Israelites in Deut. 1.10-11:

Gen. 22.17   כי־ברך אברכך והרבה ארבה את־זרעך ככוכבי השמים
                             For I will surely bless you and multiply your seed like the stars of the heavens.

Deut. 1.10–11   הרבה אתכם והנכם היום ככוכבי השמים...ויברך אתכם
                             (The LORD) has multiplied you until you are today like the stars in the heavens…
                             and may he bless you, just as he spoke to you.

In support of the view that Deut. 1.10-11 refers to Gen. 22.17, Milgrom (1976: 3) rightly argued that whenever Deuteronomy refers to its own statements it uses the participial construction 'which I am commanding' (אשר אנכי מצוה).[22] Milgrom also noted that whenever Deuteronomy refers to an antecedent tradition it uses the perfect 'just as I have/he has commanded/swore/spoken (√דבר/√נשבע/√צוה כאשר) – even as one finds with Deut. 1.11.[23]

Dtr's use of of Gen. 22.17, Exod. 18.13-27, and Num. 11.10-25 in Deut. 1.9-18 shows that such traditions were deeply impressed on his memory, for it is not as if Dtr painstakingly unrolled scrolls in order to include incidental snippets from different stories. Rather, Dtr recalled Tetrateuchal stories and even their particular wording with little forethought. But this is not to suggest that Dtr had a computer-like hypermnesia.[24] This is clear enough from the seemingly arbitrary conflation of the similar stories in Exodus and Numbers in Dtr's account. Because of their marked similarity such stories coalesced in Dtr's mind. This conclusion is akin to the manner in which later biblical writers naturally assimilated the language and themes of earlier biblical writers.[25]

Numbers 21.21-35 and Deuteronomy 2.24–3.3
This brings me to a discussion of Num. 21.21-35 and Deut. 2.24–3.3, passages that outline Israel's interaction with Sihon and Og and that share ten verbal parallels.

Num. 21.21   וישלח ישראל מלאכים אל־סיחן מלך־האמרי לאמר
                     And Israel sent messengers to Sihon king of the Amorites saying
Deut. 2.26   ואשלח מלאכים...אל־סיחן מלך חשבון דברי שלום לאמר
                     And I sent messengers…to Sihon king of Heshbon with words of peace saying

---

22.   The instances include Deut. 4.2, 40; 6.2, 6; 7.11; 8.1, 11; 10.13; 11.8, 13, 22, 27-28; 12.14, 28; 13.11, 19; 15.5; 19.9; 27.1, 4, 10; 28.1, 13-15; 30.2, 8, 11, 16.

23.   The instances include Deut. 1.11, 19, 21; 2.1, 14; 4.5; 5.12, 16, 29; 6.3, 19, 25; 9.3; 10.5, 9; 11.25; 12.21; 13.18; 15.6; 18.2; 19.8; 20.17; 24.8; 26.15, 18-19; 27.3; 28.9; 29.12[13]; 31.3; 34.9 (see also Lohfink's 1997 and 1998 treatments of the כאשר formulae in Deuteronomy and Joshua). Milgrom (1976: 4–13) rightly concluded that P antedates D because some such instances include P texts (see also Fishbane 1985: 164).

24.   For examples of memorization achievements in the ancient world see Harris (1989: 30–33, 301).

25.   See Zakovitch 1985: 174–96 and Carr 2001: 124. Although dealing with Graeco-Roman literature, Smalley (1997: 199–200) similarly asserted that authors 'break any given event into little pieces and store them all over the place…with the result that one event can have multiple labels' and that 'similar stories get mixed up with each other'. Minchin (1992: 239) similarly contended that one 'script' might be interwoven with others.

Num. 21.22
אעברה בארצך...בדרך המלך נלך
Let me pass through your land...we will go by the way of the king.

Deut. 2.27
אעברה בארצך בדרך המלך אלך
Let me pass through your land; I will go by the way of the king.[26]

Num. 20.17
לא נטה ימין ושמאול
We will not turn aside to the right or the left.

Deut. 2.27
לא אסור ימין ושמאול
I will not turn to the right or the left.

Num. 20.19
רק אין־דבר ברגלי אעברה
It is nothing, let me pass through on foot.

Deut. 2.28
רק אעברה ברגלי
Only let me pass through on foot.

Num. 21.23
ולא־נתן סיחם את־ישראל עבר בגבלו
And Sihon would not let Israel pass through his territory.

Deut. 2.30
ולא אבה סיחן מלך חשבון העברנו בו
And Sihon king of Heshbon would not let us pass by him.

Num. 21.23
ויאסף סיחם את־כל־עמו ויצא לקראת ישראל
המדברה ויבא יהצה וילחם בישראל
Sihon gathered all his people and went out to meet Israel in the wilderness. He came to Jahaz and battled against Israel.

Deut. 2.32
ויצא סיחן לקראתנו הוא וכל־עמו למלחמה יהצה
And Sihon went out to meet us, he and all his people, for battle at Jahaz.

Num. 21.35
ויכו אתו ואת־בניו ואת־כל־עמו
And they struck him and his sons and all his people.

Deut. 2.33
ונך אתו ואת־בניו ואת־כל־עמו
And we struck him and his sons and all his people.

Num. 21.25
ויקח ישראל את כל־הערים האלה
And Israel took all these cities.

Deut. 2.34
ונלכד את־כל־עריו
And we captured all his cities.

Num. 21.33-34
ויפנו ויעלו דרך הבשן ויצא עוג מלך־הבשן לקראתם הוא וכל־עמו
למלחמה אדרעי ויאמר יהוה אל־משה אל־תירא אתו
כי בידך נתתי אתו ואת־כל־עמו ואת־ארצו
ועשית לו כאשר עשית לסיחן מלך האמרי אשר יושב בחשבון
And they turned and went up the road to Bashan. And Og the king of Bashan went out to meet them, he and all his people, for battle at Edrei. And the LORD said to Moses, 'Do not fear him for I have given him and all his people and his land into your hand; and you will do to him just as you did to Sihon the king of the Amorites who dwelt in Heshbon'.

Deut. 3.1-2
ונפן ונעל דרך הבשן ויצא עוג מלך־הבשן לקראתנו הוא וכל־עמו
למלחמה אדרעי ויאמר יהוה אלי אל־תירא אתו
כי בידך נתתי אתו ואת־כל־עמו ואת־ארצו
ועשית לו כאשר עשית לסיחן מלך האמרי אשר יושב בחשבון
And we turned and went up the road to Bashan and Og the king of Bashan went out to meet us, he and all his people, for battle at Edrei. And the LORD said to me,

---

26. Following Num. 21.22, I have emended the MT's בדרך בדרך to בדרך המלך. The LXX omits the second בדרך.

'Do not fear him for I have given him and all his people and his land into your hand; and you will do to him just as you did to Sihon the king of the Amorites who dwelt in Heshbon'.

Num. 21.35   ויכו אתו...עד־בלתי השאיר־לו שריד

And they struck him...until there was no remnant left to him.

Deut. 3.3   ונכהו...עד־בלתי השאיר־לו שריד

And we struck him...until there was no remnant left to him.

In support of the secondary nature of Num. 21.21-25, Van Seters (1992: 393-98) argued that this text is a conflation of Deut. 2.26-36 and Jepthah's synoptic report in Judg. 11.19-26. Van Seters contended that where Numbers differs from Deuteronomy in three respects, Judges differs from Deuteronomy in the same way.[27] First, whereas Deuteronomy attributes to Moses the sending of the messengers (Deut. 2.26), in Numbers and Judges this action is attributed to Israel (Num. 21.21; Judg. 11.19). According to Van Seters (1992: 395), this attribution fits the context of Judges but in Numbers it represents a 'striking inconsistency', for in Num. 20.14 Moses sent messengers to Edom and in Num. 21.32 he sent spies to Jazer. '[S]triking inconsistency', however, is surely an overstatement when all that can be shown is that one account differs from two others.[28] Second, Van Seters noted that whereas Deut. 2.34-36 refers to the capture of cities, Judg. 11.21-22 refers to the capture of territory. He concluded that Num. 21.24-25 conflates these accounts because references to both the capture of territory as well as cities are problematic in Num. 21.24-25. With regard to the capture of territory, Van Seters contended that the seizing of land 'from the Arnon to the Jabbok, as far as the Ammonites' (Num. 21.24; cf. Judg. 11.22) is problematic because the Ammonites are not mentioned in the narrative prior to this. But this is hardly problematic, for with his mention of the Ammonites the narrator simply delimited the area of conquest. With regard to the capture of cities, Van Seters (1992: 396–97) argued that 'these cities' in Num. 21.25, where cities had not been previously mentioned, is a reference to the cities in Deut. 2.34-36. Van Seters here only assumed what he wished to demonstrate, for Deut. 2.34-36 itself never refers to 'these cities'. Third, Van Seters noted that whereas Deuteronomy avoids any discussion of settlement, both Judg. 11.26 and Num. 21.25 refer to it, although Num. 21.25 is inconsistent with its context. According to Van Seters (1992: 397–98), the mention of Israel settling in the region in Num. 21.25 is 'quite surprising' for shortly thereafter the narrative refers to the conquest of Jazer (21.32) and Bashan (21.33-35). But, as Bartlett (1978: 349) rightly noted, if J had the Deuteronomy account before him he could have easily overcome this problem by incorporating Deut. 2.31, which anticipates the settlement: 'See *I have begun* (החלתי) by placing Sihon and his land at your disposal'. Moreover, Van Seters' contention that Num. 21.25 contradicts 21.33-35 is based on his view that J

----

27. Most of Van Seters' arguments first appeared in an article of 1972 (see Van Seters 1972b). See also the response of Bartlett (1978) and the rejoinder by Van Seters (1980).

28. Note also that the sending of messengers that is attributed to Moses (Deut. 2.26) rather than to Israel (Num. 21.21) is consistent with Dtr's positive portrayal of Moses.

was responsible for 21.33-35; but most rightly argue that these verses represent a Deuteronom(ist)ic interpolation.[29]

The fact is that the most notable difference between Num. 21.21-35 and Deut. 2.26-37 supports the view that Dtr based his account on that of Numbers. Between Sihon's refusal to let Israel pass through his territory and the subsequent preparation for the battle, unlike the account in Numbers that of Deuteronomy includes the reason for Sihon's obstinacy as well as the divine charge to conquer Sihon.

Num. 21.23	*Deut. 2.30-32*
(23a) But Sihon would not let Israel pass through his territory.	(30) But king Sihon of Heshbon refused to let us pass through, because the LORD had stiffened his will and hardened his heart in order to deliver him into your hand – as is now the case. (31) And the LORD said to me, 'See I begin by placing Sihon and his land at your disposal. Begin the occupation; take possession of his land'.
(23b) Sihon gathered all his people and went out against Israel in the wilderness. He came to Jahaz and engaged Israel in battle.	(32) Sihon with all his men took the field against us at Jahaz.

As with Deut. 1.32-33, the reference to the hardening of Sihon finds a parallel in the Exodus story: just as the LORD had 'hardened' (קשׁה√) Pharaoh so the LORD 'hardened' (קשׁה√) Sihon.[30] There is, moreover, a close resemblance between 'and I will harden Pharaoh's heart' (ואני אקשׁה את־לב פרעה) of Exod. 7.3 and 'because the LORD your God had stiffened his will and hardened his heart' (כי־הקשׁה יהוה אלהיך את־רוחו ואמץ את־לבבו) of Deut. 2.30. Similarly, whereas the LORD had hardened Pharaoh so that he would not free Israel, the LORD hardened Sihon to deliver him over to Israel (Exod. 4.21; Deut. 2.30). It is difficult to know why J would have omitted this Exodus motif. If J had this account in Deuteronomy before him, and if J was responsible for the Exodus story itself, then his omission of the Exodus motif in Num. 21.23 is difficult to explain. A better explanation for the parallel is that Dtr relied on Num. 21.23 for Deut. 2.30-32.[31]

That Dtr relied on the Exodus story is also evident from Deut. 2.24-25:

> (24) Up! Set out across the wadi Arnon! See, I give into your power Sihon the Amorite, king of Heshbon, and his land. Begin the occupation: engage him in battle. (25) This day I begin to put the dread and fear of you upon the peoples everywhere under heaven whenever they hear you mentioned so that they shall tremble and writhe before you.

29. See Scharbert 1992: 83.

30. 'For he hardened' (כי־הקשׁה) occurs only in Exod. 13.15 and Deut. 2.30.

31. This conclusion is also supported from a verbal difference between Num. 21.23 and Deut. 2.30. Whereas in the Numbers account Sihon's refusal is worded as 'Sihon *did not let* [Israel] pass' (לא־נתן סיחן עבר), Deut. 2.30 reads 'and Sihon...*refused* to let us pass through' (ולא אבה סיחן...העברנו). Dtr's account again finds a parallel to the Exodus story: 'and [Pharaoh] *refused* to send them' (ולא אבה לשׁלחם) (Exod. 10.27). If J had this account in Deuteronomy before him, and if J was responsible for Exod. 10.27, then one would expect J's account rather than that of Dtr to be consistent with the Exodus story.

To begin with, there is a parallel between Exod. 15.14 and Deut. 2.25.

Exod. 15.14	*Deut. 2.25*
The peoples hear (שמעו עמים);	The peoples (העמים)...hear (ישמעון)...
they tremble (ירגזון);	so that they tremble (ורגזו)
writhing (חיל) grips the dwellers in Philistia.	and writhe (וחלו) before you.

Moran (1963: 340) noted that the same terminology is used in the same sequence in both passages (these are, moreover, the only two instances of this grouping). Furthermore, the command to cross the Arnon in Deut. 2.24 is reminiscent of the command to cross the Sea of Reeds in Exod. 14.15-16. In terms of the relationship between the Exodus story and Deut. 2.24-25 and 30, I argued above that Dtr based Deut. 1.30-33 on Exod. 13.21 because the verbal parallels are accompanied by two verses that explicitly refer back to the Exodus story. Because Deut. 2.24-25 and 2.30 also share parallels with the Exodus story, it is best to conclude that they too were based on the Exodus account.[32]

To this point I have contended that Dtr relied on the corresponding account in Numbers as well as the Exodus story in his retelling of Israel's encounter with Sihon. What remains to be discussed is the account concerning Og and the summary of Israel's Transjordan adventure in Deut. 3.1-3. Arguing that Dtr based his narratives on Tetrateuchal accounts does not preclude the possibility that Dtr himself may have been responsible for various Tetrateuchal passages. This appears to be the case with the account of the battle with Og in Num. 21.33-35 and the corresponding account in Deut. 3.1-3. That Dtr was responsible for Num. 21.33-35 is evident, first, from its terminology. Apart from Num. 21.33 and Deut. 3.1, the verbs פנה 'to turn' and עלה 'to go up' only occur together in Deut. 1.24. Moreover, Numbers regularly uses the verb נסע 'to set out' (11.35; 20.22; 21.4, 10-13; 22.1) rather than פנה for Israel's travels – apart from Num. 21.33, פנה is only used once for Israel's travels (Num. 17.7). Similarly, Deut. 3.1b (which, apart from person and number, is identical to Num. 21.33) is parallel to Deut. 2.32: 'And Sihon/Og king of Bashan went out to meet us, he and all his people, for war at Jahaz/Edrei'. Again, אל־תירא 'do not fear' of Deut. 3.2 is a favorite of Dtr (Deut. 1.21 [cf. 1.29]; 3.22; Josh. 8.1), as is the pair נתן ביד 'he gave into the hand' with the LORD as the subject (e.g., Deut. 1.27; 2.24, 30; Josh. 2.24). The terminology of Num. 21.33-35 is thus Deuteronomistic.[33] This conclusion does not detract from the view that Dtr patterned Deuteronomy 1–3 after the Tetrateuch, for Dtr himself was responsible for the interpolation.

Dtr's purpose for interpolating Num. 21.33-35 may have been to conform the Tetrateuchal account to his own. Numbers 21.33-35 is the only Tetrateuchal refer-

---

32.   Because Deut. 2.25 uses the second person singular some commentators have argued that it is secondary (e.g., Mayes 1979: 134, 140; Perlitt 1985: 160; cf. Noth 1981: 53–54 n. 4). But the fact that both Deut. 2.24 and 2.25 refer to the Exodus story suggests that they come from the same hand. Moreover, other instances in Deuteronomy 1–3 that refer to Tetrateuchal accounts also use the second person singular (Deut. 1.21; 2.30). See also Begg (1980), who argued that certain changes of number in Deut. 4.1-40 can be explained by a system of quotation.

33.   See also Scharbert 1992: 83.

ence to the conquest of the land north of the Jabbok, and without it the Tetrateuch would be at odds with Dtr's account. For Dtr the conquest commenced not with the crossing of the Jordan but with the crossing of the Arnon. This is implicit in Dtr's concern to have the entire Exodus generation die before the conquest: in Deut. 1.35-38 the LORD swore that, with the exception of Joshua and Caleb, the entire Exodus generation would die prior to seeing the land - and it was only with the fulfillment of this vow in Deut. 2.14-16 that the conquest could begin. What is only implicit in Deut. 1.35-38 and 2.14-16 is made explicit elsewhere. With the crossing of the Arnon the conquest began: 'Up! Set out across the wadi Arnon!… This day I begin to put the dread and fear of you upon the peoples everywhere under heaven' (Deut. 2.24-25); 'See, I begin by placing Sihon and his land at your disposal. Begin the occupation; take possession of his land' (Deut. 2.31).[34] Dtr was evidently compelled to present the conquest as having begun already with the crossing of the Arnon because he needed to provide theological justification for how Israel came to occupy the Transjordan as well as Canaan. Without Num. 21.33-35 there would be no mention of the conquest of the land north of the Jabbok in the Tetrateuch: Numbers 21 refers only to the conquest of Sihon's kingdom, which for Dtr extended from the Arnon to the Jabbok (Judg. 11.13, 22 [cf. Num. 21.24]). By interpolating the account of the conquest of Og's kingdom – which for Dtr extended from the Jabbok to Mount Hermon (as may be adduced from Deut. 3.8) – Dtr filled this lacuna and thereby brought conformity between the Tetrateuchal account and his own.

Numbers 27.12-23 and Deuteronomy 3.21-28

To this point I have limited the analysis to Deuteronomy's prologue. With the account concerning the succession of Joshua and the death of Moses in Deut. 3.21-28, however, it is necessary to discuss the relationship between Num. 27.12-23 and various texts in the epilogue to Deuteronomy – texts that are also concerned with the succession of Joshua and the death of Moses. Numbers 27.12-14 and Deut. 32.48-52 read as follows.

	Num. 27.12-14		*Deut. 32.48-52*
12	ויאמר יהוה אל־משה	48	וידבר יהוה אל־משה
			בעצם היום הזה לאמר
	עלה אל־הר העברים הזה	49	עלה אל־הר העברים הזה הר־נבו
			אשר בארץ מואב
			אשר על־פני ירחו
	וראה את־הארץ		וראה את־הארץ כנען
	אשר נתתי לבני ישראל		אשר אני נתן לבני ישראל לאחזה
13	וראיתה אתה		
		50	ומת בהר
			אשר אתה עלה שמה
	ונאספת אל־עמיך גם־אתה		והאסף אל־עמיך
	כאשר נאסף אהרן אחיך		כאשר־מת אהרן אחיך בהר ההר
			ויאסף אל־עמיו

---

34. See also Deut. 34.1-4 where the promised land includes Gilead (Noth 1981: 54; Weinfeld 1991: 175–78).

14 כאשר מריתם פי
במדבר־צן במריבת העדה
להקדישני במים לעיניהם
הם מי־מריבת קדש במדבר־צן

51 על אשר מעלתם בי בתוך בני ישראל
במי־מריבת קדש במדבר־צן
על אשר לא־קדשתם אותי בתוך בני ישראל

52 כי מנגד תראה את־הארץ
ושמה לא תבוא אל־הארץ
אשר־אני נתן בני ישראל

12 And the LORD said to Moses
'Ascend these heights of
Abarim

and view the land
which I have given to the
children of Israel.

13 And when you have seen it

then you too shall be gathered
to your kin,
just as your brother Aaron was,

14 for you disobeyed my
command –
in the wilderness of Zin,

when the community was
contentious –
to uphold my sanctity in their
sight at the water'.
Those are the waters of
Meribath-kadesh,
in the wilderness of Zin.

48 That very day the LORD spoke to Moses.
49 'Ascend these heights of Abarim to Mount
Nebo, which is in the land of Moab facing
Jericho,
and view the land of Canaan,
which I am giving the children of Israel as a
possession.

50 And die on the mountain that you ascend,
and be gathered to your kin,

as Aaron your brother died on Mount Hor
and was gathered to his kin;
51 for you both broke faith with me among the
Israelites,

at the waters of Meribath-kadesh in the
wilderness of Zin,

by failing to uphold my sanctity among the
Israelites.

52 You may view the land from a distance, but you
shall not enter it – the land that I am giving to
the Israelites'.

The traditional argument is that Deut. 32.48-52 was interpolated by P in order to make a connection between Num. 27.12-14 and Deut. 34.1*, 7-9 – texts that have almost universally been assigned to P or a P redactor. Contrary to this argument, I contend that Dtr was responsible for Deut. 32.48-52 for the following reasons: (1) because the presence of 'P language' in Deut. 32.48-52 is consistent with Dtr's use of such language elsewhere; (2) because Deut. 32.48-52 includes 'D language'; and (3), because Deut. 32.48-52 is integral to Dtr's narrative.

In support of the view that P interpolated Deut. 32.48-52 commentators have noted that in some instances where this passage differs from Num. 27.12-14 one finds language that is characteristic of P. This is true, for instance, of 'as a possession' (לאחזה) in Deut. 32.49 as well as 'Mount Hor' (הר ההר) of Deut. 32.50.[35] It

---

35. אחזה occurs elsewhere in Lev. 14.34; 25.45; Num. 32.5, 22, 29; Josh. 21.12; 22.19. הר ההר occurs elsewhere in Num. 20.22-23, 25, 27; 21.4; 33.37-39, 41; 34.7-8.

does not, however, necessarily follow that P interpolated this passage, for as I noted above Dtr cited many P texts in Deuteronomy 1–3.[36] Although there is no question that the language of passages that have traditionally been attributed to P is markedly homogenous, it has often been the case that one's presuppositions concerning the compositional history of the Tetrateuch govern the way the criterion of P language is used. This is nowhere more apparent than in Deuteronomy. The reigning assumption is 'P is later than D; it therefore follows that where P language exists in D there exists a redaction by P'. Many commentators have quickly employed this assumption by asserting that various texts in Deuteronomy that include P language represent P's attempt to round off the Pentateuch.[37] A glaring inconsistency is the failure to draw the same conclusions with regard to P language in, for instance, the story of the spies in Deut. 1.19-46. This pericope includes three striking verbal parallels with the P layer of the corresponding Tetrateuchal account (Deut. 1.25 and Num. 13.26; Deut. 1.29 and Num. 14.29; Deut. 1.39 and Num. 14.31), and one with Num. 20.1 (= Deut. 1.46) – which is also attributed to P. The fact is, like the dozens of other instances in which Deuteronomy 1–3 shares verbal parallels with the corresponding Tetrateuchal accounts, there is no evidence that such passages were interpolated. Rather, in each instance it is best to regard them as borrowings from the corresponding Tetrateuchal account by Dtr. Along these same lines, the existence of P language at the close of Deuteronomy should not be seen as a redaction by P but Dtr's use of P language.[38] This view is supported by the fact that the phrase 'in the land of Moab' (בארץ מואב) of Deut. 32.49 (which does not occur in Num. 27.12-14) occurs elsewhere in Deuteronomy (Deut. 1.5; 28.69[29.1]; 32.49).[39]

The view that Dtr was responsible for Deut. 32.48-52 is also supported by the fact that this passage is integral to Dtr's narrative, as is evident from the movement between Deut. 31.14 and 32.50, and between 32.49-50 and 34.1, 5.

36.   Throughout this work I use the word 'cite' interchangeably with 'quote'. Such terms simply refer to Dtr's adoption of Tetrateuchal terminology, phrases, clauses or complete sentences – whatever Dtr's purposes may or may not have been. For a helpful discussion of citation terminology (quotation, paraphrases, allusions, reminiscences) see Stanley 1992: 33–37.

37.   See the review of scholarship in Perlitt 1988: 65–68.

38.   See also Schmitt 1995, Perlitt 1988, and Stoellger 1993.

39.   ארץ מואב occurs only in Judg. 11.15, 18 and Jer. 48.24; and מארץ מואב occurs only in Jer. 48.33. Many commentators have also argued that בעצם היום ('on that same day') of Deut. 32.48 should be attributed to P, first, because the phrase occurs elsewhere in P texts (Gen. 7.13; 17.23, 26; Exod. 12.17, 41, 51; Lev. 23.21, 28–30); and second, because P is concerned with chronology. But the force of this argument is undermined both by the fact that the phrase also occurs in Josh. 5.11 and that Dtr was also concerned with chronology (cf. Noth 1981: 34-44). Moreover, although Deut. 32.48 refers to Deut. 1.3 (which gives the date of Moses' speech), there is no reason to attribute Deut. 1.3 to P. Indeed, consistent with Deut. 1.3 Dtr dated the commencement of the construction of the temple from the Exodus in 1 Kgs 6.1. Perlitt (1988: 69–70, 73–74) similarly argued against the view that Deut. 1.3 and Deut. 32.48 come from P or a P redactor.

The LORD to Moses (31.14) ⟶	The LORD to Moses (32.50)
'The days have drawn near for you to die'	'And die on the mountain which you ascend'

The LORD to Moses (32.49-50) ⟶	Moses' action (34.1, 5)
(49) 'Go up (עלה)...	(1) 'And Moses went up (ויעל משה)...
Mount Nebo (הר־נבו)...	Mount Nebo (הר־נבו)...
facing Jericho (על־פני ירחו)...	facing Jericho (על־פני ירחו)...
see the land (ראה את־ארץ)...	and the LORD showed him all the land (ויראהו יהוה את־כל־הארץ)...
(50) And die (ומת)'.	(5) and he died (וימת)...at the command of the LORD'.

Deut. 31.14 is the first explicit reference to the imminent death of Moses (it is anticipated in Deut. 1.37 and 3.27). But it is only with Deut. 32.50 that one learns that Moses would die on the mountain, which happened, in turn, in Deut. 34.5. More striking is the relationship between Deut. 32.49-50 and 34.1, 5. In addition to the verbal correspondence between these distant pericopes, the three divine commands in Deut. 32.49-50 are fulfilled in the same sequence in 34.1, 5. Moreover, the fact that Moses' death came 'at the command of the LORD' (Deut. 34.5) also shows that the narrator had Deut. 32.50 in mind, for this is the only place where the LORD uttered such a command. Such features suggest that Deut. 34.1, 5 was based on 32.49-50.[40]

All that remains to be shown is that Dtr rather than P was responsible for the given elements of Deut. 34.1, 5. The traditional view is that P interpolated 'Mount Nebo' of 34.1.[41] Because this name only occurs in Deut. 32.49 and 34.1, it should not be simply assumed that it is from P.[42] As for Deut. 34.5, many commentators

---

40. Note also the association between Deut. 32.52 and 34.4.

Deut. 32.52	Deut. 34.4
'For you shall see (תראה) the land...	'I will give it (אתננה) to your descendants;
but you shall not enter there (ושמה),	I have let you see (הראיתיך) with your eyes,
into the land which I am giving (נתן) the sons	but you shall not cross there (ושמה)'.
of Israel'.	

That Deut. 34.4 is Deuteronomistic is plausible from the reference to the oath to the Patriarchs in the first half of the verse (cf. Deut. 1.35; Josh. 1.6; Judg. 2.1), and from the similarity between the second half of Deut. 34.4 ('I have let you see [the land] with your eyes, but to there you will not cross') and Deut. 3.27 ('your eyes will see [the land], but you will not cross').

41. Commentators have also argued that P likewise interpolated 'from the Plains of Moab' (34.1) because 'Plains of Moab' occurs elsewhere only in P texts (Num. 22.1; 26.3, 63; 31.12; 33.48-50; 35.1; 36.13; Josh. 13.32) (see the review of scholarship in Perlitt 1988: 65–68). But this only begs the question, for if Dtr relied on P texts and language elsewhere he may have done so here as well.

42. There is no contradiction between Deut. 3.27, where the LORD instructed Moses to go up Pisgah where he would view the land, and Deut. 34.1, which includes a reference to Mount Nebo. Deuteronomy 34.1 consists of Moses' itinerary: he traveled west from the steppes of Moab to Mount Nebo, and northwest from Mount Nebo to the summit of Pisgah (see Grohman 1962: 529).

have attributed 'according to the command of the LORD' (עַל־פִּי יהוה) to P.[43] But there is little to support this conclusion. This phrase appears elsewhere in the DtrH,[44] as does 'command of the LORD' (פִּי יהוה).[45] These facts undermine any dogmatic attribution to P. That Deut. 34.5 is Deuteronomistic is evident, first, from 'and Moses the servant of the LORD died there' (וַיָּמָת שָׁם מֹשֶׁה עֶבֶד־יהוה). This is parallel to Judg. 2.8, 'and Joshua the son of Nun, the servant of the LORD, died' (וַיָּמָת יְהוֹשֻׁעַ בִּן־נוּן עֶבֶד יהוה). Apart from 2 Chron. 1.3 and 24.6, moreover, the title עֶבֶד־יהוה occurs elsewhere only in the DtrH.[46] There are therefore good reasons to attribute the given elements in Deut. 34.1, 5 to Dtr and to conclude that Deut. 32.48-52 is integral to Dtr's narrative. Contrary to the view that P interpolated Deut. 32.48-52 in order to bring cohesion to the Pentateuch, then, the best explanation is that Dtr was responsible for this passage.

This brings me to the relationship between Tetrateuchal accounts and Deut. 3.21-28, which also concerns the succession of Joshua and the death of Moses. The first point to be made is that Dtr based Deut. 3.24-25 on various texts from Exodus 14–15.[47] Deut. 3.24a is parallel to Exod. 14.31.

Exod. 14.31	*Deut. 3.24a*
And Israel saw (וַיַּרְא) the great hand (הַיָּד הַגְּדֹלָה) which the LORD did (עָשָׂה) among the Egyptians.	You have begun to show (לְהַרְאוֹת) your servant your greatness (גָּדְלְךָ) and your strong hand (יָדְךָ הַחֲזָקָה)…who can do (יַעֲשֶׂה) works like your own?

Deut. 3.24b is similarly reminiscent of Exod. 15.11:

Exod. 15.11	*Deut. 3.24b*
Who is like you, O LORD, among the gods …doing wonders?	What god is there who can do such works …as yours?

But most pronounced is the parallel between Exod. 15.16-17 and Deut. 3.24a, 25:

Exod. 15.16-17	*Deut. 3.24a, 25*
(16) Terror and dread fell upon them; through the majesty (בִּגְדֹל) of your arm they are still as stone; till your people cross over (יַעֲבֹר), O LORD, till this people cross over (יַעֲבֹר) whom you have ransomed. (17) You will bring them and plant them in your own mountain (הַר).	(24a) You have begun to show your servant the works of your majesty (גָּדְלְךָ) and your mighty hand… (25) Let me, I pray, cross over (אֶעְבְּרָה), and see the good land on the other side of the Jordan, this good mountain (הַר), and the Lebanon.

---

43. E.g., Driver 1916: 423. The phrase occurs in the following P texts: Exod. 17.1; Lev. 24.12; Num. 3.16, 39, 51; 4.37, 41, 45, 49; 9.18, 20, 23; 10.13; 13.3; 33.2, 38; 36.5.

44. Josh. 19.50; 22.9; 2 Kgs 24.3; cf. Josh. 21.3 which reads אֶל־פִּי יהוה.

45. As the object of מָרָה ('to rebel [against]'): Deut. 1.26, 43; 9.23; 1 Sam. 12.14-15; 1 Kgs 13.21 (Stoellger 1993: 32 n. 33).

46. Josh. 1.1, 13; 8.31, 33; 11.12; 12.6; 13.8; 14.7; 18.7; 22.2, 4-5; 24.29; Judg. 2.8; 2 Kgs 18.12.

47. See also Moran 1963: 341.

Given the fact that Dtr based Deut. 2.30b-31 on the Exodus story, and that he used the language of the Exodus story in Deut. 1.30 with reference to the conquest, it is best to conclude that he also based Deut. 3.24-25 on Exod. 14.31; 15.11, 16-17.

That Dtr based Deut. 3.21-28 on Tetrateuchal accounts is also evident from Deut. 3.25-27 where one reads that Moses would not enter the land because the LORD was angry with him on account of the Israelites. Concerning the LORD's anger, some have argued that although Moses did not follow the counsel of the unbelieving spies the LORD nevertheless implicated Moses in their sin as he was the leader.[48] More likely is the view that Deut. 3.26 is a reference to the LORD's anger with Moses for his transgression at the waters of Meribath–kadesh (Num. 20.22-29). In support of this view is the fact that Deut. 32.48-52 teaches that Moses would not enter the land because of his sin at the waters of Meribath-kadesh. Moreover, Deut. 1.37, which gives the same explanation as Deut. 3.25-27 concerning the LORD's anger at Moses, is followed in Deut. 1.38 by the LORD's statement that Joshua would enter the land. Significantly, these are the two subjects that are outlined in Num. 27.12-23; and since Dtr used Num. 27.12-14 for Deut. 32.48-52 it follows that the best explanation for both Deut. 1.37-38 and 3.25-27 is that they were similarly based on Num. 27.12–23.[49]

Analysis of the Remaining Accounts

To this point I have limited the analysis to the relationship between those narratives in Deuteronomy that closely correspond to narratives in the Tetrateuch. What remains to be discussed are the remaining portions of Deuteronomy 1–3, namely, Deut. 2.1-23 and 3.12-20. Deuteronomy 2.1-23 shares two verbal parallels with accounts in Numbers, and Deut. 3.4-20 shares three verbal parallels with Numbers 32.

---

48. E.g., Driver 1916: 26–27, Mayes 1979: 147.

49. That Dtr was aware of Num. 27.12-23 is also evident from Deut. 34.9. There is universal agreement that Deut. 34.9 refers to Num. 27.18, the only other text that concerns Moses' commissioning of Joshua by laying his hand(s) on him (e.g., Driver 1916: 424; Mayes 1979: 413; von Rad 1966: 210). Contrary to most commentators, however, the evidence suggests that Dtr rather than P was responsible for this verse. This is evident from the differences between Num. 27.18 and Deut. 34.9. To begin with, whereas Num. 27.18 states that Joshua was a man 'in whom was the spirit' (אשר־רוח בו), Deut. 34.9 states that Joshua 'was filled with the spirit of wisdom' (מלא רוח חכמה). As I noted above, Dtr reformulated Exod. 18.21 in Deut. 1.15 in order to emphasize the role of wisdom among Israel's leaders. Moreover, whereas in Num. 27.18 the LORD commanded Moses 'lay your hand on him' (וסמכת את־ידך עליו), Deut. 34.9 states that Joshua had the spirit of wisdom 'because Moses laid his hands on him' (כי־סמך משה את־ידיו עליו), which is consistent with Dtr's concern to present Moses positively. The fact, then, that the differences between Num. 27.18 and Deut. 34.9 are consistent with Dtr's reformulations of Tetrateuchal accounts in Deuteronomy 1–3 suggests that Dtr rather than P was responsible for Deut. 34.9 (after reviewing a century of literature, Perlitt [1988: 80] could similarly state that it was especially annoying that commentators avoided the problems of attributing Deut. 34.9 to P; see also Weinfeld 1972: 181 n. 3).

Num. 21.4

דרך ים־סוף לסבב את־ארץ אדום

the way of the Sea of Reeds to go around the land of Edom

Deut. 2.1

דרך ים־סוף...ונסב את־הר־שעיר

the way of the Sea of Reeds...and we went around the hill country of Seir

Num. 32.13

עד־תם כל־הדור

until the entire generation

Deut. 2.14

עד־תם כל־הדור

until the entire generation

Num. 32.41

יאיר בן־מנשה הלך וילכד את־חותיהם ויקרא אתהן חות יאיר

Jair son of Manasseh went and captured their villages and he named them Havvoth-jair.

Deut. 3.14

יאיר בן־מנשה לקח את־כל־חבל ארגב...
ויקרא אתם על־שמו את־הבשן חות יאיר

Jair son of Manasseh took the whole district of Argob...and he named them after his name, Havvoth-jair.

Num. 32.21

ועבר לכם כל־חלוץ

and all of your armed men cross

Deut. 3.18

חלוצים תעברו

you cross as armed men

Num. 32.26

טפנו נשינו מקננו וכל־בהמתנו יהיו־שם בערי הגלעד

Our children, our wives, our flocks, and all our livestock will be there in the cities of Gilead

Deut. 3.19

רק נשיכם וטפכם ומקנכם...ישבו בעריכם

Only your wives and your children and your flocks...will remain in your cities

In support of the proposed direction of dependence, one can explain the differences between the given texts on the basis of Dtr's concern with the land. Von Rad (1966: 39) asserted that Deuteronomy 1–3 was based not on the given Tetrateuchal accounts but on 'an account not preserved for us, which gave a considerably shorter description of the events between Horeb and the arrival in the country east of Jordan'. But the fact that Deuteronomy 1–3 is much shorter than its counterpart in Numbers only points to Dtr's selectivity. McKenzie (1967: 96) rightly contended that '[o]ne theme, and one theme only, runs through all these passages: the theme that Yahweh is giving Israel the land which he promised to the fathers'. This theme introduces the events in Deuteronomy 1–3: 'See, I place the land at your disposal. Go, enter the land that the LORD swore to your fathers, Abraham, Isaac, and Jacob, to assign to them and to their offspring after them' (Deut. 1.8). The appointment of officials in Deut. 1.9-18, which was a response to the population surge, is also akin to the land theme. The command of Deut. 1.8 is repeated at the beginning of the story of the spies in Deut. 1.19-46, which is itself concerned with the conquest of the land. Moreover, McKenzie (1967: 96) rightly noted that the people were not permitted to take the lands of Edom, Moab, or Ammon because the LORD had allocated these lands to their present inhabitants (Deut. 2.5, 9), even as he had given the land of the Amorites to Israel (Deut. 2.24; 3.2). Finally, Moses himself would not enter the good land (Deut. 3.23-28). On the traditional supposition that Dtr had only the non-P texts of Numbers 11–32 before him, Dtr omitted the following accounts that do not concern the land: the rebellion of Miriam and Aaron in Num. 12.1-16; the rebellions of Korah, Dathan and Abiram in Numbers 16; the bronze serpent in Num. 21.4-9; Balak and Balaam in Numbers 22–24; and apostasy in Moab in Num. 25.1-5.[50] Two further accounts that are not paralleled in Deuteronomy 1–3 must also be explained. Dtr did not include the defeat of Arad the Canaanite king in Num. 21.1-3 because that account is inconsistent with the commencement of the conquest after the death of the Exodus generation (Deut. 1.34-36; 2.14-16). Similarly, Dtr did not include the itinerary of the wilderness wanderings in Num. 21.10-20 because for him the only wilderness wandering traditions of import took place at Kadesh (Deut. 1.19–46) – for it was from Kadesh that the people refused to take the land.[51]

This brings me to Deut. 2.1-23 and 3.4-20. One may again explain the differences between these accounts and their Tetrateuchal counterparts on the basis of Dtr's concern with the land. With regard to Deut. 2.1-23, whereas Num. 20.14-21 has Israel requesting permission from the Edomites to enter their land (Num. 20.14-17), in Deuteronomy the LORD instructed Israel to pass through Edom (Deut. 2.3-4). Again, whereas in Numbers Edom came out against Israel and Israel turned away (Num. 20.20-21), in Deuteronomy the Edomites were afraid of Israel (Deut. 2.4). Similarly, whereas in Num. 21.13-20 Israel's Transjordan itinerary is outlined, in Deut. 2.9-23 Israel's encounter with Moab and Ammon is similar to the previously discussed encounter with Edom. All of these differences can be explained as the result of Dtr's understanding of the conquest. For Dtr, nations possessed their lands only because the LORD had allotted given tracts of land to such nations. This was true of Edom (Deut. 2.5), Moab (Deut. 2.9), and Ammon (Deut. 2.19). This was equally true for Israel: just as the Edomites dispossessed the Horites because the LORD willed them to do so (Deut. 2.9, 12), so Israel later dispossessed the Canaanites in accordance with the will of the LORD (Deut. 2.12). Because these lands had been allotted to Edom, Moab and Ammon, it followed for Dtr that Israel was prohibited from engaging them in battle.

The differences between Deut. 3.4-20 and Numbers 32 – passages that concern the apportioning of the Transjordan to the two and a half tribes – can also be explained on the basis of Dtr's view of the conquest. Whereas in Numbers Moses castigated these tribes for requesting to stay in the Transjordan, the account in Deuteronomy does not mention this conflict and it explicitly states that the LORD had given them the land. As I argued above, for Dtr the conquest commenced not with the crossing of the Jordan, but with the crossing of the Arnon. Because the Transjordan was a part of the promised land, Dtr had no place for a tradition that had Moses chastising the two and a half tribes for wishing to occupy the Transjordan.

---

50. That Dtr was nevertheless familiar with such accounts is evident from the fact that Deuteronomy and the DtrH explicitly refer to them elsewhere: Miriam (Deut. 24.9); Dathan and Abiram (Deut. 11.6); the bronze serpent (2 Kgs 18.4); Balaam (Deut. 23.4-6; Josh. 13.22; 24.9-10). The lone exception is the apostasy in Moab, but, as I will show, Dtr used this account in his depictions of the spies sent to Jericho (Joshua 2) and Eli's sons (1 Samuel 2).

51. The wilderness wanderings are only referred to in Deut. 1.19 and 2.1.

Conclusions

A perennial difficulty in Deuteronomistic studies is distinguishing between Dtr and his sources. Noth (1981: 128-33), for instance, argued that for the most part Dtr left his sources intact. According to Noth (1981: 128), Dtr 'spoke in his own person only at certain exceptional points, letting the old traditions speak for themselves instead. He did so even when these old traditions told of events that did not fit in with his central ideas'. In his analysis of Deuteronomy 1–3, however, Noth (1981: 46) concluded that although Dtr based much of these chapters on the given JE accounts he freely adapted his sources: Dtr 'at all times related the incidents which he select[ed] from his own point of view and thus somewhat independently of his source or sources'. More specifically, although Noth (1981: 49) argued that Deut. 1.9-18 was taken from Exod. 18.13-27 and Num. 11.10-25, he could conclude that Dtr 'expresse[d] them in his own way' and rearranged them. With regard to the account of the spies in Deut. 1.19-46, Noth (1981: 50) similarly argued that Dtr 'put this whole section in his own words and is responsible for the nuances of the story'. As for the Transjordan expedition in Deut. 2.1-25, Noth (1981: 53) concluded that Dtr's departure from the account concerning Edom in Num. 20.14-21 was the result of his revisionist historiography: '[i]t is obviously better to connect [the divine prohibition concerning warfare against Edom] with Dtr's tendency towards a systematic theological interpretation of history such as one can clearly see in Deuteronomy 2 and 3'; similarly, it was Dtr's contention that Edom was not part of the promised land 'that lies behind Dtr's deviation from Num. 20.14-21'. Noth's conclusions regarding Dtr's use of the JE traditions in Deuteronomy 1–3 thus stand in marked contrast to his conclusions regarding Dtr's general procedure through the rest of the DtrH. Given Dtr's free use of his Tetrateuchal sources in Deuteronomy 1–3, the operating assumption must not be that Dtr tended to leave his sources untouched.[52]

This conclusion is substantiated by the nature of the literary parallels shared by Tetrateuchal accounts and Deuteronomy 1–3. The literary parallels are infrequently verbatim and extensive. The lone exception to this is the nearly equivalent Num. 21.33-35 and Deut. 3.1-3, which, as I argued above, likely marks Dtr's attempt to harmonize his understanding of the conquest of the Transjordan with that of the Tetrateuch. The remaining verbal parallels show that in those instances where Dtr cited synoptic Tetrateuchal accounts he was not constrained to follow them to the letter. There is, moreover, nothing to suggest that in every departure from the given Tetrateuchal accounts Dtr was trying to conform them to his particular ideology or bias. Rather, Dtr's citations were simply the product of his impressive, yet fallible memory. Consistent with this observation is the fact that the verbal parallels do not typically appear in the same order as in their Tetrateuchal counterparts, as a perusal of the literay parallels shows.

Related to how Dtr used his sources is the criterion of Deuteronomistic language, which is appealed to for identifying Dtr's work. Noth (1981: 18) stated:

---

52. See also Brettler 1995: 77.

> The linguistic evidence remains the most reliable basis for attributing parts of the various traditions to Dtr... The limited variety of expression has led to frequent repetition of the same simple phrases and sentence constructions, in which the 'Deuteronomistic' style is easily recognized. The characteristics of this style, its vocabulary, diction and sentence structure, are, therefore, undisputed; we need not consider them in detail.

The fact that Noth rarely used this criterion makes this statement curious. In his thorough analysis of Noth's argument from Deuteronomistic language, Talstra (1993: 24, 25–31) noted that in every instance that Noth appealed to this argument in Deuteronomy he was referring to putative interpolations in Dtr's work; and that this argument is rarely used elsewhere in Noth's work. Talstra (1993: 25, 32) rightly concluded that '[t]he characterization "sicherste Grundlage" [most reliable] seems a somewhat bold assertion' and that this argument 'does not have the decisive importance which Noth awards to it at the beginning of his study'. If Noth can be criticized for failing to use the ostensibly compelling criterion of Deuteronomistic language, much of subsequent scholarship can be criticized for similarly failing to address the limitations of this criterion. Such limitations are evident from the lack of agreement among scholars concerning Deuteronom(ist)ic language in the Tetrateuch. Although there is some measure of agreement over the identification of texts in the Tetrateuch that include Deuteronom(ist)ic language, to date there is no consensus concerning the nature and extent of such language. A distinction cannot be made between proto-Deuteronom(ist)ic and Deuteronom(ist)ic language, or between Deuteronom(ist)ic and post-Deuteronom(ist)ic language. There is, similarly, nothing approaching a consensus over the extent of Deuteronom(ist)ic language in the DtrH itself.[53] Can a distinction be made between the language used by Dtr^1, Dtr^2, DtrG, DtrP, DtrN, or other putative redactions? Is it possible to distinguish between the language of such redactions and the sources that were redacted? Again, judging from the diversity of opinion at present the answer to such questions is 'No'; and the criterion therefore has limited value.[54] This contention is readily supported by the above analysis of Deuteronomy 1–3. If the Tetrateuchal accounts were not extant it would be impossible to identify Dtr's source material, for in the dozens of instances that Dtr cited the Tetrateuch he did so without creating disjunctions.[55] Another limitation of the criterion of Deuteronom(ist)ic language is that context determines the selection of words.[56] Weinfeld (1972: 3) listed more than 200 lexical items that recur in the

---

53.   See Talstra 1993: 53–68; Vervenne 1994; and Ausloos 1997.

54.   See the survey of scholarship by Talstra (1993: 68–78), the remarks of McKenzie (1994b: 299, 301–302), and the essays in Schearing and McKenzie (1999).

55.   This is equally true of the 20 times that the Deuteronomist(s) cited the Tetrateuch in Deuteronomy 9–10 (Exod. 24.12 = Deut. 9.9; Exod. 24.18 = Deut. 9.9; Exod. 34.28 = Deut. 9.9; Exod. 31.18 = Deut. 9.10; Exod. 32.7-8 = Deut. 9.12; Exod. 32.9 = Deut. 9.13; Exod. 32.10 = Deut. 9.14; Exod. 32.15 = Deut. 9.15; Exod. 32.19 = Deut. 9.17; Exod. 34.28 = Deut. 9.18; Exod. 32.20 = Deut. 9.21; Exod. 32.11 = Deut. 9.26; Exod. 32.13 = Deut. 9.27; Num. 14.16 = Deut. 9.28; Exod. 32.11 = Deut. 9.29; Exod. 34.1 = Deut. 10.1a; Exod. 34.2 = Deut. 10.1b; Exod. 34.1 = Deut. 10.2; Exod. 34.4 = Deut. 10.3; Exod. 34.28 = Deut. 10.4 (references compiled by Driver [1916: 112]).

56.   See Halpern 1988: 194–96.

DtrH, yet he could state that '[o]nly those recurrent phrases that express the essence of the theology of Deuteronomy can be considered "deuteronomic"'. But surely it is reductionistic to suppose that every Deuteronomistic text must express 'the theology' of Dtr. Contending that those narratives that do not use Deuteronomistic language cannot be Deuteronomistic amounts only to a *non sequitur*, for they may simply pertain to matters that are not expressly theological. The contention that context determines the selection of words is nowhere more evident than in Deuteronomy 1–3, for although these chapters are rightly attributed to Dtr, they contain a paucity of so-called Deuteronomistic language. Only thirteen examples from Weinfeld's impressive list are present in Deuteronomy 1–3,[57] and four of these examples cannot be regarded as uniquely Deuteronomistic: one of the examples includes the phrase 'he followed the LORD fully' (מלא אחרי יהוה) in Deut. 1.36, which also occurs in Num. 32.12 and is one of Dtr's many citations of the Tetrateuch in Deuteronomy 1–3; three of the thirteen examples occur outside the DtrH;[58] and only the remaining nine examples consist of lexical data that are unique to the DtrH.[59] Other uniquely Deuteronomistic terms were not used by Dtr in Deuteronomy 1–3 simply because it was not amenable to the context.[60] The fact, then, that there is no concensus concerning the nature and extent of Deuteronom(ist)ic language, and that context determines word selection, lessens the force of the criterion of Deuteronomistic language. This is not to say that the criterion is without value, only that it rarely furnishes definitive conclusions.

More fruitful than tracing Deuteronomistic language is identifying Tetrateuchal language in Deuteronomy 1–3. Dtr had absorbed the lexica of Dtr's Tetrateuch, such that in his recounting of Tetrateuchal accounts he was given to using a host of their terms and phrases. There was, moreover, little deliberation on Dtr's part in using Tetrateuchal language. Dtr did not need to look at a scroll to borrow its language, for the language of his Torah was deeply embedded in his mind. This is evident from the random and seemingly arbitrary nature of the verbal parallels. Rather than only being limited to central terms and expressions, Dtr was wont to use many incidental linguistic features of the given Tetrateuchal accounts – even with little regard for the sequence in which such features appear.

The conclusions that I arrived at in this chapter set the stage for the subsequent chapters. I concluded that in every instance where Deuteronomy 1–3 corresponds to an account in the Tetrateuch the Tetrateuchal account is primary. This conclusion is in line with my contention that Dtr was responsible for drawing the parallels shared by narratives in the Tetrateuch and his history. I also concluded that Dtr freely adapted the given Tetrateuchal accounts in accordance with his concerns, as is evident from his high view of Moses, his emphasis on wisdom, his use of the Exodus story, and his concerns with the conquest and the land. The fact that each of these concerns are also present in the given narratives in the Former Prophets

---

57.   The thirteen examples come in the following sections of Weinfeld's list: III 16; V 19; VI 4, 8, 10–13, 15–16, 16a; VII 2a, 9; VIII 4.

58.   VI 11, 13; VIII 4.

59.   III 16; VI 8, 10, 12, 15, 16, 16a; VII 2a, 9.

60.   Eslinger (1989: 123 n. 1) made a similar argument concerning Solomon's prayer in 1 Kings 8.

supports my contention that Dtr rather than his sources was responsible for the given parallels. Dtr's use of the Tetrateuch in Deuteronomy 1–3 is thus the Archimedean point by which the nature of the parallels in the Former Prophets can be determined: because there is a marked consistency between Dtr's use of the Tetrateuch in Deuteronomy 1–3 and in the Former Prophets, Dtr rather than his sources should be regarded as the creator of the parallel features between narratives in the Former Prophets and the Tetrateuch. Finally, the free and creative manner in which Dtr used Tetrateuchal accounts shows that such accounts had a formative role to play in his understanding of history and life.[61] Indeed, they were Torah.

61. The contention that Dtr could not have manipulated Tetrateuchal traditions if he regarded them as Torah is anachronistic. Even while biblical writers adapted antecedent accounts to fit their needs, they held them in the highest regard. Fishbane (1980: 361) rightly argued:

> an exegetical consciousness is, simultaneously, a constructive and deconstructive consciousness; for it both asserts and denies the authority of the text in question. The very cognition of the insufficiency of a textual authority – i.e., its lack, failure, or irrelevance to a present moment – is profoundly and dialectically bound up with a reassertion of its sufficiency, insofar as the revision is not presented as self-validating but rather finds its authority in the text-unit which elicited the exegetical response in the first place.

See also Levinson (1997: esp. 46). Bloch (1978: 34–35) was similarly on the mark with her contention that 'midrash' exists within the Bible itself.

Chapter 2

THE GENESIS OF THE PARALLEL NARRATIVES

I concluded in Chapter 1 that Dtr's Torah had a formative influence on his histori-ography. In this chapter I briefly discuss the Deuteronomic antecedents to Dtr's use of his Torah. I then argue that the parallel narratives are the product of literary dependence rather than oral convention; and I outline eight criteria for determining the direction of dependence between the parallel narratives.

An inevitable consequence of a national catastrophe is the transformation of a society's story. Tales are spun, myths created, and revisions made to earlier tradi-tions – all to make a society's story plausible in the face of woe. Coupled with the introduction of a new story is the adaptation or even repudiation of older stories.[1] The acceptance and rejection of stories are not typically coterminous actions, nor are the stories that vie for attention always mutually exclusive. Stories wax and wane in popularity and influence, and they converge and adapt as they compete for greater acceptance.[2] Judah's story took center stage with the collapse of 587 BCE and the loss of land, king and temple. This catastrophe engendered an intellectual revolution in Judah, and Judean crisis literature was born.[3] Some exilic voices rein-terpreted or repudiated the stories of old involving the inviolability of Zion, Judah's possession of the land, or the presence of God in the temple. Other exilic voices regrouped to find direction in the nation's sacred traditions.

Common to those exilic communities that espoused the views of the Deuterono-mists was a high regard for the nation's sacred traditions. The Deuteronomists recalled such traditions not simply for antiquarian reasons but because they had binding power for the present. The Exodus, for instance, was a stimulus for ethical behavior: the people were to ensure that those under them did not work on the sabbath, for they themselves had been delivered from servitude in Egypt (Deut. 5.12-15); they were to release their servants with generosity every seventh year, for the people themselves were redeemed from Egypt (Deut. 15.12-15); and they were to care for the poor as they were also poor in Egypt (Deut. 24.17-18, 20-22). In recall-ing the Exodus the Deuteronomists were not simply bringing to mind a great act of

1.   MacIntyre (1989: 140) rightly argued that '[w]hen an epistemological crisis is resolved, it is by the construction of a new narrative which enables the agent to understand *both* how he or she could intelligibly have held his or her original beliefs *and* how he or she could have been so drastically misled by them'.
2.   See McConnell 1986.
3.   See Römer 1997.

past redemption. They believed that the Exodus was a story that any oppressed generation might experience anew:

> You have but to bear in mind what the LORD your God did to Pharaoh and all the Egyptians: the wondrous acts that you saw with your own eyes, the signs and the portents, the mighty hand, and the outstretched arm by which the LORD your God liberated you. *Thus will the LORD your God do to all the peoples you now fear* (Deut. 7.18-19).

Given the ubiquity of the Exodus motif in the Hebrew Bible, the above examples should occasion no surprise. But what strikes the reader is the frequent use of seemingly marginal traditions, which the Deuteronomists nevertheless often used as motivations for obedience: the people were to recall how the LORD destroyed those who followed Baal-peor (Deut. 4.3-4); they were not to try the LORD as they had done at Massah (Deut. 6.16; cf. 9.22); they were to remember the manna episode (Deut. 8.2-3) as well as that of Dathan and Abiram (Deut. 11.6); they were to remember how the LORD struck Miriam (Deut. 24.9), and how Amalek mistreated them on their journey (Deut. 25.17-18).[4] Although less predominant than the place given to the Exodus story, these traditions were nevertheless integral to the Deuteronomists' consciousness.

Deuteronomy's existential appeal is consistent with this interpretation. Von Rad (1962: 231) astutely observed that Deuteronomy 'wipes out some seven centuries squandered in disobedience, and places Israel once again in the wilderness, with Moses speaking to her'.[5] 'It was not', Moses said, 'with our fathers that the LORD made this covenant, but with us, the living, every one of us who is here today' (Deut. 5.3). Nor was it with the new generation's children who experienced the marvellous deeds of the LORD in Egypt and the wilderness, but the new generation itself (Deut. 11.2-7). Every generation was to situate itself in Egypt, Horeb and the wilderness. 'I made this covenant', the LORD said, 'with its sanctions, not with you alone, but both with those who are standing here with us this day before the LORD our God and with those who are not with us here this day' (Deut. 29.13[14]-14[15]). Consonant with these existential appeals is the emphasis on the offspring of the Exodus generation. The children experienced both the oppression and deliverance from Egypt[6] and the revelation at Horeb;[7] the children worshiped the calf,[8] and refused to enter the promised land;[9] Moses charged the children to possess the Transjordan;[10] and the children witnessed and experienced the rebellions in the wilderness.[11] Rather

---

4.   See Doron 1978: 61–77 and Sonsino 1980.
5.   Peckham (1999: 304) similarly stated that in Deuteronomy 'the past and the present are contemporary and integral'.
6.   Deut. 4.35, 37; 6.12; 7.8, 18; 8.14; 15.15; 16.1, 3, 12; 23.8[7]; 24.9, 18; 25.17-18; 26.6-8; 29.1.
7.   Deut. 4.9-12, 33; 5.3, 23–27.
8.   Deut. 9.21.
9.   Deut. 1.26-27.
10.   Deut. 3.18.
11.   Deut. 4.3; 6.16; 8.2-4, 15-16; 9.7; 29.4[5]-5[6].

than being punctiliar episodes bound to the past, for the Deuteronomists the sacred traditions were ontologically wed to the ongoing experience of Israel.[12]

Not later than the seventh century many such sacred traditions had been coalesced to form a nascent Tetrateuch. This Tetrateuch in turn became the locus of Dtr's historiography. The existence of a Tetrateuch in Dtr's time is suggested in part by the fact that parallel narratives in the DtrH share features with two or more redactional layers of composite accounts in the Tetrateuch. That is to say, when an account in the DtrH shares parallels with two or more redactional layers of the corresponding Tetrateuchal account, it is reasonable to conclude that redaction of the Tetrateuch occurred before the composition of the DtrH. The existence of a Tetrateuch in Dtr's time is also suggested by his particular use of Israel's traditions. Dtr conflated stories, cited synoptic accounts with little regard for chronological sequence, and everywhere assumed knowledge of essential storylines. This is apparent, for instance, from his free use of the Exodus story in Deuteronomy 1–3: Dtr alluded to the Exodus story in Moses' reproof to the wilderness generation for failing to enter the promised land (Deut. 1.30, 32-33); using language from the Song of the Sea, Dtr had the LORD assure Moses that the peoples would fear encroaching on Israel (Deut. 2.25), and he had Moses praise the LORD for his deeds (Deut. 3.24-25); finally, Dtr patterned the stubbornness of Sihon after that of Pharaoh (Deut. 2.30). As I will show, this creative use of the Exodus story similarly pervades the Former Prophets: Dtr contrasted many national deliverers with Moses; foreign kings who threatened Israel were Pharaoh *redivivus*; and divine deliverances were but types of the Exodus. Such creative and divergent uses of Tetrateuchal stories were the product of Dtr's intimate knowledge of them. Tetrateuchal stories formed the bedrock of Dtr's consciousness, and they initiated those mnemonic processes that guided his historiography. For Dtr, Tetrateuchal stories were Torah.

More generally, Dtr's use of his Torah as a repository of schemata is to be understood in relation to his paradigmatic historiography. One sees, for instance, the paradigmatic nature of various episodes in Deuterononomy 1–3: the LORD would fight for Israel 'just as' he had done for them against Egypt (Deut. 1.30); the descendants of Esau dispossessed the Horites 'just as' Israel had done to the inhabitants of Canaan (Deut. 2.12); the LORD obliterated the Rephaim 'just as' he had done for the descendants of Esau when he destroyed the Horites (Deut. 2.20-22); 'just as' Moses purchased food and water from the descendants of Esau and the Moabites, so he urged Sihon of Heshbon to provide him with food and water (Deut. 2.28-29); the LORD assured Moses that he would overcome Sihon 'just as' he had defeated Og (Deut. 3.2); Israel destroyed Sihon 'just as' they had destroyed Og (Deut. 3.6); and 'just as' the LORD defeated Sihon and Og, so he would defeat the kings of the Cisjordan (Deut. 3.21). One also sees Dtr's paradigmatic historiography at work at a macro-level. This is true of the recurring five-fold sequence of events in Judges:

---

12.   In his analysis of זכר ('to remember') Childs (1962) drew similar conclusions regarding the Deuteronomists' reliving of traditions. 'To remember', Childs (1962: 74) stated, 'was to actualize the past, to bridge the gap of time and to form a solidarity with the fathers'. 'Actualization', in turn, was 'the process by which a past event is contemporized for a generation removed in time and space from the original event' (1962: 85). Cf. Hyatt 1970: 169.

the Israelites did evil before the LORD (2.11; 3.7, 12; 4.1; 6.1; 13.1); such evil led to the anger of the LORD and the consequent deliverance into the hands of foreign oppressors (2.14; 3.8; 4.2; 10.9); the Israelites then cried out to the LORD (3.9, 15; 6.6-7; 10.10); the LORD heard their cries and raised up a deliverer (2.16; 3.9, 15; 10.1, 12); and a period of peace ensued (3.11, 30; 8.28).[13] A similar paradigm concerns Jeroboam's contravention of the Deuteronomic law of centralized worship and its consequences. Dtr sentenced all of the kings of Israel simply because they 'walked in the way of Jeroboam son of Nebat'.[14] Dtr's use of Torah as a source of schemata was thus consonant with his paradigmatic historiography.

A common explanation for the parallel narratives is that they are the product of convention. This explanation does not, however, explain peculiar similarities within the parallel narratives – for convention lends itself to general patterns rather than the recurrence of particular lexemes that have little to do with narrative structure. Consider, for example, the parallels shared by Abram's battle against the Mesopotamian kings in Genesis 14 and Joshua's defeat of Canaanite kings in Joshua 10.[15] In both accounts a coalition of kings united against a rebellion (Gen. 14.1-9; Josh. 10.3-4). Following the rebellion there was a capture or impending threat: the Mesopotamian kings captured Lot, and the Canaanite kings were poised to defeat the Gibeonites (Gen. 14.10-12; Josh. 10.5). The hero of the story (Abram, Joshua) then heard of the crisis, pursued, and defeated the coalition (Gen. 14.13-16; Josh. 10.6-39). Theoretically, the conventional explanation might do justice to such parallels as they are general and pertain to the basic outline of a military campaign. But a closer analysis of the stories reveals various particularities on which the conventional explanation falters. The warfare in Gen. 14.15 and Josh. 10.9-10, for instance, bears striking resemblances.

Gen. 14.15   ויחלק עליהם לילה...ויכם...וירדפם
            and he deployed against them at night...and he smote them...and he pursued them

Josh. 10.9–10   ויבא אליהם...כל־לילה...ויכם...וירדפם
            and he came upon them...all night...and he smote them...and he pursued them

Unlike the previous examples, the parallels here are very specific. In addition to the fact that these are the only instances where ויכם and וירדפם appear together, in both cases the word string is prefaced by reference to attack at night. But the most striking parallel shared by these stories are the names 'Melchizedek (מלכי־צדק) of Salem' and 'Adonizedek (אדני־צדק) of Jerusalem' (Gen. 14.18; Josh. 10.1, 3). Such specificity suggests literary dependence rather than shared convention. Supporting this conclusion is the fact that the story in Joshua shares parallels with more than one layer of the redactionally composite Genesis 14. Commentators have argued that the account of Melchizedek in Gen. 14.18-20 is an interpolation.[16] Significantly,

13.   See the discussions in Lindars 1995: 98–101 and Trompf 1979: 219–24.
14.   See 1 Kgs 15.34; 16.19, 26; 22.53[52]; 2 Kgs 3.3; 10.29, 31; 13.2, 6, 11; 14.24; 15.9, 24, 28 (see von Rad 1953).
15.   Greenstein 1990: 168.
16.   See, for example, Van Seters 1975: 299 and Westermann 1985: 189–90.

'Melchizedek of Salem' (Gen. 14.18) is a part of the interpolation while the remaining parallels occur outside the Melchizedek pericope.[17]

In support of the conventional explanation of various parallel narratives is Alter's (1981: 51) argument for the existence of 'type-scenes', which he defined as 'fixed constellation[s] of predetermined motifs' that a narrator could adapt to complement the concerns of the greater narrative. An example for Alter (1981: 52) is the so-called 'betrothal' type-scene in which a bridegroom meets a girl at a well, either the man or girl draws water from the well, the girl rushes home with news of the man's arrival, and a betrothal follows (Gen. 24.10-61; 29.1-20; Exod. 2.15-21; Ruth). In a later work Alter (1983: 119-20) argued for an annunciation type-scene, which consists of the plight of barrenness, the annunciation from a visiting man of God or messenger concerning the promise of a son, and the conception or birth of the promised son (Gen. 18.9-15; 25.19-26; Judg. 13.2-24; 1 Sam. 1.4-20; 2 Kgs 4.8-17). Alter (1983: 128) concluded that the examples of the annunciation type–scene cannot be the product of the transmission of a single story, whether oral or written, because variations in the handling of the repeated motifs are deliberate. Alter (1983: 128) also contended that the type-scenes cannot be explained simply on the basis of allusion as they lack requisite textual signals that allude to an antecedent story. Alter (1983: 128–29) concluded that the best explanation for the existence of the annunciation type-scene is that it was 'an accepted common framework of narrative situation which the writer could…modify for the fictional purposes at hand'. Against Alter, in the following paragraphs I contend that both the promise of a son to Manoah and his barren wife (Judg. 13.2-24), and the promise of a son to the barren Shunemite woman (2 Kgs 4.8-17) are the product of Dtr's reliance on the divine promise of a son to Abraham and Sarah in Genesis 18.

In his discussion of the annuciation type-scene Alter failed to note other passages in the DtrH that share many parallels with Genesis 18 *and that have nothing to do with an* '*annunciation*'. Parallels exist, for instance, between the divine revelation to Abraham in Genesis 18 and the Bethlehemite's interactions with the Levite in Judges 19: both Abraham and the Bethlehemite urged their guests (the messengers,

---

17. David's battle against the Amalekites in 1 Samuel 30 also shares the structure of Genesis 14. As a fugitive told Abram that invaders had seized Lot together with the wealth of Sodom (Gen. 14.11–13), so an Egyptian slave told David that the Amalekites – who had seized David's wives – had burned Ziklag (1 Sam. 30.11-15). As Abram then pursued the four kings who had plundered the five kings and had taken Lot captive (Gen. 14.14), so David then pursued the Amalekites who had plundered Ziklag and had taken his wives captive (1 Sam. 30.10, 16). As Abram successfully recovered all the possessions of the five kings, together with Lot, the women, and the rest of the people (Gen. 14.16), so David was able to recover the things that the Amalekites had taken, together with his wives and the people (1 Sam. 30.17-19). As the king of Sodom then brusquely told Abram to give him the people and keep the possessions for himself (Gen. 14.21), so churlish men of David told him that the men who did not accompany them into battle against the Amalekites were not to receive any of the plunder, but only their family members who had been taken (1 Sam. 30.22). As Abram replied to the king of Sodom that he would only keep enough possessions to give to those who accompanied him in the battle (Gen. 14.24), so David replied to the selfish men that 'the share of those who remain with the baggage shall be the same as the share of those who go down to battle' (1 Sam. 30.25).

the Levite) to receive their hospitality (Gen. 18.1-5; Judg. 19.1-9); and as Abraham 'saw' (וירא) the messengers and ran 'to meet them' (לקראתם), so the Bethlehemite 'saw [the Levite]' (ויראהו) and was glad 'to meet him' (לקראתו) (Gen. 18.2; Judg. 19.3). Gideon's encounter with a 'messenger' of the LORD in Judg. 6.11-24 also shares parallels with Genesis 18.[18] Abraham's encounter with three 'men' who turned out to be the LORD and two 'messengers' is similar to Gideon's encounter with the 'messenger' of the LORD (Judg. 6.11-24), for in both instances the identity of such supra–humans is ambiguous. In Genesis the supra-human is identified as a man as well as the LORD himself (compare Gen. 18.1-2, 13, 22; and 19.1), and in Judges the messenger of the LORD is later similarly identified as the LORD himself (Judg. 6.11-12, 14, 20).[19] In both cases, moreover, the supra–human 'appeared' (וירא) to Abraham and Gideon at (an) 'oak(s)' (אלה) (Gen. 18.1; Judg. 6.11-12). Abraham and Gideon similarly began their conversations to the supra-human(s) with 'My Lord(s)' (אדני) followed by 'if I have found favor in your eyes' (אם־נא מצאתי חן בעיניך; Gen. 18.3; Judg. 6.13, 15, 17). The supra–humans thereupon accepted the invitations of Abraham and Gideon to stay for meals, which they ate 'under' (תחת) a tree (Gen. 18.4–8; Judg. 6.19). A further parallel exists between Abraham's final intercession for Sodom and Gideon's request concerning the fleece: 'Let not my Lord be angry, but let me speak only once' (אל־נא יחר לאדני ואדברה אך־הפעם; Gen. 18.32); 'Let not your anger burn against me, but let me speak only once' (אל־יחר אפך בי ואדברה אך הפעם; Judg. 6.39).[20] The parallels between Genesis 18 and Judges 19, then, are of the same ilk as those between Genesis 18 and Judges 6 (which has nothing to do with an annunciation). The best explanation is that they, too, are the product of Dtr's reliance on Genesis 18.

Both the story of the annunciation and Manoah in Judg. 13.2-24 as well as Elisha's promise of a son to the Shunemite woman in 2 Kgs 4.8-17 are similarly dependent on the divine promise of a son to Abraham and Sarah in Genesis 18. With regard to Judg. 13.2-24, this passage also shares parallels with Genesis 11 and 17. As Sarai 'was barren and had no child (עקרה אין לה ולד)', so Manoah's wife 'was barren and had no child (עקרה ולא ילדה)' (Gen. 11.30; Judg. 13.2). A divine promise of a son was then given to Sarai and Manoah's wife (Gen. 18.9-15; Judg. 13.3-7). As the LORD 'appeared' (וירא), promised Abraham progeny, and then 'ascended' (ויעל), so the messenger of the LORD 'appeared' (וירא), promised Manoah and his wife a son, and then 'ascended' (ויעל) (Gen. 17.1, 22; Judg. 13.3, 20). Finally, as Abraham pled with the messengers to eat a meal, so Manoah pled with the messenger of the LORD to eat a kid (Gen. 18.5; Judg. 13.15).[21] As with the

18. See also the analysis by Greenstein 1990: 168.
19. Cf. Gen. 16.9-13; 22.15-16; 31.10-13; 48.15-16; Exod. 23.20-22.
20. 'But let me speak only once' (ואדברה אך הפעם) occurs only in these two instances.
21. That Dtr drew these parallels is evident from the redactionally composite nature of Genesis: Judg. 13.2-24 shares three parallels with passages that have traditionally been assigned to J (Gen. 11.30 = Judg. 13.2; Gen. 18.9-15 = Judg. 13.3–7; Gen. 18.5 = Judg. 13.15) and two that have traditionally been assigned to P (Gen. 17.1 = Judg. 13.3; Gen. 17.22 = Judg. 13.20). Because the story in Judges shares parallels with more than one redactional layer in Genesis, the best explanation for the given parallels is that Dtr based Judges 13 on Genesis 18.

above examples, Dtr based the Manoah story on Genesis 18 rather than a generic type scene.[22] Elisha's promise of a son to the Shunemite woman in 2 Kgs 4.8-17, the other proposed type–scene, is similarly dependent on the divine promise of a son to Abraham and Sarah in Genesis 18. The two accounts share the following features: in both a woman prepared a meal for the visitor(s) (Gen. 18.6; 2 Kgs 4.8); the visitor(s) then promised that the woman would have a son in the 'spring time' (כעת חיה; Gen. 18.10, 14; 2 Kgs 4.16-17);[23] and the woman, who heard this promise while she was in the 'doorway' (פתח), regarded the promise as unbelievable (Gen. 18.10, 12; 2 Kgs 4.15-16). The fact that the common denominator of the Levite, Gideon, Manoah and Shunemite stories is Genesis 18, pinpoints Genesis 18 as the base text.[24] Like other Tetrateuchal accounts, then, Dtr used Genesis 18 in diverse ways. It served as the basis for annunciation stories, for Gideon's encounter with a supra-human, and, as I will show in Chapter 5, for the depiction of Israel as a new Sodom in Judges 19.

Having argued above that the parallel narratives are due to literary dependence rather than convention, in the remainder of this chapter I discuss the eight criteria that I use to determine the direction of dependence between them. I do so on the basis of the parallels that exist between various Tetrateuchal accounts, and Joshua 1–5 and 1 Samuel 1–8.

There are four parallel accounts between the Tetrateuchal Moses and the depiction of Joshua in Joshua 1–5.[25] First, both Numbers 13 and Joshua 2 concern the sending of men to scout the promised land. As Moses 'sent' (וישלח) spies who were to 'see' (ראה√) 'the land' (הארץ) and the cities, so Joshua 'sent' (וישלח) spies to 'see the land' (ראו את־הארץ) and Jericho (Num. 13.17-19; Josh. 2.1). Upon their return, the spies 'reported to [Moses/Joshua]' (ויספרו־לו) their findings (Num. 13.27-29; Josh. 2.23). But whereas Moses' spies negatively reported that the people could not succeed in taking the land, Joshua's spies positively reported that the LORD had given them all the land (Num. 13.31-33; Josh. 2.24).

Second, there is a parallel between the crossing of the Sea (Exodus 14–15) and the crossing of the Jordan (Joshua 3–4), a connection that Joshua explicitly drew: 'For the LORD your God dried up the waters of the Jordan before you until you crossed, *just as* the LORD your God did to the Sea of Reeds, which he dried up for

22. Note also the parallels between Jacob's tussle with a 'man' after crossing the Jabbok (Gen. 32.23[22]-33[32]) and the conclusion to the Manoah story (Judg. 13.2-24). In response to Jacob's request to know the man's name, the angel of the LORD replied, 'Why do you ask my name? (למה זה תשאל)' (Gen. 32.30[29]), and in response to Manoah's request the angel of the LORD replied with precisely this question – its only other occurence (Judg. 13.18); and as Jacob thereupon said, 'I have seen God face to face and my life has been preserved', so Manoah then said, 'We shall surely die for we have seen God' (Gen. 32.31[30]; Judg. 13.22).

23. 'Spring time' (כעת חיה) only occurs in these two passages.

24. Akin to this is a standard argument used in Gospel studies: simply put, the priority of Mark over Matthew and Luke is evident from the fact that Matthew and Luke do not agree with each other in wording or order against Mark. Mark is the common denominator of the synoptics and is therefore the base text.

25. See also Fishbane 1985: 358-59; Hulst 1965: 162-88; Wenham 1971: 146; and Zakovitch 1991: 60-67.

us until we crossed' (Josh. 4.23).[26] The timing of the corresponding events is also parallel. Like the deliverance from Egypt, the crossing of the Jordan took place on the tenth day of the first month (Josh. 4.19; Exod. 12.1-3, 41, 51). Each account, moreover, represents the point at which the people placed their confidence in their leader. After the crossing of the Sea 'the people believed in the LORD and in Moses his servant' (Exod. 14.31), and before the crossing of the Jordan the LORD stated, 'this day I will begin to exalt you before all Israel that they might know that *just as* I was with Moses so I will be with you' (Josh. 3.7; cf. 4.14). The descriptions of the miracles are also similar: the waters became 'heaps' (נד; Exod. 15.8; Josh. 3.13, 16),[27] turned to 'dry ground' (חרבה; Exod. 14.21; Josh. 3.17), and thereafter returned to their normal course (Exod. 14.27; Josh. 4.18). Finally, in each instance the reaction of the nations is similar. As the peoples of Edom, Moab and Canaan were terrified by the crossing of the Sea, so the kings on both sides of the Jordan 'lost heart and no spirit was left in them' because of the crossing of the Jordan (Exod. 15.15-16; Josh. 5.1).[28]

The third parallel between Moses and Joshua concerns the circumcisions that they instituted. As Moses commanded that people be circumcised prior to participating in the Passover, so Joshua had the Israelites circumcised before participating in the Passover (Exod. 12.43-50; Josh. 5.2-9). Joshua's reference to the circumcision at Gilgal as the 'second' circumcision makes this parallel explicit (Josh. 5.2).[29] For Dtr the first circumcision took place prior to the Exodus (Exod. 12.48-50), as is evident from his contrast of the two circumcisions: 'Now whereas all the people who came out of Egypt had been circumcised, none of the people born after the Exodus, during the desert wanderings, had been circumcised (Josh. 5.5)'.[30] Moreover, in keeping with the first Passover celebration 'the Israelites offered the Pass-

---

26. Lohfink (1997, 1998) persuasively argued for an 'antitype-type' pattern in Deuteronomy 1–3 and Joshua that uses the clauses כאשר עשה, 'just as he did' and ככל כאשר עשה, 'according to all that he did'. Such clauses consistently serve to unite Tetrateuchal and Deuteronomistic accounts.

27. This term occurs elsewhere only in Ps. 78.13, where it is also used with reference to the piling up of the Sea of Reeds.

28. As I demonstrated in Chapter 1, there are similarly many links between Deuteronomy 2–3 and Exod. 15.11, 16-17.

29. The LXX of Josh. 5.2-6, which, unlike the MT, does not refer to a 'second' circumcision (Josh. 5.2), and which states that not all of the Exodus generation was circumcised (Josh. 5.5), may have been based on a different *Vorlage* than the MT – for there is no reason why the LXX's *Vorlage* would have omitted such material (Auld 1979: 8–10). However, because the MT's version contains a number of Deuteronomistic features it is tenable to conclude that the LXX's account is pre-Deuteronomistic. The reference to a second circumcision in the MT is consistent with Dtr's concern to pattern the conquest story after the Exodus story (Josh. 5.2). Only the MT states that 'all the men of war died' (Josh. 5.4), which is consistent with Deut. 2.14-16. Finally, whereas the LXX states that the wilderness travels lasted for 42 years, consistent with Deut. 1.3 and 2.14 the MT states that such travels lasted for 40 years (Josh. 5.6).

30. That Dtr did not regard the first circumcision as that of Joshua and his family in Genesis 17 is evident from 'the second circumcision of *the sons of Israel*' (5.2). Of the roughly 900 times that the term 'Israel' occurs in the DtrH it never refers to the people prior to the conquest. Rather, the DtrH always refers to the pre-conquest generations as the 'fathers' (approximately 80 times).

over sacrifice on the fourteenth day of the month, toward evening' (Josh. 5.10; Exod. 12.6, 18).

Fourth, Joshua's meeting of the captain of the LORD's host is reminiscent of Moses' encounter with a being (Exod. 3.1-5; Josh. 5.13-15). The messenger of the LORD, who is also identified as God, said to Moses from the burning bush, 'Remove your sandals from your feet, for the place where you stand is holy ground' (Exod. 3.5). Nearly verbatim to this, the 'commander of the army of the LORD' said to Joshua, 'Remove your sandal from your foot for the place where you stand is holy' (Josh. 5.15). These accounts also have similar functions. The Exodus account, which prefaces the promise of deliverance from Egypt, is a divine guarantee of deliverance; and the Joshua story, which prefaces the promise of conquest of Jericho, is a divine guarantee of conquest.

Before discussing the issue of the direction of dependence, one must determine whether the above parallels are the product of shared oral or literary tradition. It has been asserted that one can detect a conventional spy story in Numbers 13, Deut. 1.19-46, Joshua 2, Josh. 7.2-5, Judg. 1.22-26, Judg. 18.2-10, and 2 Sam. 17.17-22.[31] This view fails to appreciate the literary nature of such pericopes. It is clear enough, for instance, that a literary relationship exists between Numbers 13 and Deut. 1.19-46. Before positing a conventional spy story on the basis of Numbers 13, one should therefore first seek to determine if there also exists literary dependence between Numbers 13 and Joshua 2. The same caution applies to using the other 'spy story' texts to posit a convention. All such spy stories are in the DtrH, and prior to arguing for a generic convention it would therefore be prudent to determine if some or all such accounts are not simply the product of Deuteronomistic tendency. Others have argued on the basis of Joshua 3–5 and related Tetrateuchal passages that it is possible to outline a ritual conquest celebrated at Gilgal: the people sanctified themselves, the ark was carried to the sanctuary at Gilgal, the dammed Jordan acted as the Sea of Reeds, twelve stones were set up at the sanctuary, the soldiers were circumcised, the Passover was celebrated, and the commander of the LORD's army appeared at the sanctuary.[32] As with the hypothesized spy convention, this thesis fails to appreciate the literary context of Joshua 3–5, for the parallels shared by the conquest story in Joshua and corresponding Tetrateuchal accounts exist together with other parallels. As I noted above, there are parallels between the ventures of Moses' spies (Numbers 13) and Joshua's spies (Joshua 2); as Moses set up twelve pillars 'for the twelve tribes of Israel', so Joshua had twelve stones removed from the Jordan 'corresponding to the number of the tribes of Israel', which he set up in the middle of the Jordan (Exod. 24.4; Josh. 4.7-9); as Moses held out the rod of God until the Amalekites were defeated, so Joshua held out his sword until the forces of Ai were exterminated (Exod. 17.8-13; Josh. 8.18-19, 26); as the LORD hardened Pharaoh's heart in order that he might defeat the Egyptians, so the LORD hardened the hearts of the Northern kings that Joshua might defeat them (Exod. 14.4, 8; Josh.

31. E.g., Zakovitch 1990: 75–98 and Fields 1997.
32. E.g., Cross 1973: 103–11.

11.20);[33] at a place 'on the way' Zipporah circumcised Moses' son with a 'flint knife', even as Joshua circumcised the Israelites with 'flint knives' because all those who were born 'on the way' in the wilderness had not been circumcised (Exod. 4.24-25; Josh. 5.2-5);[34] as Balaam's ass saw the messenger of the LORD standing in the way 'and his sword was drawn in his hand' (וחרבו שלופה בידו; Num. 22.23), so Joshua saw a man standing before him 'and his sword was drawn in his hand' (וחרבו שלופה בידו; Josh. 5.13); and Joshua's intercession on behalf of Israel after its defeat at Ai is reminiscent of Moses' intercession on behalf of Israel after the spies swayed the people with their unfavorable report (Num. 14.13-16; Josh. 7.9).[35] The 'conquest ritual' hypothesis takes no account of the fact that such parallels appear before, within and after the putative 'conquest ritual'. A better hypothesis is that the given parallels are due to the marked influence that antecedent Tetrateuchal texts had on Dtr.

Having argued that the parallels between Joshua 1–5 and Tetrateuchal accounts are due to literary dependence, in the remainder of this chapter I focus on the criteria for ascertaining the direction of dependence between the parallels.

Criterion 1: Cross-reference
When a narrative in the Former Prophets explicitly refers to the corresponding Tetrateuchal account, the narrative in the Former Prophets was likely based on the given Tetrateuchal account. Cross-references from Joshua to Exodus include explicit comparisons between Moses and Joshua. The Transjordan tribes stated that they would obey Joshua just as they had obeyed Moses and they declared 'only may the LORD your God be with you just as he was with Moses' (Josh. 1.17). After this the LORD stated to Joshua that he would exalt him before all Israel 'so that they shall know that I will be with you just as I was with Moses' (Josh. 3.7), and upon crossing the Jordan 'the LORD exalted Joshua in the sight of all Israel, so that they revered him all his days just as they had revered Moses' (Josh. 4.14). Another cross-reference concerns the crossings of the Sea and the Jordan: 'For the LORD your God dried up the waters of the Jordan before you until you crossed, just as the LORD your God did to the Sea of Reeds, which he dried up before us until we crossed' (Josh. 4.23). There is also a reference to the Exodus story. In her speech to the spies Rahab stated, 'for we have heard how the LORD dried up the waters of the Sea of Reeds' (Josh. 2.10). As elsewhere, Dtr made these cross-references to help readers recognize the parallels between the Exodus and conquest stories.

33.   These are the only instances in which the LORD is the agent of the verb חזק ('to harden') with לב ('heart') as the object. Cf. Exod. 4.21; 9.12; 10.20, 27; 11.10.

34.   See also Alter 1992: 119.

35.   'When the Egyptians, from whose midst you brought up this people in your might, hear the news, they will tell it to the inhabitants of that land....If then you slay this people to a man, the nations who have heard your fame will say, "It must be because the LORD was powerless to bring that people into the land"' (Num. 14.13-16); 'When the Canaanites and all the inhabitants of the land hear of this, they will turn upon us and wipe out our very name from the earth. And what will you do about your great name?' (Josh. 7.9).

Criterion 2: Assumed Knowledge

When a narrative in the Former Prophets presupposes knowledge that is furnished in the corresponding Tetrateuchal account, the narrative in the Former Prophets was likely based on the given Tetrateuchal account.[36] Dtr's reference to the circumcision at Gilgal as the 'second circumcision' (Josh. 5.2) assumes knowledge of what was in Dtr's mind was the first circumcision, which took place prior to the Exodus (Exod. 12.43-50). The statement of the captain of the LORD's host, 'Now (עתה) I have come' (Josh. 5.14), is similarly the fulfillment of the LORD's promise to send a messenger before Israel to drive out the inhabitants of Canaan (Exod. 23.20).[37] Finally, Dtr emphasized the point that on the day following the celebration of the Passover, which took place four days after having crossed the Jordan (Josh. 4.19; 5.10), the divine provision of manna ceased (Josh. 5.11-12). This assumes knowledge of Exod. 16.35: 'And the Israelites ate manna forty years, until they came to a settled land; they ate the manna until they came to the border of the land of Canaan'.

Criterion 3: Multiple Occurrence

When two or more narratives in the Former Prophets share parallels with a single Tetrateuchal narrative, and it can be shown that one such narrative in the Former Prophets is derivative, the other narrative(s) in the Former Prophets is/are likely also derivative. Consistent with this criterion, like Deut. 1.34-36, 39 and 2.14-16, Joshua 2 shares parallels with Numbers 13–14. Because the given passages in Deuteronomy were demonstrably based on Numbers 13–14, it is plausible that Joshua 2 was also based on Numbers 13–14. Similarly, because the reference to the death of those who heeded the counsel of the spies in Josh. 5.4-6 assumes knowledge of Deut. 1.34-36, 39 and 2.14-16 (passages which Dtr based on Numbers 13–14), it is again tenable to conclude that Dtr was also dependent on Numbers 13–14 for Josh. 5.4-6.

Criterion 4: Thematic Congruence

When the concern of a narrative in the Former Prophets is consistent with, or complemented by, the parallels with the corresponding Tetrateuchal account, the narrative in the Former Prophets was likely based on the given Tetrateuchal account. This criterion is both difficult to use and tremendously helpful: difficult insofar as it is directly tied to the subjective task of interpretation; helpful insofar as the parallel narratives often clearly complement Dtr's general narrative concerns.

The parallels shared by Joshua and Moses complement Joshua's consistent faithfulness to Mosaic legislation. Joshua's faithfulness is already anticipated in the LORD's first speech to Joshua:

> But you must be very strong and resolute to do all the teaching that my servant Moses enjoined upon you. Do not deviate from it to the right or to the left, that you

36. Cf. Carr 2001: 124.

37. See 2 Kgs 19.25 where the adverb עתה is also used with reference to the fulfillment of an earlier divine decree: 'Have you not heard? Of old I planned that very thing. I designed it long ago. Now (עתה) I have fulfilled it'.

may be successful wherever you go. Let not this teaching depart from your lips, but
recite it day and night, that you may observe faithfully all that is written in it. Only
then will you prosper and only then will you be successful (Josh. 1.7-8).[38]

In line with this passage are the many instances in which Joshua carried out previous Mosaic commands. In Numbers 32 and Deut. 3.18-20 Moses commanded the
Transjordan tribes to aid the Cisjordan tribes in the conquest before settling in the
Transjordan. That Joshua was carrying out the command of Moses is made explicit
by his words to the people, 'Remember what Moses the servant of the LORD en-
joined upon you' (Josh. 1.13) as well as the people's response, 'We will obey you
just as we obeyed Moses' (Josh. 1.17). Again, in Deuteronomy 27–28 Moses commanded the people to construct an altar on Mount Ebal and recite a series of blessings and curses from Mounts Gerizim and Ebal, a command that Joshua fulfilled
(Josh. 8.30-35). As with the previous example, Dtr made the connection explicit:
'There was not a word of all that Moses had commanded that Joshua failed to read
in the presence of the entire assembly of Israel' (Josh. 8.35). In Deut. 20.16-18 the
LORD commanded Moses, with respect to the law of warfare, 'everything that
breathes shall not live' (לא תחיה כל־נשמה). In fulfillment of this, Joshua killed the
inhabitants of Hazor: 'nothing that breathed remained' (לא נותר כל־נשמה; Josh.
11.11; cf. 11.14). Dtr again made the connection explicit: 'Just as the LORD had
commanded his servant Moses, so Moses had charged Joshua, and so Joshua did;
he left nothing undone of all that the LORD had commanded Moses' (Josh. 11.15).
In Deut. 9.1-3 the LORD promised Israel that they would dispossess the Anakites,
and they did so (Josh. 11.21-22). As elsewhere, Dtr recalled the Deuteronomic
promise: 'Thus Joshua conquered the whole country just as the LORD had promised
Moses' (Josh. 11.23). In fulfillment of Num. 34.13, in Josh. 14.1-2 Dtr introduced
the section regarding the allotment to the nine and a half tribes with the standard
'just as the LORD had commanded through Moses'. In Deut. 19.1-10 Moses commanded the people to set aside cities of refuge, and Joshua was told by the LORD to
do so 'as [the LORD] had spoken through Moses' (Josh. 20.2). Finally, in Num.
35.1-8 the LORD commanded Moses to have cities set aside for the Levites, and in
Josh. 21.1-40 this was fulfilled by Joshua. As with all the other instances, Dtr made
the connection explicit: 'so the Israelites, in accordance with the LORD's command,
assigned to the Levites [the cities]' (Josh. 21.3; cf. 21.2).

Joshua's consistent faithfulness to Mosaic legislation is consistent with the many
parallels between Joshua and Moses. The thematic congruence between the story of
Joshua 1–5 and the parallels shared between Tetrateuchal accounts and these chapters therefore supports the prosed direction of dependence.

The criterion of thematic congruence is similarly helpful concerning Dtr's depiction of the generation under Joshua as a new, obedient Israel. Dtr made a clear dis-

    38.   Some have argued that Josh. 1.7-9 was interpolated (e.g., Noth 1981: 62 n. 1; cf. Rofé 1993:
78–85). Mayes (1979: 273–74), however, is correct in his assertion that Josh. 1.7-8 bears a close
resemblance to Dtr's interpolation in Deut. 17.18-19, and the motif of not turning to the right or the
left with reference to the Torah occurs elsewhere only in the DtrH (Deut. 17.20; Josh. 23.6; cf. Deut.
28.14). See also Boling and Wright 1982: 123–24.

tinction between the righteous generation under Joshua's leadership and the un-righteous generations that preceded and followed.[39] With regard to the generation under Joshua, as Dtr praised Joshua for his obedience to Moses so he praised Israel for its obedience to Joshua: 'the Reubenites, the Gadites, and the half-tribe of Manas-seh went across armed before the Israelites, as Moses had charged them' (Josh. 4.12); 'they revered [Joshua] just as they had revered Moses' (Josh. 4.14); 'the people served the LORD during the lifetime of Joshua and the lifetime of the older people who lived on after Joshua and who had witnessed all the marvelous deeds that the LORD had wrought for Israel' (Judg. 2.7). Dtr highlighted this emphasis on the obedience of the generation under Joshua by distinguishing it from the following generations. Whereas Joshua's generation 'served the LORD' (Judg. 2.7), the suc-ceeding generations 'did what was offensive to the LORD' (Judg. 2.11). Dtr also dis-tinguished the generation under Joshua from the generation under Moses because, like the period of the judges, the generation under Moses was corrupt. This concern is already present in Deut. 1.37-39 where one reads that only the generation under Joshua would see the land (cf. Deut. 2.14-16).

Complementing the depiction of the generation under Joshua as a new Israel are the parallels shared between Tetrateuchal accounts and Joshua 1–5: in marked con-trast to the travesty of Numbers 13, in Joshua 2 the spies stated the LORD had given all the land into their hands and that the inhabitants of the land were quaking before them; the crossing of the Jordan marked the birth of a new Israel (Josh. 3.1–5.1); with the passing of the disobedient generation there came the second circumcision and the celebration of the Passover (Josh. 5.2-12); and with the appearance of the promised messenger the business of conquering Canaan could at last proceed (Josh. 5.13-15). As with the example concerning the parallels between Joshua and Moses, the criterion of thematic congruence here supports the proposed direction of depend-ence: Dtr drew the parallels between the generations under Moses and Joshua to complement his depiction of the generation under Joshua as being new and obedient.

I will base the remaining four criteria that I use for determining the direction of dependence on the parallels that exist between 1 Samuel 1–8 and corresponding Tetrateuchal accounts.

There are many parallels between the life of Samuel in 1 Samuel 1–8, and Moses in Exodus 1–14 and Numbers 11.[40] First, their early years are similar. After having been suckled by their mothers (Exod. 2.1-9; 1 Sam. 1.20-23), these figures were brought up in official establishments: Moses with Pharaoh's daughter in the court of Pharaoh and Samuel under Eli's tutelage in Shiloh (Exod. 2.10; 1 Sam. 1.24–3.19). More specifically, prior to embarking on their careers both Moses and Samuel 'grew up' (גדל√; Exod. 2.10, 11; 1 Sam. 2.21; 3.19).

Second, there are parallels between the prophetic offices of Moses and Samuel. Indeed, Samuel was 'a prophet like Moses' in fulfillment of the LORD's promise that he would raise up a prophet like Moses (Deut. 18.18). In response to Hannah's statement that she would bring Samuel to Shiloh after he had been weaned,

---

39. For the clean break between the generations see also von Rad 1965: 109–10.
40. See also the analysis of Garsiel 1985: 44–57.

Elkanah said to Hannah 'only may the LORD fulfill his word' (1 Sam. 1.23). Because there is no earlier word of the LORD in the MT of 1 Samuel, most commentators have followed the LXX's ἀλλὰ στήσαι κύριος τὸ ἐξελθὸν τοῦ στόματητός σου and 4QSamᵃ's אך יקם יהו]ה היוצא מפיך] ('only may the LORD fulfill what has come from your mouth').[41] As Walters (1988: 411–12) contended, a better solution is to find the antecedent in the LORD's promise to Moses to 'raise up a prophet from among [the] people like yourself' (Deut. 18.18). This interpretation alone does justice to the prophetic language of 1 Sam. 1.23, for in every instance in the DtrH where the LORD is the subject of the verb קום and דבר is the object, the concern is with the fulfillment of prophecy.[42] The calls and commissions of Moses and Samuel also parallel one another. In both instances the LORD called (ויקרא) to the prophet, addressing each with double vocatives (Exod. 3.4; 1 Sam. 3.10). Finally, as God then spoke words of judgment against the king of Egypt to Moses, so he then outlined his judgment against the house of Eli to Samuel (Exod. 3.19-20; 1 Sam. 3.11-14).

The third parallel between the lives of Moses and Samuel is found in the early chapters of Exodus, particularly the plagues narrative in chs. 5–12, and the early chapters of 1 Samuel, particularly the ark narrative in chs. 4–6.[43] Both accounts concern God's possession (Israel/ark) that an enemy (Egypt/Philistia) held, and the resultant series of plagues that ensued to force the return of the possession to Canaan. Prior to outlining the more specific parallels, I will discuss the explicit cross-references to and various citations of the plagues narrative in the ark narrative. The Philistine priests and diviners referred to the plagues narrative twice – first with the declarative, 'These are the same gods who struck the Egyptians with every kind of plague in the wilderness' (1 Sam. 4.8), and then with the instructive, 'Don't harden your hearts as the Egyptians and Pharaoh hardened their hearts' (1 Sam. 6.6). Coupled with these references, the Philistines cited the plagues narrative four times. Whereas God said to Moses that he would favorably dispose the Egyptians toward Israel, 'so that when you go, you will not go emptily (ריקם)' (Exod. 3.21), the Philistine priests and diviners counseled the Philistines, 'If you are going to send the Ark of the God of Israel away, do not send it away emptily (ריקם)' (1 Sam. 6.3). Similarly, whereas the LORD stated that Pharaoh would 'send' (ישלח) Israel and they would 'depart' (תלכון) (Exod. 3.20-21), relying yet again on Exod. 3.21 the Philistine priests and diviners stated that the Egyptians 'sent them (וישלחום) and they departed (וילכו)' (1 Sam. 6.6), and that 'you will send [the ark] and it shall depart (ושלחתם אתו והלך)' (1 Sam. 6.8).[44] Again, whereas the LORD stated 'you may recount in the hearing of your sons…how I made a mockery of the Egyptians (התעללתי במצרים)' (Exod. 10.2), the Philistine priests and diviners stated 'he made a mockery of [the Egyptians]' (התעלל בהם; 1 Sam. 6.6). The Ekronites also cited the plagues narrative when the ark entered their town: parallel to Pharaoh's request of Moses and Aaron, 'Plead with the LORD to remove the frogs from me and my

41. E.g., McCarter 1980: 56; and Klein 1983: 3.
42. 2 Sam. 7.25; 1 Kgs 2.4; 6.12; 8.20; 12.15 (see also 1 Sam. 3.12).
43. The following analysis is from Harvey 2001: 73–76.
44. Miller and Roberts 1977: 55, 103 n. 11.

people' (Exod. 8.4), is the Ekronites' exclamation that 'they have moved the ark of the God of Israel to me to kill me and my people' (1 Sam. 5.10; cf. 5.11).[45]

The specific parallels between the plagues narrative and the ark narrative include the following.[46] (1) The refusal of Pharaoh/the sons of Eli to heed the voice of the LORD/Eli stemmed from the LORD's desire to punish them. The LORD hardened the heart of Pharaoh so that he would not let the people go (Exod. 4.21), so that he might display his signs (Exod. 7.3; 10.1), and so that he might gain glory (Exod. 14.4). Hophni and Phinehas similarly ignored Eli's plea to reform 'for the LORD was resolved that they should die' (1 Sam. 2.25). (2) As Pharaoh's courtiers exhorted Pharaoh 'Let the men go to worship the LORD their God', so the priests and diviners counseled the Philistines 'Send [the ark] off, and let it go on its own way' (Exod. 10.7; 1 Sam. 6.8 [cf. 5.8, 11]). (3) There is also a parallel between the summoning of the leaders: 'And Pharaoh…summoned (ויקרא) the wise men and the sorcerers' (Exod. 7.11); 'The Philistines summoned (ויקראו) the priests and the diviners' (1 Sam. 6.2). (4) What escaped one plague was struck by another: the locusts consumed what was left after the plague of hail (Exod. 10.5, 12, 15); and the Ekronites who escaped death were stricken with tumors (1 Sam. 5.12). (5) As Moses told Pharaoh to provide animals for the burnt offerings, so the Philistines provided the cows for the burnt offering when the ark returned to Israel (Exod. 10.25; 1 Sam. 6.14). (6) Just as the Egyptians were persuaded to release Israel after a series of plagues, so the Philistines were persuaded to release the ark after a series of plagues. (7) In both instances 'the hand of the LORD' (יד־יהוה) was instrumental in bringing the plagues (Exod. 9.3; 1 Sam. 5.6).[47] (8) Upon release from Egyptian bondage, Israel received 'objects of gold' (כלי זהב) from the Egyptians (Exod. 3.22; 11.2; 12.35), and upon release from Philistia, the ark received 'objects of gold' (כלי הזהב) from the Philistines (1 Sam. 6.8, 11). (9) Outcries are mentioned. This is true of those who were struck by the plagues in each account (Exod. 11.6; 12.30; 1 Sam. 5.10-12); and as the Hebrews' 'outcry went up' (ותעל שועתם) to God so the Ekronites' 'outcry went up' (ותעל שועת) to the skies (Exod. 2.23; 1 Sam. 5.12).[48] (10) As a result of the plagues, the Egyptians, Moses and the Philistines came to a 'knowledge' of the LORD (Exod. 7.5, 17; 8.6[10], 18[22]; 9.14, 29; 10.2; 1 Sam. 6.3).[49]

45. The phrase 'me and my people' only occurs in these three instances: ממני ומעמי (Exod. 8.4); להמיתני ואת־עמי (1 Sam. 5.10); אתי ואת־עמי (1 Sam. 5.11).

46. Much of what follows is from Bourke 1954: 96–99; Daube 1963: 73–88; Garsiel 1985: 51–54; and Damrosch 1987: 188–91. See also Zakovitch 1991: 52–53 and Nohrnberg 1995: 342–44.

47. Exod. 3.20; 7.4; 14.31; 1 Sam. 5.7, 9, 11; 6.3, 5, 9. See also Roberts 1971, and Miller and Roberts 1977: esp. 48.

48. In only these two instances does the clause (ם)ותעל שועת occur.

49. Following the LXX and 4QSamᵃ, some have argued that the MT's ונודע לכם ('and he will make himself known to you') of 1 Sam. 6.3 should be emended to ונכפר לכם ('when you have been ransomed'), primarily because of the interrogative למה that immediately follows (e.g., McCarter 1980: 129). But כפר never occurs in the niphal stem. A better explanation is to take ונודע לכם reflexively, 'he will make himself known to you' (*NJPS*; cf. Exod. 6.3 and Isa. 19.21 where the *niphal* of ידע is used reflexively with יהוה/אלהים as the subject), and למה as introducing an undesirable alternative, 'otherwise his hand will not turn away from you' (see 1 Sam. 19.17; Qoh. 5.5; Waltke and O'Connor 1990: 18.3c).

Similar to this is the parallel between 'I [Pharaoh] do not know (לא ידעתי) the LORD' (Exod. 5.2) and '[Hophni and Phinehas] did not know (לא ידעו) the LORD' (1 Sam. 2.12). (11) Each episode consists of a confrontation between the God of Israel and the enemy's god(s): as the LORD punished 'all the gods of Egypt' by means of the plague on the firstborn, so his defeat of Dagon included plagues on the people (Exod. 12.12; 1 Sam. 5.2-7; 6.5). (12) Finally, neither Israel nor the ark reached a final resting place: Israel stayed in the desert for 40 years and the ark remained at Kiriath-jearim for 20 years (Num. 14.34; 1 Sam. 7.2).

The fourth parallel between Moses and Samuel pertains to Israel's victory over both the Egyptians and the Philistines (Exodus 14; 1 Samuel 7).[50] Both narratives are concerned with divine deliverance from an oppressor – Israel from Egypt and the Philistines respectively. The two narratives share the following order of events. Both Pharaoh and the Philistines were told of Israel's whereabouts and then went out to them. Upon hearing that Israel had fled, Pharaoh gathered his men and pursued them (Exod. 14.5-9), and 'when the Philistines heard that the Israelites had assembled at Mizpah the lords of the Philistines marched out against Israel' (1 Sam. 7.7). In both accounts the Israelites consequently became terrified and appealed to the LORD/Samuel for assistance.

Exod. 14.10	*1 Sam. 7.7–8*
וייראו מאד ויצעקו בני־ישראל אל־יהוה	וייראו מפני פלשתים ויאמרו בני־ישראל אל־שמואל אל־תחרש ממנו מזעק אל־יהוה
they were greatly frightened and the Israelites cried out to the LORD	they were frightened of the Philistines and they implored Samuel, 'Do not neglect us and do not refrain from crying out to the LORD'

Through the ministration of Moses/Samuel the LORD then brought victory to Israel: Moses held out his rod over the sea and the waters divided (Exod. 14.21); and upon sacrificing and crying out the LORD responded to Samuel (1 Sam. 7.9-10). Finally, the LORD then 'confused' (המם) the enemy and defeated them 'on that day' (ביום ההוא) (Exod. 14.24, 30; 1 Sam. 7.10).

The fifth parallel between Moses and Samuel concerns rebellions against the LORD (Numbers 11; 1 Samuel 8).[51] In Num. 11.4-6 the people complained about the manna and lack of meat, while in 1 Sam. 8.1-5 the people noted the failings of Samuel's sons and demanded a king. These stories record this complaint or request in the same way. As the complaint of the people was 'evil in the eyes of Moses' (ובעיני משה רע; Num. 11.10), so the request for a king was 'evil in the eyes of Samuel' (וירע הדבר בעיני שמואל; 1 Sam. 8.6). In both accounts the prophet then prayed to the LORD: Moses expressed his frustration to the LORD over Israel's complaint, and Samuel prayed regarding the people's request for a king (Num. 11.10-15; 1 Sam. 8.6). Although the LORD fulfilled such pleas, the consequences were disastrous: after being deluged with quail, the people were struck by a plague

---

50.   The following analysis is from Harvey 2001: 73–76.
51.   The following analsis is from Harvey 2001: 77–78.

(Num. 11.31-34); and after the LORD told Samuel to heed the demand of the people, Samuel warned the people of oppression under a monarchy (1 Sam. 8.7, 11-18). In both instances the complaint/request of the people amounted to 'rejecting' the LORD: 'for you have rejected the LORD' (כי מאסתם את־יהוה; Num. 11.20); 'for they have rejected me' (כי אתי מאסו; 1 Sam. 8.7).[52] Finally, as the people wailed for lack of food 'in the ears of the LORD' (באזני יהוה; Num. 11.1, 18), so Samuel reiterated the request of the people 'in the ears of the LORD' (באזני יהוה; 1 Sam. 8.21).[53]

Three criteria used in the discussion of Joshua 1–5 in support of the proposed direction of dependence also apply to 1 Samuel 1–8: the criteria of cross-reference, multiple occurrence and thematic congruence.

With regard to the criterion of cross-reference, in 1 Samuel 1–8 various characters explicitly refer to the corresponding Tetrateuchal accounts. As I noted, this is true of the Philistines (1 Sam. 4.8) as well as the Philistine priests and diviners (1 Sam. 6.6), who both refer to the Exodus story. Similarly, as I argued above , Numbers 11 shares striking parallels with 1 Samuel 8. Dtr furthered this parallel by referring to Israel's rebellious tendency: 'Like everything else they have done ever since I brought them out of Egypt to this day – forsaking me and worshiping other gods – so they are doing to you' (1 Sam. 8.8). The best explanation for such allusions and cross-references is that Dtr made them to call the reader's attention to the corresponding Tetrateuchal accounts.

Concerning the criterion of multiple occurrence, I argued above that Dtr based the appointment of officials in Deut. 1.9-18 in part on Num. 11.10-25. It is therefore reasonable to conclude that Dtr also drew the parallels between Numbers 11 and 1 Samuel 8.

The criterion of thematic congruence also supports the proposed direction of dependence. With 1 Samuel 5–6 the narrative shifts its focus from the disaster at Shiloh to the movement of the ark from Philistia to Israel. But the movement of the ark only provides the skeleton of the narrative, for the principal concern of these chapters is not the ark but the LORD's supremacy over the Philistines, their god, and Israel.[54] 1 Samuel 5.1-5 outlines the LORD's supremacy over Dagon where, after the Philistines placed the ark in the temple of Dagon, in two consecutive mornings Dagon was in obeisance before the ark.[55] The LORD's supremacy over the Philistines and Israel is similarly evident from their relationship with the ark, which they both viewed as possessing inherent power. The Israelites cried, 'Why did the LORD put us to rout today before the Philistines? Let us fetch the ark of the covenant of the LORD from Shiloh; thus he will be present among us and will deliver us from the hands of our enemies' (1 Sam. 4.3). The Philistines similarly lamented, 'God has come to the camp... Woe to us! Nothing like this has ever

---

52. The verb מאס 'to reject' with people as the subject and the LORD as the object occurs only in these two instances (Stanley D. Walters, personal communication).

53. This phrase only occurs in these instances.

54. Referring to 1 Samuel 4–6 as 'the ark narrative' is a misnomer as the central concern of these chapters is not the ark but the supremacy of the LORD over the Philistines, their god, and Israel (see also Miller and Roberts 1977: 60).

55. See also Smelik 1992: 48–49.

happened before. Woe to us! Who will save us from the hand of these mighty gods?' (1 Sam. 4.7-8).[56] Both the Philistines and the Israelites were misguided, for the ark ironically became their nemesis – the Philistines were struck by plagues for possessing the ark (1 Sam. 5.6-12), and the LORD struck the men of Beth-shemesh for looking into the ark (1 Sam. 6.19). The LORD thus stands above the manipulations of the Philistines and Israel.[57]

In the ark narrative one finds that both the Philistines and Israel are presented as new Egypts that challenged the sovereignty of God. With regard to the Philistines, this is evident from those two instances in which they explicitly compared their circumstances to those of the Egyptians of old (1 Sam. 4.8; 6.6). The movement of the ark from Philistia to Israel, which parallels the movement of Israel from Egypt to the promised land, also supports the equation 'Philistia = Egypt'. But the same holds true for Israel. In the plagues narrative it was Israel that was oppressed by Egypt and in need of deliverance. Dtr inverted the schema afforded by the plagues narrative, for it was the ark that was mistreated by Israel and it was the ark that needed to be delivered. The Philistines' curious statement, 'these are the gods who struck the Egyptians with every sort of plague in the wilderness' (1 Sam. 6.9) is suggestive of this equation between Israel and Egypt. Whereas the Philistine's statement 'every kind of plague' is an allusion to Egypt, the incongruous 'in the wilderness' is an allusion to the plagues that the LORD punished Israel with in the wilderness. Contrary to the text-critical conclusion that this text is corrupt,[58] it is apparent that Dtr had the Philistines draw the stunning conclusion that Israel had become a new Egypt.

The criterion of thematic congruence also applies to 1 Samuel 8. Here Samuel evidently regarded the request for a king as a slight against himself, but the LORD assured him that 'it is not you that they have rejected; it is me they have rejected as their king' (1 Sam. 8.7). Again, the request 'Let our king rule over us and go out at our head and fight our battles' (1 Sam. 8.20) was an implicit rejection of the LORD's leadership in war, for according to Deuteronomic legislation the LORD was Israel's military leader.[59] The LORD had demonstrated as much in his victories over Dagon (1 Sam. 5.1-5) and the Philistines (1 Sam. 7.2-14). Consistent with 1 Samuel 8, in

---

56. See also Hertzberg 1964: 52; Willis 1971: 301–302; and Smelik 1992: 46.

57. In addition to their common view of the ark, there exists a parallel four-fold sequence between the Philistines and the Israelites in their dealings with the ark. (1) As the ark was taken to Philistia (1 Sam. 4.11–5.1), so it was later taken to Beth–shemesh (1 Sam. 6.10-12). (2) Both the Philistines and the Israelites were punished for their sin involving the ark: the LORD 'struck' (ויך) the Ashdodites because the Philistines had taken the ark from Israel (1 Sam. 5.6, 9; cf. 5.2); and the LORD 'struck' (ויך) the men of Beth-shemesh who looked into the ark (1 Sam. 6.19). (3) As 'the men of Ashdod' then asked, 'What shall we do with the ark of the God of Israel?' (1 Sam. 5.7-8), so 'the men of Beth-shemesh' asked, 'Who can stand in attendance on the LORD, this holy God? And to whom shall he go up from us?' (1 Sam. 6.20). (4) Finally, whereas the men of Ashdod then 'sent' (וישלחו) people to ask what they should do with the ark (1 Sam. 5.8), the Israelites thereupon 'sent' (וישלחו) messengers to the inhabitants of Kiriath-jearim and told them to take the ark into their keeping (1 Sam. 6.21).

58. E.g., McCarter 1980: 104.

59. Deut. 20.1-4; cf. Josh. 10.14, 42; 23.3, 10; Judg. 4.14; 2 Sam. 5.24.

Numbers 11 the people rejected the LORD by complaining. Dtr's purpose in patterning 1 Samuel 8 after the rejection of the LORD in Numbers 11 was to underline the fact that the predisposition of the Exodus generation to reject the LORD was equally present in Samuel's generation. Dtr invited this interpretation in 1 Sam. 8.8, 'Like everything else they have done ever since I brought them out of Egypt to this day – forsaking me and worshiping other gods – so they are doing to you'. In patterning 1 Samuel 8 on Numbers 11 Dtr also evidently had a Moses/Samuel parallel in mind, for Samuel's role as intercessor in 1 Samuel 8 is the same as that of Moses in Numbers 11.[60] This interpretation is supported by the fact that the given narratives in 1 Samuel 1–8 follow the same sequence as the corresponding accounts in Moses' life: early life and call (Exodus 1–3; 1 Samuel 1–3); plagues narrative and ark narrative (Exodus 5–12; 1 Samuel 4–6); defeat of Egyptians/Philistines (Exodus 14; 1 Samuel 7); and the people's rebellion against the LORD (Numbers 11; 1 Samuel 8). More specifically, Dtr drew the Moses/Samuel parallel to align Samuel with the prophetic office established by Moses. As I noted above, Samuel was a prophet like Moses. This is in accord with the close relation between Mosaic teaching and the prophetic word in the DtrH: the prophetic word is inseparable from the teaching of Moses (e.g., 1 Kgs 14.6-16; 2 Kgs 22.14-20); it was the channel through which the Deuteronomic blessings and curses were fulfilled;[61] and all prophets were to follow the Mosaic pattern (Deut. 18.15-22) as Moses was the pre-eminent prophet, for 'never again did there arise in Israel a prophet like Moses' (Deut. 34.10).[62] In light of this association between Moses and the prophetic office, then, Dtr drew the Moses/Samuel parallel to present Samuel as a model prophet.

I turn now to a discussion of the remaining four criteria that I use in determining the direction of dependence between the parallels.

Criterion 5: Source Criticism

When an account in the Former Prophets shares parallels with two or more redactional layers of the corresponding Tetrateuchal account, the narrative in the Former Prophets was likely based on the given Tetrateuchal account.[63] As Harvey (2001: 80–81) argued, the ark narrative shares verbal parallels both with the non-P and P layers of Exodus 1–14. With regard to the non-P layer, 'vessels of gold' of Exod. 3.22 and 12.35 is cited in 1 Sam. 6.8; 'me and my people' of Exod. 8.4 is cited in 1 Sam. 5.10–11; and 'I do not know the LORD' of Exod. 5.2 is cited in 1 Sam. 2.12.

---

60. There may have been a Deuteronomic tradition that associated Moses and Samuel as great intercessors, for the LORD could say to Jeremiah that 'even if Moses and Samuel were to stand with me I would not be won over to that people' (Jer. 15.1).

61. Von Rad (1953: 78–81) noted eleven prophecies and their fulfillments in the DtrH: Josh. 6.26 and 1 Kgs 16.34; 2 Sam. 17.13 and 1 Kgs 8.20; 1 Kgs 11.29-39 and 1 Kgs 12.15; 1 Kgs 13.2 and 2 Kgs 23.16–18; 1 Kgs 14.6–16 and 1 Kgs 15.29; 1 Kgs 16.1-4 and 1 Kgs 16.12; 1 Kgs 21.21-22 and 1 Kgs 21.29; 1 Kgs 22.17 and 1 Kgs 22.29-36; 2 Sam. 1.6 and 2 Kgs 1.17; 2 Kgs 21.10-15 and 2 Kgs 24.2; 2 Kgs 22.15-20 and 2 Kgs 23.30. See also Wyatt 1979: 61 n. 42.

62. Blenkinsopp (1992: 232) is correct in his contention that this statement is 'probably a warning against interpreting [the promise in Deut. 18.15-18] in such a way as to put prophetic mediation on the same level as that of Moses'. See also Otto 1998.

63. See also Carr 2001: 125.

As for the P layer, 'the outcry went up' of Exod. 2.23 is cited in 1 Sam. 5.12; and 'Pharaoh summoned [two groups of officials]' of Exod. 7.11 is cited in 1 Sam. 6.2.[64] The ark narrative thus shares four verbal parallels with the non-P layer and two verbal parallels with the P layer of Exodus 1–14. It therefore follows that the ark narrative was based on the plagues narrative.[65]

Criterion 6: Incongruity
When a narrative in the Former Prophets includes a feature that is grammatically or contextually incongruous, but this same feature is grammatically and contextually sound in the corresponding Tetrateuchal account, it is best to conclude that the narrative in the Former Prophets was based on the given Tetrateuchal account.[66] This criterion is similar to the criterion of cross-reference because it often marks the author's attempt to draw the reader's attention to an antecedent account. Other incongruities are the product of the author's melding his source with a given Tetrateuchal account where the source and the Tetrateuchal account shared the same or similar verbal features. It is no coincidence that such incongruous features in the Former Prophets regularly include a text-critical issue. In fear of the ark, for instance, the Philistines cried, 'they have moved the ark of the God of Israel to me to kill *me and my* people' (1 Sam. 5.10, 11). Here the use of the first person singular rather than the expected first person plural[67] is Dtr's attempt to call the reader's attention to the plagues narrative, for the plagues narrative records Pharaoh's words to Moses and Aaron, 'Plead with the LORD to remove the frogs from *me and my* people' (Exod. 8.4[8]). The Philistines' curious statement, 'these are the gods who struck the Egyptians with every sort of plague in the wilderness' (1 Sam. 6.9) is also incongruous – the Egyptians were struck by plagues in Egypt, and it was Israel that was struck in the wilderness. Contrary to the text-critical conclusion that this text is corrupt,[68] the Philistine's statement 'every kind of plague' is an allusion to Egypt, and the incongruous 'in the wilderness' is an allusion to the plagues that Israel experienced in the wilderness. Again, in response to the Philistines' concern over the troublesome ark their priests and diviners counseled them to send 'five golden mice…for the same plague which struck all of *them* and your lords' (1 Sam. 6.4). This also represents Dtr's attempt to call the reader's attention to the plagues narrative, for the reader expects the second rather than the third person. Because of this incongruity most commentators have followed the LXX which reads 'you',[69] but in light of the many parallels shared by the two narratives such an emendation is unwarranted.

64. For the source-critical identifications see Childs (1974) and Durham (1987).

65. The criterion of source criticism also applies to the parallels shared by Moses and Joshua that I discussed above. Dtr's reference to the 'second circumcision' (Josh. 5.2) assumes knowledge of the circumcision prior to the Exodus (Exod. 12.43-50). Exodus 12.43-50 is usually assigned to P while other parallels are from non–P layers (see Durham 1987: 170–71).

66. See also Carr 2001: 111.

67. Presumably to correct its *Vorlage*, the LXX reads 'us and our'.

68. E.g., McCarter 1980: 104.

69. E.g., McCarter 1980: 129; Hertzberg 1964: 55.

The fact, then, that features are grammatically incongruous in Samuel but fitting in the parallel Tetrateuchal accounts supports the posited direction of dependence.[70]

Criterion 7: Deuteronomistic Tendency

When various features of an account in the Former Prophets are found in other narratives in the DtrH that are demonstrably based on corresponding Tetrateuchal narratives, it is best to conclude that such an account in the Former Prophets was based on the given Tetrateuchal account. This criterion is also consistent with the proposed direction of dependence, for, like the depiction of Joshua and several other characters in the Former Prophets, in 1 Samuel 1–8 one finds that Samuel is presented as a new Moses.

Criterion 8: Context

When a narrative in the Former Prophets exists in a complex of narratives that are demonstrably dependent on Tetrateuchal accounts it is best to conclude that the account in the Former Prophets is derivative. On the basis of several criteria, I argued that Dtr based 1 Samuel 4–6 and 8 on the corresponding Tetrateuchal accounts. The criterion of context suggests that Dtr may have also based the remaining parallels in 1 Samuel 1–3 and 7 on the corresponding Tetrateuchal accounts, as these passages in 1 Samuel exist in a complex of other narratives that are demonstrably based on the given Tetrateuchal accounts.

Throughout this work I use the above eight criteria to show that in every instance Dtr based the given accounts in the Former Prophets on the corresponding Tetrateuchal accounts. The greater the degree to which one or more of these criteria are met the more confident one can be that the given narratives in the Former Prophets were based on the corresponding Tetrateuchal accounts.[71]

---

70. Van Seters (1986) dated the plagues narrative after Dtr. But he failed to note the fact that the ark narrative – which shares a wealth of parallels with the plagues narrative – explicitly refers to the plagues narrative.

71. After submitting six criteria for determining the direction of dependence between synoptic accounts, Carr (2001: 126) was similarly cautious: a text 'tends' to be later than its parallel when it fulfills one or more of the six criteria, and such criteria require 'judicious use'.

Chapter 3

DTR'S TORAH-CONSCIOUSNESS

As I type these words I do not consciously think of the location of the keys to depress, for as a consequence of my knowledge of the keyboard's layout my fingers have become an extension of my thoughts. Michael Polanyi (1962) referred to such action as 'tacit knowledge' – an intuitive know-how that is the product of saturation in an activity or process. Akin to this is Dtr's use of his Torah. Dtr inhabited his Torah, every parallel narrative that he drew was the product of his saturation in Torah, and Dtr could mirror its stories on thematic or verbal levels with little forethought.[1] Using examples mostly from 1 and 2 Samuel, in this chapter I argue that the parallels that Dtr drew came naturally out of his Torah-consciousness.

Consonant with Dtr's patterning the rejection of the LORD in 1 Samuel 8 on the rejection of the LORD in Numbers 11, there are miscellaneous echoes to Numbers 11 in 1 Samuel 6–10 that are best explained as the product of Dtr's intimate knowledge of his Torah. A verbal parallel, for instance, exists between Numbers 11 and 1 Samuel 6: while the meat was still in the mouths of rebellious Israel 'the LORD struck the people with a very great plague (ויך יהוה בעם מכה רבה מאד)' (Num. 11.33); and as a consequence of looking into the ark 'the LORD struck the people with a great plague (הכה יהוה בעם מכה גדולה)' (1 Sam. 6.19).[2] As Harvey (2001: 78–79) noted, there are also parallels between Numbers 11 and 1 Samuel 10. To begin with, both Num. 11.20 and 1 Sam. 10.18-19 refer to the people's dissatisfaction in spite of the fact that they had come out of Egypt. In each case, moreover, the people had thereby 'rejected' (מאס) the LORD/God.[3] A further parallel concerns the subject of prophecy. In the Numbers account 70 elders prophesied (Num. 11.25), as did Eldad and Medad, who were not among the 70 and upon whom 'the LORD put his spirit' (Num. 11.26, 29). In Samuel a band of prophets similarly prophesied (1 Sam. 10.5, 10), as did Saul, who, although he was not one of the prophets, was gripped by 'the spirit of the LORD' (1 Sam. 10.6, 10). Because Eldad and Medad were 'prophesying' (√נבא), Joshua was constrained to object to Moses (Num. 11.27-28).

---

1. Crites (1997: 30) similarly contended that 'stories, and the symbolic worlds they project, are…like dwelling places'. See also Allan 1993.

2. Some commentators have here followed the LXX because of the MT's redundancy: 'and he struck the men of Beth-shemesh…and he struck the people…for the LORD struck the people' (e.g., Driver 1966: 59). A better explanation is that the MT's redundancy is the result of the incorporation of Num. 11.33.

3. This verb only occurs with the LORD or God as the object in these verses and previously discussed 1 Sam. 8.7.

Moses nevertheless countered Joshua's objection by stating that he wished that all the LORD's people were prophets (Num. 11.29). The bystanders in Samuel were similarly perplexed by Saul's 'prophesying' (√נבא; 1 Sam. 10.11), but an individual suggested that Saul himself was not only among the prophets but that he was their 'father' (1 Sam. 10.11-12). The finale finds Moses re-entering the camp and Saul entering the shrine (Num. 11.30; 1 Sam. 10.13).[4]

In addition, then, to patterning complete narratives after Tetrateuchal accounts, the effect that such narratives had on Dtr are seen in those citations of Tetrateuchal accounts that precede and follow the given narratives in the DtrH. That Dtr consciously sought to equate the rejection of the LORD in 1 Samuel 8 with the rejection of the LORD in Numbers 11, for instance, is clear enough. But what of the remaining parallels before and after 1 Samuel 8? The best explanation is that while composing the accounts that precede and follow the birth of the monarchy, the lexicon and themes of the Numbers 11 story were predominant in Dtr's mind. This is typical. When Dtr's citations of Tetrateuchal accounts do not occur within a given parallel narrative, they neverthess appear in close proximity to this parallel narative. Dtr's diverse use of Numbers 11 suggests that Tetrateuchal accounts were not static rubrics that he sedulously followed. They were, rather, living and adaptable stories that provided Dtr with the conceptual framework that defined his historiography.

That Dtr's Torah was inseparable from his consciousness is also evident from his conflation of Tetrateuchal schemata.[5] The rape of Tamar in 2 Samuel 13 shares

---

4.   The proposed direction of dependence between the random parallels of Numbers 11 and 1 Samuel 6–10 is supported by two criteria. First, the criterion of context: because such parallels are interspersed within complexes of parallels that are demonstrably based on the corresponding Tetrateuchal accounts, it is most likely that they too were based on the corresponding Tetrateuchal accounts. Second, there is the criterion of source criticism. Source critics have argued that Num. 11.4-35 consists of two layers. The first layer (11.4-15, 18-24a, 31-35) pertains to the people's complaint regarding the lack of meat and the subsequent plague. The second layer (11.16-17, 24b-30) concerns prophecy and the selection of 70 elders (for a review of scholarship see Sommer 1999). To be sure, the account in 1 Samuel 8 only shares verbal parallels with the first layer (Num. 11.10 = 1 Sam. 8.6; Num. 11.18 = 1 Sam. 8.21; Num. 11.20 = 1 Sam. 8.7). But other Deuteronomistic accounts share parallels with both layers of Numbers 11. Deuteronomy 1.9-18 shares one verbal parallel with the first layer of Numbers 11 (Num. 11.14 = Deut. 1.9) and one with the second layer (Num. 11.17 = Deut. 1.12). 1 Samuel 6–10 also shares verbal parallels with each layer of Numbers 11. As I argued above, this is true of 1 Sam. 6.19 and Num. 11.33; 1 Sam. 10.18-19 and Num. 11.20; and 1 Sam. 10.5 and Num. 11.27. Various accounts in the DtrH, then, share verbal parallels with each layer of Num. 11.4-35: the Deuteronomistic accounts share five verbal parallels with the first layer (Num. 11.10 = 1 Sam. 8.6; Num. 11.14 = Deut. 1.9; Num. 11.18 = 1 Sam. 8.21; Num. 11.20 = 1 Sam. 8.7; Num. 11.20 = 1 Sam. 10.19; Num. 11.33 = 1 Sam. 6.19) and two verbal parallels with the second layer (Num. 11.17 = Deut. 1.12; Num. 11.27 = 1 Sam. 10.5). The best explanation for such data is that Dtr relied on Num. 11.10–35 for the given Deuteronomistic accounts. This conclusion also holds for different source–critical analyses of Numbers 11. Noth (1968: 83), for example, argued that vv. 14-17, 24b-30 are the only insertions into an otherwise unified text. Seebass (1978) argued for no less than four sources. And Van Seters (1992: 227–29) argued that J interwove the two traditions.

5.   Note again Dtr's conflation of Jethro's advice to Moses (Exod. 18.13-27) and the appointing of 70 elders (Num. 11.10-25) in Moses' appointment of elders (Deut. 1.9-18).

parallels with four accounts in Genesis: Lot's interaction with the men of Sodom (Genesis 19); the rape of Dinah (Genesis 34); the incestuous relationship of Tamar and Judah (Genesis 38); and the near-seduction of Joseph (Genesis 39).

There are two parallels shared by the rape of Tamar and Lot's interaction with the men of Sodom. As Lot said to the perpetrators 'my brothers, do not commit evil' (Gen. 19.7), so Tamar pled with Amnon her brother, 'do not do this vile thing' (2 Sam. 13.12). Similarly, as Lot 'shut the door after him (והדלת סגר אחריו)' (Gen. 19.6), so after telling his servants to send Tamar away, Amnon told them to 'latch the door after her (ונעל הדלת אחריה)' (2 Sam. 13.17).

The parallels shared by the rapes of Dinah and Tamar are more extensive.[6] Both stories pertain to the rape of the daughter of a Hebrew leader – Dinah the daughter of Jacob, and Tamar the daughter of David.[7] In both accounts the rapists were princes: Hamor the son of Shechem chief of the Hivites, and Amnon son of David (Gen. 34.2; 2 Sam. 13.1). As Dinah's brothers protested that intermarrying with the Shechemites would be a 'disgrace' (חרפה; Gen. 34.14), so Tamar protested to Amnon that she would not be able to rid herself of her 'disgrace' (חרפתי; 2 Sam. 13.13). The descriptions of the rapes also mirror one another: Shechem 'lay with her and ravished her' (וישכב אתה ויענה; Gen. 34.2), and Amnon 'ravished her and lay with her' (ויענה וישכב אתה; 2 Sam. 13.14). The similarities between the responses of Jacob's sons and David to the rapes are striking: 'when [Jacob's sons] heard... they were very angry' (כשמעם...ויחר להם מאד; Gen. 34.7), and David 'heard...and he was very angry' (שמע...ויחר לו מאד; 2 Sam. 13.21). The verdicts regarding the vileness of the rapes are likewise parallel. Whereas Gen. 34.7 reads, 'he had committed an outrage in Israel...a thing not to be done' (כי־נבלה עשה בישראל...וכן לא יעשה), in 2 Sam. 13.12 Tamar cried, 'for such a thing is not done in Israel; don't commit this outrage' (כי לא־יעשה כן בישראל אל־עשה את־הנבלה הזאת). Just as Jacob 'kept quiet' (החרש; Gen. 34.5) upon hearing of Dinah's rape, so Absalom told Tamar to 'keep quiet' (החרישי; 2 Sam. 13.20) after Amnon had raped her. In both accounts, moreover, the brother(s) deceived the transgressor before murdering him: Simeon and Levi told Hamor and his clan that they must be circumcised, and Absalom invited Amnon to a feast on the pretext of hospitality (Gen. 34.13-17; 2 Sam. 13.23-27). Finally, Freedman (1997: 492) rightly noted that the avenging brothers suffered similar fates for their misdeeds: Dinah's brothers forfeited their father's blessing while Absalom was banished from his father David.

Embedded within these parallels are those between the two Tamars.[8] Both accounts outline sexual misconduct toward women with the name Tamar: Onan failed to carry out his levirate duty to Tamar (Gen. 38.8-9) while Judah, the father of Onan, treated Tamar as a prostitute (Gen. 38.12-18); and Amnon raped Tamar (2 Sam. 13.11-14). The transgressors' names as well as their relation to the given Tamars are also similar. Onan (אונן) was the brother-in-law of Tamar, and Amnon (אמנון) was the half–brother of Tamar (Gen. 38.8; 2 Sam. 13.1). Again, Judah's

---

6.   See also Zakovitch 1985: 189–90.

7.   Freedman (1997: 492) similarly noted that 'in each case this is the only daughter whose name we know and of whom we have any direct information'.

8.   See also Rendsburg 1986.

wife, who is referred to as the 'daughter of Shua' (בת־שׁוּעַ; Gen. 38.12), finds a close parallel with David's wife, the 'daughter of Sheba' (בת־שׁבע; 2 Sam. 11.3).[9]

Finally, Dtr's conflation in 2 Samuel 13 also includes parallels with the near-seduction of Joseph by Potiphar's wife (Genesis 39).[10] Perhaps the strongest association that links the Tamar and Joseph stories is the reference to the 'ornamented tunic' (כתנת פסים) that Tamar rent (2 Sam. 13.18-19). The only other occurrences of this term are in the Joseph story where one finds that Joseph's father Jacob made his son an 'ornamented tunic' (Gen. 37.3, 23, 32). Moreover, as Potiphar's wife sought to seduce Joseph 'day after day' (יום יום; Gen. 39.10) only to have Joseph tell her that he would not do 'this great evil' (הרעה הגדלה הזאת; Gen. 39.9), so Amnon pined for Tamar 'morning by morning' (בבקר בבקר; 2 Sam. 13.4) only to have Tamar refer to her post-rape sending away as 'this great evil' (הרעה הגדלה הזאת; 2 Sam. 13.16). As Potiphar's wife said to Joseph 'Lie with me' (שׁכבה עמי; Gen. 39.7, 12), so Amnon said to Tamar 'Lie with me' (שׁכבי עמי; 2 Sam. 13.11).[11] Both Joseph and Tamar nevertheless declined the propositions (Gen. 39.8-10; 2 Sam. 13.12-13).[12]

Immediately following the conflation in 2 Samuel 13, in his account of the fratricide of Amnon (2 Samuel 14) Dtr relied on the story of the fratricide of Abel.[13] Cain and Absalom hated their brothers. Whereas Cain was consumed by jealousy, Absalom wanted to avenge his sister (Gen. 4.3-5; 2 Sam. 13.32). As Cain thereupon killed Abel 'in the field' (בשׂדה), so the Tekoite stated in her tale that one brother (= Absalom) killed another (= Amnon) 'in the field' (בשׂדה) (Gen. 4.8; 2 Sam. 14.6).[14] As Cain then feared for his life and appealed to the LORD (Gen. 4.14), so the Tekoite feared for the life of her son and appealed to David (2 Sam. 14.11). Lyke (1997: 26 n. 4) rightly noted that as Cain declared that his 'guilt' (עוני) was too great too bear (Gen. 4.13), so the Tekoite declared that the 'guilt' (העון) would be on her (2 Sam. 14.9). The murderers then received protection. The LORD put a mark on Cain, and David promised the woman of Tekoa that her son would not be put to death (Gen. 4.15; 2 Sam. 14.11). As Cain was nevertheless to be a

---

9. Cf. 1 Chron. 3.5 where David's wife is referred to as 'daughter of Shua' (בת־שׁוּעַ). For other possible parallels see Rendsburg 1986: 438–46.

10. See also Auld 2000.

11. There is here continuity between Dtr's use of Genesis 34 and 39 in 2 Samuel 13, for in his use of both of these Genesis stories Dtr relies on the motif of 'to lie with': Amnon 'lay with' Tamar (2 Sam. 13.14) and Shechem 'lay with' Dinah (Gen. 34.2), even as, using imperatives, Amon told Tamar to 'lie with' him (2 Sam. 13.11) and Potiphar's wife told Joseph to 'lie with' her (Gen. 39.7, 12).

12. Although occurring after Genesis 39, Alter (1992: 114) noted that there is a striking parallel between Joseph's command to send out men prior to identifying himself before his brothers, and Amnon's command to send out men following his rape of Tamar: 'send out every man from me (הוציאו כל־אישׁ מעלי)' (Gen. 45.1; 2 Sam. 13.9). This word string is unique to these two passages.

13. See also Blenkinsopp 1964: 449; 1966: 51; and Brueggemann 1968: 164–67.

14. For a comparison of Gen. 4.8 and 2 Sam. 14.6 see Lyke (1997: 25–26). Dtr may also have had Gen. 4.8 in mind in the story of David and Jonathan in the field. As Cain said to Abel 'Let us go into the field' (following the LXX) prior to murdering him, so Jonathan said to David 'Let us go into the field' (1 Sam. 20.11) prior to discovering the murderous scheme of Saul.

wanderer 'upon the face of the earth' (מֵעַל פְּנֵי הָאֲדָמָה; Gen. 4.12), so the woman of Tekoa would not have a remnant 'upon the face of the earth' (עַל־פְּנֵי הָאֲדָמָה; 2 Sam. 14.7).[15] Finally, as Cain was exiled to the land of Nod so Absalom was not permitted to leave his house (Gen. 4.16; 2 Sam. 14.24).

Typical of the indelible imprint of Dtr's Torah upon his consciousness is Dtr's conflation of four accounts (Genesis 19, 34, 38 and 39) into one (2 Samuel 13), which is immediately followed by parallel narratives involving Genesis 4 and 2 Samuel 14. Every note in the cacophany of parallels in 2 Samuel 13–14 had already been sounded by the harmony of Dtr's Torah. Dtr lived and breathed his Torah, such that he could effortlessly blend its schemata.[16]

The fact that parallel narratives are regularly linked by incidental features such as relative clauses or lone prepositional phrases also suggests that the process was altogether spontaneous and natural for Dtr. As I have shown with Deuteronomy 1–3, the story of Joshua, and 1 Samuel 4–6, Dtr buttressed obvious parallels by his refrain that the LORD would do for someone in the Former Prophets 'just as' he had done for someone in a Tetrateuchal account. But more often than not the parallels are less striking. One typically finds parallels that are only secondary to the given narratives – incidental features, relative clauses, or lone prepositional phrases. Such data suggests that the process was altogether spontaneous and natural for Dtr.

The story of David in 1 Samuel 16–19, which is replete with seemingly random features, supports this contention. In 1 Samuel 16–17 Dtr patterned David after Joseph.[17] The following thematic parallels are present. Both Joseph and David were shepherds (Gen. 37.2; 1 Sam. 16.11, 19); both were selected over their brothers by the LORD to rule – Joseph dreamt that his brothers and parents would bow down to him (Gen. 37.5-11) and Samuel anointed David rather than any of his brothers (1 Sam. 16.6-13); and both were sent by their fathers to their elder brothers to inquire after their welfare (Gen. 37.13-14; 1 Sam. 17.17-18), but the brothers were

15. This phrase is used with reference to exile only in these instances.

16. By drawing the given parallels, Dtr made the point that the sordidness of the men of Sodom, the Shechemites, Judah and Potiphar's wife was equally present in the lives of David's sons. Dtr underscored the consequence of such sordidness by following the conflation with the parallels between Genesis 4 and 2 Samuel 14. Dtr's concern is latent in Nathan's exchange with David in 2 Samuel 12.7-12. David there exclaimed (following the LXX, see Carlson 1964: 152–57), 'He shall pay for the lamb *seven* times over' (2 Sam. 12.6) and Nathan responded with, 'You are the man… Therefore the sword shall never depart from your house… I will make a calamity rise against you from within your own house' (2 Sam. 12.7, 10-11). This exchange is the hermeneutical key to the stories in 2 Samuel 13–14, for the trouble that David later had with his sons was the consequence of his sin with Bathsheba. The very name Bathsheba is suggestive of this, for the consequence of David's sin with the 'Daughter of *Seven*' was complete retribution (so Coxon 1981; and Garsiel 1987: 129–30). The tragic story of David's sons clearly comes as the fulfillment of David's own words 'he shall pay for the lamb *seven* times over'. Indeed, David saw Bathsheba from his roof (2 Sam. 11.2), and from that same roof Absalom had sexual relations with David's concubines (2 Sam. 16.21-22). David's exclamation is also reminiscent of the LORD's promise to Cain: 'if anyone kills Cain, *sevenfold* vengeance shall be taken on him' (Gen. 4.15). David's exclamation 'he shall pay for the lamb *seven* times over' is therefore ironic, for in contrast with the Genesis story David thereby sentenced himself to *sevenfold* retribution.

17. See also Garsiel 1985: 120–21; and Alter 1981: 117.

hostile toward them (Gen. 37.18-28; 1 Sam. 17.28). Coupling these thematic parallels are verbal parallels. Both Joseph and David are said to be 'prudent' (נבון; Gen. 41.33, 39; 1 Sam. 16.18); and in both cases one reads that Joseph and David were handsome – in Gen. 39.6 Joseph is described as יפה מראה, as is David in 1 Sam. 17.42. Using incidental features, Dtr similarly patterned David's quest for a wife (1 Samuel 18–19) after Jacob's quest for a wife (Genesis 29). As Laban gave his eldest daughter Leah to Jacob (Gen. 29.23-26), even though Jacob loved his younger daughter Rachel (Gen. 29.18), so Saul offered his older daughter Merab to David (1 Sam. 18.17), even though David was loved by Saul's youngest daughter Michal (1 Sam. 18.20). Augmenting such thematic parallels are the following verbal parallels. After Jacob had worked for seven years he asked Laban for his wife for 'my days have been filled' (מלאו ימי; Gen. 29.21). Laban nevertheless deceived Jacob who had to work double his quota for Rachel (Gen. 29.27). Like Jacob, David was pleased with becoming the king's son-in-law, 'but the days [before he could take Michal] had not been filled' (ולא מלאו הימים; 1 Sam. 18.26), and David similarly doubled Saul's demand of 100 Philistine foreskins for Michal by providing Saul with 200 foreskins (1 Sam. 18.25-27). Following their marriages, Jacob and David 'fled' (ויברח) from their fathers-in-law (Gen. 31.21; 1 Sam. 19.12). As Laban then pursued Jacob because 'he was told (ויגד) that Jacob had fled' (Gen. 31.22), so Saul sent messengers to seize David because 'he was told (ויגד) that David was at Naioth' (1 Sam. 19.19-20). As Rachel then deceived Laban by remaining seated on his 'teraphim' (תרפים; Gen. 31.31-35), so Michal deceived Saul's men by placing 'teraphim' (תרפים) in David's bed (1 Sam. 19.11-17). A final verbal resemblance between the two accounts concerns Jacob's question to Laban, 'Why have you deceived me? (למה רמיתני)' (Gen. 29.25), which is parallel to Saul's question to Michal, 'Why have you deceived me so? (למה ככה רמיתני)' (1 Sam. 19.17). Although the questions come in different contexts, the fact that רמיתני occurs only in one other instance (1 Sam. 28.12) makes the correspondence striking.[18] Such seemingly random features in 1 Samuel 16–19 suggest that they are not the result of conscientious and studied patterning. They are, rather, the product of a mind steeped in Torah.

The integrality of Dtr's Torah to his consciousness is also evident from the metonymic function of specific words. Single words function as tags to alert readers to

---

18. The criterion of incongruity supports the proposed direction of dependence. The parallel clause 'my days have been fulfilled/but the days had not been fulfilled' is fitting in Gen. 29.21 but problematic in 1 Sam. 18.26. Whereas in Genesis it clearly refers to the time that Jacob had to wait for his bride, in the Samuel account it has no expressed antecedent. Some have therefore suggested that it introduces 1 Sam. 18.27 ('When the time had not yet been fulfilled...') (e.g., Hertzberg 1964: 129; Klein 1983: 185; *NJPS*). Others have simply stated that it is obscure (e.g., Driver 1966: 154), or that the LXX, which does not include the phrase, best represents the original (e.g., McCarter 1980: 316). The most tenable explanation is that, as elsewhere, the incongruous clause arose from the parallel that Dtr drew with Genesis 29–31. The proposed direction of dependence also finds support from the criterion of thematic congruence. Consistent with the parallels between Joseph and David, Dtr drew these parallels to emphasize further David's rise to prominence despite his circumstances: like Jacob, David had to overcome the machinations of his father-in-law if he was to rise to power.

Torah stories. This may be seen, for example, with Dtr's use of the term 'Jebusite' in the story of David's purchase of Araunah's threshing floor (2 Sam. 24.18-25). Dtr patterned this account on the story of Abraham's purchase of a burial plot in Canaan for Sarah (Genesis 23).[19] In both cases a central figure in the history of Israel (Abraham and then David) offered to purchase land from one of the pre-Israelite inhabitants of Canaan (Ephron the Hittite and then Araunah the Jebusite). The owner of the land then offered the site at no cost, but reverse haggling never-theless ensued. As Abraham insisted on paying Ephron for the burial plot, so David demanded to pay Araunah for the threshing floor. Immediately following the pur-chase of the sites at the beginning of the subsequent narratives, there exists a strik-ing verbal parallel: as 'Abraham was old and advanced in years' (Gen. 24.1), so 'David was old and advanced in years' (1 Kgs 1.1). Dtr's purpose for drawing the given parallels can be understood with reference to the significance of the acquisi-tions of Abraham and David. Abraham's purchase of a burial plot is an anticipation of the later conquest of the land, for while the LORD had promised Abraham the land (Gen. 12.7), by the end of Genesis all that his family possessed was the given burial plot.[20] The reader must wait until Joshua before seeing the fulfillment of the promise of land. Whereas Abraham's purchase from a Hittite is thus anticipatory of the conquest of the promised land, David's purchase of the threshing floor from a Jebusite marks the culmination of the conquest – for the temple that Solomon later built at this site is the one place in the promised land that the LORD chose for himself. Equally important as the geographical significance of the site is the nation-ality of Araunah, for in every list of the pre-conquest inhabitants of Canaan – al-though each list differs in number – the 'Jebusites' are always the final enemy.[21] McDonough (1999: 129) correctly asserted that David's purchase of the threshing floor from a 'Jebusite' is thus 'a symbolic representation of the final enemy to be conquered in the holy land'.

Similar to the appellation 'Jebusite', the names 'Abimelech', 'Hamor', and 'Shechem' in Judges 9 also function as tags that pertain to the threat of foreigners possessing the land. The only other Abimelech in the Hebrew Bible is the Philistine king who disagreed with Isaac over land rights (Genesis 26). Similarly, 'Hamor the father of Shechem' – who vied for power against 'Abimelech' (Judg. 9.28) – finds his reflex in 'Shechem the son of Hamor' (Gen. 34.2) who raped Dinah. Dtr used the tags 'Abimelech', 'Hamor', and 'Shechem' in Judges 9 in order to call the reader's attention to accounts in Genesis that also pertain to the threat of foreigners ruling over the land: just as Abimelech squabbled over land rights with Isaac (Genesis 26), and just as Simeon and Levi's murder of Shechem caused Jacob to fear that the inhabitants of Canaan would expel the Israelites from the land (Genesis 34), so the rule of the half-breed Abimelech threatened Israel's dominance over the land

19.   See also McDonough 1999.

20.   The significance of Abraham's acquisition of the burial plot is underscored by the refrain that various patriarchs and their wives were buried in the field of Ephron the Hittite in the cave of Macpelah east of Mamre (Gen. 25.9-10; 49.29-32; 50.13).

21.   Ten nations are mentioned in Gen. 15.19-21; six in Exod. 23.23 and 34.11; and seven in Deut. 7.1.

(Judges 9).[22] Single words from Dtr's Torah thus functioned metonymically for Dtr, conjuring up as they did complete Torah narratives – and worlds of meaning with them.

In the above examples, I asserted that individual words from Dtr's Torah could bear wider significance. The majority of parallel features shared by Tetrateuchal and Deuteronomistic accounts, however, are seemingly arbitrary: unique prepositional phrases, odd gramatical constructions, linguistic and thematic convergences, etc. But they, too, are the product of Dtr's Torah-consciousness, for while individual parallel features may seem to be arbitrary, a group of such parallel features often discloses Dtr's intent. The story of David and Nabal (1 Samuel 25) and the bracketing stories of David's sparing of Saul (1 Sam. 23.19–24.23 and 26.1-25) are particularly instructive in this regard. David's sparings of Saul are parallel not only to each other but also to the intervening account of Nabal. All three accounts, moreover, share parallels with the story of Jacob and Laban (Genesis 27–33). Dtr's purpose in drawing such parallels is evident from the given collages of parallel features, rather than from individual parallel features.

I begin by noting the parallels between David's sparings of Saul.[23] In 1 Sam. 23.19 David was fleeing from Saul when the Ziphites reported to him 'Is not David hiding (הלוא דוד מסתתר) with us in the strongholds of Horesh in Gibeah of Hachilah (בנבעת החכילה) south of Jeshimon?' Using precisely the same language, in 1 Sam. 26.1 David was fleeing from Saul when the Ziphites reported to him 'Is not David hiding (הלוא דוד מסתתר) in Gibeah of Hachilah (בנבעת החכילה) which faces Jeshimon?' Saul then selected 'three thousand chosen men' (שלשת אלפים איש בחור[י]) of Israel 'to search for David' (לבקש את־דוד) (1 Sam. 24.3[2]; 26.2). Following this, David had the opportunity to kill Saul, and David's men/Abishai thereupon told David that the LORD had delivered Saul into his hands (1 Sam. 24.5[4]; 26.8). David nevertheless refused to harm 'the LORD's anointed', choosing rather to take something that belonged to Saul (1 Sam. 24.6[5]-7[6]; 26.9-12). David then confronted Saul: Saul was seeking a 'single flea' (פרעש אחד) (1 Sam. 24.15[14]; 26.20), and David's refusal to kill Saul is evidence of his innocence (1 Sam. 24.9[8]-12[11]; 26.17-24). At this point Saul confessed his guilt, told David that he would prosper, and departed (1 Sam. 24.17[16]-23[22]; 26.21-25). A further parallel is the emphasis on providence: in the first account the LORD delivered Saul into David's hands (1 Sam. 24.11[10], 19[18]), while in the second account 'a deep sleep from the LORD' fell upon Saul's men (1 Sam. 26.12). Whatever their pre-history might have been,[24] 1 Samuel 24 and 26 were subsequently arranged and edited to augment the principal concerns of 1 Samuel 16–31, the rise of David and the correlated demise

---

22. There is an emphasis in the Judges story on the 'racial purity' of the leader (8.31; 9.2-3, 26-28).

23. For the parallels between 1 Samuel 24 and 26 see also Koch (1969: 133–37), Culley (1976: 49–54) and Klein (1983: 236–37).

24. The classic form-critical explanation for the parallels between these chapters comes with the study of Koch (1969: 132–48) who argued that the accounts represent different versions of a single tradition.

of Saul.[25] This theme is central to 1 Samuel 24 and 26, which portray David as a righteous hero and Saul as a desperate has-been. More specifically, these chapters are concerned with David's certain accession to the throne and his blood-guilt-lessness.[26] Concerning David's accession, Saul declared to David 'I know that you will become king and that kingship over Israel will remain in your hands' (1 Sam. 24.21[20]), and he told him 'you shall achieve and you shall prevail' (1 Sam. 26.25). As for David's innocence, although in both chapters his men told him that the LORD had delivered Saul into his hands, David was determined to let the LORD alone avenge him (1 Sam. 24.13[12], 16[15]; 26.10-11). By reiterating essentially the same story, then, Dtr emphasized the pre-eminence of David over Saul.

This interpretation of 1 Samuel 24 and 26 is supported by the parallels shared by these chapters and the intervening story of David and Nabal.[27] In all three stories a prominent man treated David unjustly and David had the opportunity to kill him. Rather than avenging himself, David nevertheless trusted the LORD to avenge him (1 Sam. 24.7[6]; 25.33-34 [cf. 25.26, 31]; 26.10-11). David had thus received 'evil' (רעה) for 'good' (טובה): Saul unjustly pursued David (1 Sam. 24.13[12]-14[13], 18[17]), and Nabal did not repay David for his protection (1 Sam. 25.21). There is also an emphasis on providence. In ch. 24 the LORD delivered Saul into David's hands (1 Sam. 24.11[10], 19[18]), in ch. 25 the LORD kept David from violence against Nabal (1 Sam. 25.32, 39), and in ch. 26 'a deep sleep from the LORD' fell upon Saul's men at the instance of the LORD (1 Sam. 26.12). Like chs. 24 and 26, moreover, ch. 25 is also concerned with David's accession to the throne. This is clear from Abigail's pivotal speech to David: Abigail declared that the LORD would grant David an 'enduring house' (1 Sam. 25.28) and that the LORD would accomplish for him all that he had promised by appointing him 'ruler over Israel' (1 Sam. 25.30).[28] Finally, in all three acounts David is referred to as the 'son' of Saul/Nabal (1 Sam. 24.17[16]; 25.8; 26.17), and in the latter two accounts reference is made to the descendants of David's enemy: Saul pled with David not to destroy his descendants (1 Sam. 24.22[21]), and David relented from killing every male of Nabal's line (1 Sam. 25.34). The three stories in 1 Samuel 24–26 thus teach the same thing – David was the legitimate king of Israel. Dtr reinforced this teaching by retelling the same story and by highlighting the worthiness of David.[29]

25.   In this regard Brettler (1991: 102, 108) rightly contended that '[a] major vehicle for asserting the legitimacy of David is emphasizing the illegitimacy of Saul' and that '[a]lmost every chapter of the long unit [1 Sam. 14.52–2 Sam. 8.15] can be seen as fitting into the ideological program of legitimating David at Saul's expense'. Gordon (1980: 39) similarly stated that '[t]he motif to which all else in these chapters [1 Sam. 16.14–2 Sam. 5.10] is subservient is that of David's progress towards the throne'.

26.   Lemche (1978: 2) rightly argued that the primary purpose of these chapters was '(a) to legitimate David's succession to the throne which rightly belonged to the house of Saul, and (b) to acquit David of charges brought against him for complicity in the disaster that ruined Saul's family'.

27.   Koch (1969: 137) incorrectly argued that ch. 25 'has nothing to do with' ch. 24.

28.   Nabal's address (1 Sam. 25.10-11) is similarly replete with direct and subtle references to David's ancestry and Bethlehem (Garsiel 1985: 126–29; 1987: 189).

29.   As Gordon (1980: 45) argued, it is likely that ch. 25 also pertains to the demise of Saul as

Intertextuality between the Tetrateuch and the Former Prophets and within the Former Prophets themselves converges in 1 Samuel 24–26, for in addition to sharing common storylines these three accounts share parallels with the story of Jacob and Laban (Genesis 27–33). Many correspondences exist between 1 Samuel 24 and 26, and Genesis 27.[30] Such stories involve a 'son' who supplanted another son by receiving a 'blessing' from the father. Jacob deceived his brother Esau by stealing the 'blessing' (ברך√) of his father Isaac (Genesis 27). Similarly, David, whom Saul referred to as 'my son' (1 Sam. 24.17[16]; 26.17, 21, 25) and who referred to Saul as 'my father' (1 Sam. 24.12[11]), took Jonathan's place as the successor to Saul and he received a 'blessing' (ברך√) from Saul (1 Sam. 26.25).[31] The blessings that Jacob and David received from their 'fathers' are similar insofar as they both concern their respective reigns. Whereas Isaac intoned 'Let peoples serve you, and nations bow to you' (Gen. 27.29), Saul said 'May you be blessed my son David. You shall achieve and you shall prevail' (1 Sam. 26.25). Other parallels concern the 'voice' of principal characters. As Isaac queried over what seemed to be Jacob's 'voice' (קול; Gen. 27.22), so Saul asked David, 'Is that your 'voice' (קול), my son David?' (1 Sam. 24.17[16]; 26.17). Similarly, as 'Esau lifted up his voice and wept' (וישא עשו קלו ויבך) upon hearing of the deception (Gen. 27.38), so 'Saul lifted up his voice and wept' (וישא שאול קלו ויבך) upon being confronted by David (1 Sam. 24.17[16]).[32]

This brings me to the parallels that David in 1 Samuel 25 shares with Jacob in Genesis 29–31.[33] To begin with, 1 Samuel 25 is reminiscent of Esau's statement to Jacob, 'It was a foolish thing for you to do. I have it in my power to do you harm; but the God of your father warned me last night' (Gen. 31.28-29). Laban's charge that Jacob was 'foolish' (הסכלת) is similar to Abigail's charge that 'Nabal is his name and folly (נבלה) is with him' (1 Sam. 25.25). Laban's statement that he could have harmed Jacob if God had not warned him is likewise parallel to David's contention that he would have killed Nabal and his line if Abigail had not dissuaded him (Gen. 31.29; 1 Sam. 25.32-33). The outline of the stories is also parallel. As Jacob served Laban the wealthy shepherd by tending his flocks, so David served Nabal the wealthy shepherd by protecting his possessions (Gen. 30.29; 1 Sam. 25.21). Both Jacob and David sought remuneration for such service. Jacob requested from Laban a selection from his flocks, and David requested livestock from Nabal (Gen. 30.25-33; 1 Sam. 25.5-8). Both Jacob and David were nevertheless denied.

'Nabal reads like a diminutive Saul'. The primary points that make Nabal a reflex of Saul include their parallel functions in chs. 24–26 (as above); Abigail's wish that all David's enemies fare like Nabal, David's foremost enemy (1 Sam. 25.26); and Saul's confession that he had 'played the fool' (הכסלתי) (1 Sam. 26.21), which is an allusion to 'Nabal' (נבל) the fool (1 Sam. 25.25). See also Biddle 2002: 625–26.

30. I am reliant for most of the following parallels on Damrosch (1987: 211–12).

31. These are the only instances where David is referred to as the 'son' of Saul and Saul is referred to as the 'father' of David.

32. Dtr's use of the defectively spelled קל is here the consequence of his precise use of the Torah story, for in the dozens of instances in his history that he used this word Dtr employed the full spelling קול.

33. See also Garsiel 1985: 130–32.

Laban initially consented but acted deceptively, while Nabal brusquely rejected the request (Gen. 30.34-35; 1 Sam. 25.9-11).[34] In spite of such rejection both Jacob and David nevertheless succeeded in attaining goods from Laban/Nabal: the speckled and spotted goats miraculously multiplied under Jacob's care, and Abigail brought David provisions (Gen. 30.37-43; 1 Sam. 25.18, 27). In the end, Jacob wed 'beautiful' (יפת־תאר) Rachel the daughter of Laban, even as David wed 'beautiful' (יפת תאר) Abigail the widow of Nabal (Gen. 29.17; 1 Sam. 25.3). Both accounts, moreover, note that such success was the result of divine intervention. Although Laban kept the streaked and spotted goats for himself (Gen. 30.35), the LORD intervened and Jacob came to own large flocks of streaked and spotted goats (Gen. 30.37-43; 31.4-16); and although David was determined to kill the males in Nabal's household (1 Sam. 25.22, 34), the LORD intervened by sending Abigail to dissuade David (1 Sam. 25.32-33; cf. 25.29). More specific parallels include the following: the names of the wealthy shepherds are clever inversions of each other – 'Laban' (לבן) and 'Nabal' (נבל);[35] and the sentence 'Laban went to shear his sheep (לגזז את־צאנו)' (Gen. 31.19) is close to 'and [Nabal] was shearing his sheep (בגזז את־צאנו)' (1 Sam. 25.2).

There are also many parallels shared by Genesis 32–33 and 1 Samuel 25 that concern Esau and David, and Jacob and Abigail.[36] As Esau met Jacob with 'four hundred men' so David set out against Nabal with 'about four hundred men' (Gen. 32.7[6]; 33.1; 1 Sam. 25.13). Nevertheless, as Esau did not avenge himself against his deceptive brother, so David did not avenge himself against Nabal (Gen. 33.1-17; 1 Sam. 25.32-35). A more specific parallel is the description of both Esau and David as 'ruddy' (אדמוני).[37] Jacob and Abigail also share parallels. On their way to meet Esau/David both Jacob and Abigail counseled their attendants to 'pass on ahead' (עברו לפני) (Gen. 32.17[16]; 1 Sam. 25.19). Both of these characters then sought to appease the anger of Esau/David with gifts (Gen. 32.14[13]-22[21]; 33.1-11; 1 Sam. 25.18, 27), which they specifically referred to as a 'blessing' (ברכה) (Gen. 33.11; 1 Sam. 25.27). With regard to the encounter itself, in both cases there is an emphasis on the obeisance of Jacob and Abigail before Esau and David: Jacob 'bowed low to the ground (וישתחו ארצה) seven times' before Esau (Gen. 33.3), and Abigail 'threw herself face down before David, and bowed low to the ground (ותשתחו ארץ), and fell at his feet' (1 Sam. 25.23-24). Finally, in both narratives

---

34. These denials both stemmed from the materialism of the antagonists. Concerning the materialism of Laban see Alter (1981: 53, 56). For the materialism of Nabal see Levenson (1978: 15) and Fokkelman (1986: 481).

35. Although Dtr was particularly adept at creating name-plays to form parallels with Tetrateuchal accounts, he also did so with similar-sounding words. Just as, for instance, Abimelech 'looked down through the window and saw' (בעד החלון וירא ...וישקף) Isaac *fondle* Rebekah (Gen. 26.8), so Michal 'looked down through the window and saw' (בעד החלון ותרא ...נשקפה) David whirling (2 Sam. 6.16) – which David describes as '*dancing*' (2 Sam. 6.21). Buttressing the parallel of 'looking down through the window and seeing', there thus exists a word-play between Isaac 'fondling' (*tsakhek*) Rebekah and the similar sound of David 'dancing' (*sikhak*).

36. I adapted some of the following from Garsiel 1985: 132.

37. This term only occurs with reference to these characters (Gen. 25.25; 1 Sam. 16.12; 17.42).

Jacob and Abigail repeatedly addressed Esau and David as 'my lord',[38] and they referred to themselves as 'servant' (עבד) and 'maidservant' (שפחה, אמה).[39]

Dtr's intentions are apparent upon considering parallel features together rather than individually. Consistent with his emphasis on David's rise and Saul's correlated demise, Dtr patterned the stories of 1 Samuel 24–26 after those of Jacob and Laban – stories that are similarly concerned with the ascendancy of a protagonist. Even though Dtr's use of the Jacob and Laban stories was here sweeping – insofar as he did not use explicit cross-references but relied solely on general correspondences – the calculated nature of Dtr's use of the Jacob story is nevertheless evident from the fact that the parallels that 1 Samuel 24 and 26 share with the Jacob story are limited to the account of Jacob's deception of Isaac (Genesis 27). This is unlike 1 Samuel 25, which is at a further remove from the plot of 1 Samuel 24 and 26, and which shares parallels with segments that span more of the Jacob cycle. The commonality of the plot of 1 Samuel 24 and 26 together with their sole use of Genesis 27 is thus indicative of Dtr's calculated use of Tetrateuchal accounts. This is also suggested by the surprising turn in the parallels between 1 Samuel 25 and the Jacob cycle, for while Dtr here patterned David mainly after Jacob, David also shares parallels with Esau. In Genesis 32–33 Esau, who had been cheated by Jacob and who approached Jacob with 'four hundred men', did not avenge himself. This is parallel to 1 Samuel 25 where David, who had been cheated by Nabal and who had approached Nabal with 'about four hundred men', did not avenge himself. Dtr freely adapted the schema: Esau, rather than Jacob, became David's counterpart because Dtr wished to emphasize David's blood-guiltlessness. Dtr's use of the Jacob story in 1 Samuel 24–26 thus shows that parallel features must be understood together rather than individually. This dichotomy between the seemingly random nature of individual parallel features and their collective significance is suggestive of the profound imprint that Torah had on Dtr's consciousness. While composing his stories Dtr adopted individual linguistic and thematic features of his Torah schemata in a seemingly random manner, but when one views such features together as a whole one may detect Dtr's narrative concerns.

In this chapter I argued that every parallel feature that Dtr drew was the product of his intimate knowledge of his Torah, a mental dwelling place that defined the nature and course of history.[40] Torah, with its myriad of schemata, infused Dtr's mind, such that he could conflate Torah accounts and randomly draw verbal or thematic parallels to them with ease. In the remaining chapters I place greater emphasis on interpreting the parallel narratives.

---

38.   Gen. 32.5[4]; 33.8, 13-15; 1 Sam. 25.24-31.
39.   Gen. 32.5[4], 19[18], 21[20]; 33.5, 14; 1 Sam. 25.24-25, 27-28, 31, 41.
40.   'Mental dwelling place' is Polanyi's (1962: 202) terminology.

Chapter 4

INVERSION OF TORAH SCHEMATA

The lexica of sacred traditions mold the thought patterns of those who embrace them. This is particularly true of Jews who meditate on Tanakh, Christians who are inspired by the Gospel, and Muslims who are shaped by the Quran. It is no less true of the impression that Dtr's Torah had on him. Given such influence, Dtr himself was not always conscious of the interpretive significance of the parallels that he drew.[1] We may nevertheless be confident that we have discovered Dtr's intent when we find different Tetrateuchal accounts being used in the same way. Although Tetrateuchal schemata for Dtr were fluid and malleable, there is nevertheless a marked consistency in the ways that Dtr used such schemata. A general feature of many parallel narratives, for instance, is their inversive quality – Dtr often upset or even subverted Tetrateuchal schemata.

Typical of Dtr's inversive use of Tetrateuchal accounts is the story of the Danites' migration (Judges 18), which Dtr told through the lens of Israel's failure to enter the land (Numbers 13). Both the wilderness generation and the Danites were without land (Num. 13.2; Judg. 18.1). As Moses sent twelve men representing the twelve tribes to scout the land that Israel was to possess (Num. 13.2, 17), so the Danites sent five spies representing their clan into the land prior to seizing it (Judg. 18.2). As the twelve spies sent by Moses reported that the land flowed with milk and honey (Num. 13.27), so the five spies commissioned by the Danites declared that 'the land is very good...spacious and nothing is lacking there' (Judg. 18.9-10). As Caleb urged the people to go up and possess the land (Num. 13.30), so the five spies encouraged the people to go to the land to possess it (Judg. 18.9). The northernmost point to which the twelve spies traveled was Rehob (רחב; Num. 13.21), even as the northernmost point of the Danites' travels was Beth-rehob (בית־רחוב; Judg. 18.28). Although both the twelve spies and the five Danites gave reports of the land and its inhabitants, whereas the report of the spies was negative, that of the Danites was positive (Num. 13.28-29, 31-33; Judg. 18.9-10).[2] Finally, whereas the wilderness generation

---

1. Hays' (1989: 33) treatment of Paul's use of Scripture is particularly instructive in this regard: 'To limit our interpretation of Paul's scriptural echoes to what he intended by them is to impose a severe and arbitrary hermeneutical restriction...later readers will rightly grasp meanings of the figures that may have been veiled from Paul himself'.

2. As I noted above, this is precisely one of the parallels between Numbers 13 and Joshua 2: whereas Moses' spies gave a negative report, Joshua's spies gave a positive report.

included 600,000 men of military age (Num. 1.45-46; 2.32; 11.21), the migrating Danites consisted of 600 men 'girt with weapons of war' (Judg. 18.11, 16-17).[3]

The promised land for the Danites had become Laish rather than the land that Moses had allotted to them (Josh. 19.40-48; Judg. 1.34). The Danites' search for land in fact brought them beyond the boundaries of the promised land, as is evident from the introduction to the narrative which reads, 'the tribe of Dan was seeking a territory in which to settle, for to that day no territory had fallen to them *in the midst of the tribes of Israel*' (Judg. 18.1).[4] The Danites went outside their allotted territory and even outside Israel in search of a home, and their conquest of Laish consequently underlines their failure to take the territory that was initially allotted to them.[5] By patterning Judges 18 after Numbers 13, Dtr presented the migration of the Danites as an inverted conquest.[6] This is particularly evident from the report of the Danite spies, which is replete with language that is applied elsewhere to the conquest of the promised land:

> Let us go at once and attack them! For we have seen the land and it is very good (הארץ...טובה מאד), and you are sitting idle! Don't delay to go, to enter, and to possess the land (לרשת את־הארץ). When you come, you will come to an unsuspecting people, for God has given it into your hand (כי־נתנה אלהים בידכם); and the land is spacious (והארץ רחבת ידים) and nothing on earth is lacking there (18.9-10).

---

3. The criterion of multiple occurrence suggests that Dtr drew the parallels. I argued above that Dtr reworked the story of the spies in Numbers 13–14 in Deut. 1.6-8, 19-46. I similarly argued that Numbers 13 was Dtr's basis for the mission of the spies in Joshua 2. It is therefore reasonable to assume that Dtr was also responsible for the parallels between Numbers 13 and Judges 18.

4. The emphasis is on נחלה ('territory'), which appears only at the end of the sentence (Boling and Wright 1975: 258).

5. Dtr also underscored the illegitimacy of the Danites' conquest of Laish by emphasizing the innocence of the Laishites over against the militaristic Danites. Whereas the Laishites were 'dwelling carefree' (Judg. 18.7) and 'tranquil and unsuspecting' (Judg. 18.7, 27; cf. 18.10), in three instances the text reads that the Danites were 'girt with weapons of war' (Judg. 18.11, 16-17). Moreover, the Danites broke the Deuteronomic law of warfare (Deut. 20.10-14). Laish lay outside the promised land, and according to the Deuteronomic law of warfare the Israelites were to offer such towns terms of peace. If the people of such towns rejected the offer only the men were to be killed – the women, children and spoil were to be kept. There is no mention of an offer of peace, the people of Laish were put to the sword, and the city was burned (Judg. 18.27). Dtr similarly underlined the Danites' error in conquering Laish by basing this story on the story of Simeon and Levi's destruction of Shechem in Genesis 34. In both instances Israelites illegitimately destroyed a foreign city. Verbal parallels accompany this thematic parallel. Both Shechem son of Hamor and the Danite spies told their people that the land was 'spacious' (רחבת ידים; Gen. 34.21; Judg. 18.10). Similarly, as Jacob 'kept quiet' (√חרש) upon hearing of the rape of his daughter Dinah (Gen. 34.5), so when the priest asked the men why they were taking the idol, the ephod, and the teraphim, the men told the priest to 'keep quiet' (√חרש) (Judg. 18.19). (Again typifying the imprint of Torah schemata on Dtr's consciousness, I noted in Chapter 3 that Dtr likewise based Absalom's directive to Tamar to 'keep quiet' [√חרש] after her rape [2 Sam. 13.20] on Jacob's silence [Gen. 34.6].) Finally, just as Simeon and Levi attacked 'unsuspecting' (בטח) Shechem (Gen. 34.25), so the Danites destroyed 'unsuspecting' (בטח) Laish (Judg. 18.7, 10, 27).

6. Bauer (1998) similarly argued that Judges 18 is thereby an 'anti-narrative'.

The description of Laish as a 'very good' land is akin to the report of Joshua and Caleb (Num. 14.7), and this same description frequently occurs in Deuteronomy with reference to the promised land.[7] The Danite spies' statement concerning the 'spaciousness' of the land and the hyperbolic 'nothing on earth is lacking [in Laish]' is similarly reminiscent of descriptions of the promised land.[8] Again, the spies exhorted the Danites 'to possess the land' – a clause that frequently occurs elsewhere with reference to the conquest of the promised land.[9] Finally, the expression that God had 'given' the land occurs with reference to the promise of land to the Patriarchs;[10] it is found in the report of Joshua and Caleb;[11] and it occurs in Deuteronomy and Joshua with reference to the conquest.[12] By patterning Judges 18 after Numbers 13, and by having the Danite spies refer to Laish with language that usually applies to the promised land, Dtr thus made the point that the Danite migration to Laish amounted to an inverted conquest.

Before proceeding to the identity of the apostate Levite in Judges 18, it is important to note the parallels that Dtr drew with the stories of Jacob's flight from Laban in Genesis 31–33 in Judges 18. Whereas Jacob left Padan Aram to go to Cannan, the Danites left Canaan to go to Laish. As Jacob placed his family and possessions ahead of himself before Esau's arrival (Gen. 33.1-2), so the Danites placed their children and possessions ahead of themselves before the coming of Micah (Judg. 18.21). Upon intercepting Jacob, Laban confronted him for having taken his daughters (Gen. 31.26) and his 'gods' (את־אלהי; Gen. 31.30). Micah similarly intercepted the Danites and confronted them for having taken his priest and his 'gods' (את־אלהי; Judg. 18.24).[13] Consistent with the inversive nature of the parallels between Numbers 13–14 and Judges 18, Dtr inverted the schema afforded by the Jacob story – for the Danites' departure from the promised land to the foreign land of Laish is the inverse of Jacob's journey from the foreign land of Padan Aram to the promised land.

7.　E.g., Deut. 1.25, 35; 3.25; 6.18; 9.6; 11.17.

8.　E.g., Exod. 3.8; Num. 13.23, 27; Deut. 8.7-10.

9.　E.g., Deut. 9.4; 11.31; Josh. 1.11; 18.3; Judg. 2.6.

10.　E.g., Gen. 12.7; 15.7, 18; 24.7; 28.13.

11.　Num. 14.8.

12.　Deut. 1.25; 3.18, 20; 34.4; Josh. 1.11, 13; 21.43. God's 'giving of the land' to the Danites also suggests that the Danites viewed the conquest as a holy war. For the use of the motif elsewhere see von Rad 1991: 42–44. For the ironic use of holy war language in Deuteronomy 1–3 see Lohfink 1960: 110–14, 119–20; and Moran 1963: 334–39.

13.　As elsewhere, Dtr here used Tetrateuchal accounts at the same points: as I noted above, Rachel deceived Laban by remaining seated on his 'teraphim' (תרפים; Gen. 31.31-35), and Michal similarly deceived Saul's men by placing 'teraphim' (תרפים) in David's bed (1 Sam. 19.11-17). So also, as Laban confronted Jacob for having taken his 'gods' (את־אלהי; Gen. 31.30), Micah confronted the Danites for having taken his 'gods' (את־אלהי; Judg. 18.24). Again, on their way to meet Esau, Jacob counseled his attendants to 'pass on ahead' (עברו לפני) (Gen. 32.16[17]), even as on her way to meet David, Abigail counseled her attendants to 'pass on ahead' (עברו לפני) (1 Sam. 25.19). Similar to this, as Jacob placed his family and possessions ahead of himself before Esau's arrival (Gen. 33.1-2), so the Danites placed their children and possessions ahead of themselves before the coming of Micah (Judg. 18.21).

Akin to the Danites' inverted conquest is the identity of the apostate Levite. By associating the Levite with Moses the conclusion to the story underlines the gravity of the Danites' offence:

> (30) The Danites set up the sculptured image for themselves; and Jonathan son of Gershom son of *Moses*, and his descendants, served as priests to the Danite tribe until the land went into exile. (31) They maintained the sculptured image that Micah had made throughout the time that the House of God stood at Shiloh.

Throughout the story the Levite served as a priest to the unfaithful Danites. The story's conclusion, however, is shocking in its contention that it was Jonathan the grandson of Moses who served as priest to the Danites – the apostate Levite was Moses' grandson.[14] Worshiping an idol is a travesty; but utterly scandalous is the fact that descendants of Moses encouraged just this. The Levite was thus an 'anti-Moses', and descendants of Moses perpetuated the Danite apostasy to the demise of Israel.

As with Dtr's upsetting of the Numbers 13 schema in Judges 18, Dtr particularly enjoyed inverting the Moses schema. Moses had promised that the LORD would 'raise up a prophet like me' (Deut. 18.15), yet Dtr stated that by his time 'a prophet had not arisen like Moses' (Deut. 34.10). This unfulfilled expectation teasingly weaves its way through the DtrH and is programmatic. Although many leaders in the DtrH are remarkably similar to the Tetrateuchal Moses, they all fall short of their exemplar in different ways. Such leaders may be mottled images of Moses, they may follow Moses up to the point of delivering Israel only to fail, or, worse yet, they may follow Moses only to become apostate like Moses' brother Aaron.[15]

I will first consider the parallels between Moses and Elijah. As the LORD was to give Moses' generation 'flesh to eat in the evening and bread in the morning', so at the behest of the LORD ravens provided Elijah with 'bread and meat every morning and bread and meat every evening' (Exod. 16.8 [cf. 16.12]; 1 Kgs 17.6).[16] As Moses later gathered the people to Sinai where the LORD made a covenant with them, so Elijah gathered the people to Carmel in his defense of the covenant (Exod. 19.17; 1 Kgs 18.19). As Moses then built an altar and set up twelve pillars for the twelve tribes in his ratification of the covenant, so Elijah built an altar of twelve stones for the twelve tribes in his competition with the prophets of Baal (Exod. 24.4; 1 Kgs 18.31). Following this construction, both Moses and Elijah prayed to the God of 'Abraham, Isaac, and Israel' (Exod. 32.13; 1 Kgs 18.36), which is a rare triad.[17] Cross (1973: 192) correctly observed that the aftermath of the scenes on Sinai and

---

14. This was too much for the proto-Massoretic scribes who emmended the original 'Moses' to 'Manasseh' (מְנַשֶּׁה). Tov (1992: 57) is on the mark in his proposal that the addition of the suspended *nun* was 'meant to correct an earlier reading which ascribed the erecting of the idol in Dan to one of the descendants of Moses'. See also the verbal associations between the story of Moses' betrothal to Zipporah (Exod. 2.21-22) and the account of the young Levite and Micah (Judg. 17.7-11) in Garsiel (1987: 137).

15. At the end of this chapter, see Table 1, Moses and his Deuteronomistic Counterparts.

16. See also the emphasis on the never-ending supply of food and water in the Elijah–Elisha accounts (1 Kgs 17.8-16; 2 Kgs 3.15-20; 4.1-7; 4.42-44) (Carroll 1969: 411–12).

17. This triad occurs elsewhere only in 1 Chron. 29.18 and 2 Chron. 30.6 (Allison 1993: 40).

Carmel are also similar: Moses' imperative 'Whoever is for the LORD come here!', which precedes the slaughter of the idolaters, is parallel to Elijah's imperative, 'If the LORD is God, follow him; but if Baal, follow him!', which precedes his command to slay the prophets of Baal (Exod. 32.26-28; 1 Kgs 18.21, 40). The people's subsequent response to the fire from the LORD with the inauguration of the Aaronic priesthood (Lev. 9.24) similarly finds a close parallel to the people's response to the fire from the LORD in the Elijah story (1 Kgs 18.38-39). Leviticus 9.24a reads, 'And fire went out from before the LORD and consumed the burnt offering and the fat parts on the altar'; and 1 Kgs 18.38 reads, 'And the fire of the LORD fell and consumed the burnt offering, the stones, and the earth; and it licked up the water that was in the trench'. Again, and as Allison (1993: 40) observed, Lev. 9.24b reads, 'And all the people saw, and they shouted, and fell upon their faces', while the nearly verbatim 1 Kgs 18.39a reads, 'And all the people saw, and fell upon their faces'. The only difference between Lev. 9.24b and 1 Kgs 18.39a comes with the additional 'and they shouted' of Lev. 9.24b. Close to this, however, is the people's exclamation in 1 Kgs 18.39b, 'The LORD, he is God; the LORD, he is God!'

1 Kings 19 similarly shares many parallels with Tetrateuchal accounts of Moses' deeds. Moses' fast of forty days and nights while he was on Sinai parallels Elijah's fast of forty days and nights while he traveled to Horeb (Exod. 34.28 [cf. 24.18]; 1 Kgs 19.8). Moreover, as Moses witnessed a theophany from a rocky cleft on Sinai, so the word of the LORD came to Elijah in a cave on Horeb (Exod. 33.21-22; 1 Kgs 19.9); and as the LORD commanded Moses, 'Station yourself on the rock', so he commanded Elijah, 'Stand on the mount' (Exod. 33.21; 1 Kgs 19.11). Fohrer (1957: 56) rightly noted that in both instances the LORD's glory/name 'passed by' (עבר√) – such that the prophet was either shielded from seeing the LORD, as with Moses (Exod. 33.22), or he wrapped his mantle about his face, as with Elijah (1 Kgs 19.11, 13). The natural violence that accompanied the theophany of Exodus 19 and 1 Kings 19 is also similar. In Exodus the LORD appeared amid thunder, lightning, dense cloud, fire and smoke, while in Kings the theophanic whisper came after the great and mighty wind, the earthquake, and the fire (Exod. 19.16-18; 1 Kgs 19.11-12). Finally, both Exodus 34 and 1 Kings 19 are concerned with the LORD's maintenance of the covenant. The Sinaitic covenant, which was broken by the worship of the golden calf in Exodus 32, was re-established in Exodus 34. Similarly, though Elijah could say 'the Israelites have forsaken your covenant, torn down your altars, and put your prophets to the sword' (1 Kgs 19.10, 14), the LORD assured him that Israel's relationship to himself would nevertheless continue (1 Kgs 19.15-18). Other parallels include the following: just as Moses crossed the Sea of Reeds by means of his rod, so Elijah crossed the Jordan by means of his mantle (Exod. 14.16; 2 Kgs 2.8); and just as Joshua succeeded Moses (Num. 27.15-23), so Elisha succeeded Elijah (1 Kgs 19.16; 2 Kgs 2.9-14).[18]

18.   See also DeVries 1985: 209–10. The criteria of multiple occurrence and source criticism support the posited direction of dependence. With regard to multiple occurrence, I argued above that Dtr patterned the incident concerning the twelve stones of Josh. 4.7-9 after Exod. 24.4, where Moses 'set up an altar at the foot of the mountain, with twelve pillars for the twelve tribes of Israel'. The fact that 1 Kgs 18.31 is likewise parallel to Exod. 24.4 suggests that Dtr was also

As with Samuel, Dtr drew the above parallels between Moses and Elijah to emphasize the positive nature of Elijah's prophetic ministry.[19] But in keeping with his contention that 'never again did there arise in Israel a prophet like Moses', Dtr was careful not to equate Elijah with Moses. This is evident from two differences between Moses and Elijah in the accounts concerning the covenant. First, Moses requested to die because he wanted the LORD to pardon the people for worshiping the golden calf: 'Now, if you will forgive their sin [well and good]; but if not, erase me from the record which you have written' (Exod. 32.32). This is in contrast to Elijah, who, after having been frightened by Jezebel's plan to kill him, asked to die because he lamented his failure: 'Now, O LORD, take my life for I am no better than my fathers' (1 Kgs 19.4).[20] The second difference between Moses and Elijah pertains to the theophanies. After the description of awesome visual and audible violence, 'God answered [Moses] in thunder (בקול)' (Exod. 19.19). Dtr freely adapted this schema to underline the point that Elijah was not equal to Moses, for according to 1 Kgs 19.11-12 'the LORD was not in' the wind, the earthquake, or the fire but in a 'still, small voice' (קול דממה דקה).[21] Like Joshua, then, Elijah was not a prophet like Moses.[22]

responsible for the parallel between 1 Kgs 18.31 and Exod. 24.4. This contention is buttressed by the greater continuity between Josh. 4.8 and 1 Kgs 18.31 than between these passages and Exod. 24.4. Whereas both Josh. 4.8 and 1 Kgs 18.31 refer to twelve 'stones', Exod. 24.4 refers to twelve 'pillars'. Again, both Josh. 4.8 and 1 Kgs 18.31 define the symbolic action in the same way – 'according to the number of the tribes of the children of Israel/Jacob' – while Exod. 24.4 reads, 'according to the twelve tribes of Israel'. With regard to the criterion of source criticism, I noted above that 1 Kgs 17.6 ('bread and meat every morning and bread and meat every evening') is parallel to Exod. 16.8 ('flesh to eat in the evening and bread in the morning'). This verse from Exodus has traditionally been assigned to P (Childs 1974: 274–76). I also noted above the striking verbal correspondence between the people's response to the fire from the LORD in 1 Kgs 18.38-39 and Lev. 9.24. This verse from Leviticus has likewise traditionally been assigned to P. All the other parallels that Elijah shares with Moses come from non-P sections of the Tetrateuch.

19. See also Carroll 1969: 413; and Wilson 1980: 198.

20. Zakovitch 1991: 72. Elijah's confession that he was no better than his fathers may be a subtle criticism of his prophetic forbears who similarly failed to fulfill the Mosaic schema.

21. Childs 1980: 135. Garsiel (1987: 25) arrived at a similar conclusion on the basis of a contrast between Obadiah and Elijah:

> Obadiah remains within the establishment and among his people, taking pains to save the prophets from being cut off (*krt*) by Jezebel and participating in the efforts to save the beasts from being cut off (*krt*). Elijah, on the other hand, is far away from his people, by the brook Cherith (*kryt*), detached from all the suffering and enjoying a relatively better life. In this implied comparison, the author conveys an ironical criticism of Elijah's behavior in his capacity as a spiritual leader.

22. There are also notable parallels between Elijah and Jacob. The link between these personages is first evident from 1 Kgs 18.31: 'Then Elijah took twelve stones, corresponding to the number of the tribes of the sons of Jacob – to whom the word of the LORD had come: 'Israel shall be your name'. In addition to this reference to Jacob, 'Israel shall be your name' (ישראל יהיה שמך) is exactly parallel to God's promise to Jacob in Gen. 35.10. Another cross-reference to Jacob is present in Elijah's use of the rare triad in his prayer to 'the LORD God of Abraham, Isaac, and *Israel*' (1 Kgs 18.36). Other parallels include the following: prior to meeting Esau Jacob was 'left

I turn now to the parallels shared by Moses and Gideon.[23] As the Egyptians oppressed Israel in the time of Moses and the Israelites 'cried (ויזעקו) out to the LORD', so in the time of Gideon the Midianites oppressed Israel whose 'cry' (ויזעקו) rose up to God (Exod. 2.23; Judg. 6.6).[24] The connection between Moses and Gideon is further suggested by Gideon's references to the deliverance from Egypt in his question 'Where are all his wonders about which our fathers told us, saying, "Truly the LORD brought us up from Egypt"?' (Judg. 6.13). Gideon's reference to 'all his wonders' (כל־נפלאתיו) is parallel to the LORD's statement to Moses that he was to smite Egypt 'with all [his] wonders' (בכל נפלאתי; Exod. 3.20). The link with the deliverance from Egypt is furthered by the oracle of an unnamed prophet: 'I brought you up out of *Egypt* and freed you from the house of bondage. I rescued you from the *Egyptians*' (Judg. 6.8-9). The calls of Moses and Gideon also share parallel features. As 'the messenger of the LORD appeared to [Moses]' (וירא מלאך יהוה אליו; Exod. 3.2), so 'the messenger of the LORD appeared to [Gideon]' (וירא אליו מלאך יהוה; Judg. 6.12).[25] Both figures were afraid to look at the theophany (Exod. 3.6; Judg. 6.22). As God nevertheless said to Moses, 'I will send you', so he said to Gideon, 'have I not sent you?' (Exod. 3.10; Judg. 6.14). Both Moses and Gideon regarded themselves as unequal to the task of delivering Israel but the LORD nevertheless assured them of his presence – the LORD said to both Moses and Gideon 'for I will be with you' (כי־אהיה עמך) (Exod. 3.12; Judg. 6.16).[26] Again, both Moses and Gideon received signs from the LORD as confirmations that he would grant them success: the LORD gave signs to Moses (Exod. 4.1-9), and Gideon requested miracles from the LORD (Judg. 6.36-40). The divine commissioning of Moses and Gideon is also parallel. As the LORD commanded Moses to fight the Midianites, so he called Gideon to deliver Israel from the Midianites (Num. 31.2; Judg. 6.14). Moses did so in response to the Midianite seduction of Israel in Numbers 25, while Gideon did so in keeping with the sin-opression-deliverance cycle in Judges.[27] Finally, 'Jether' (יתר) was the name of both Moses' father-in-law and the son of

by himself' (וינתר...לבדו; Gen. 32.24[25]), and Elijah complained that 'I am left by myself' (ואותר אני לבדי; 1 Kgs 19.10, 14; cf. 18.22); to end the wrestling match the mysterious man 'struck Jacob's hip' (וינע בכף־ירכו; Gen. 32.25[26]), and to awaken Elijah a messenger 'struck him' (נגע בו; 1 Kgs 19.5).

23. I adapted many of the following parallels from Zakovitch 1991: 67–69; Klein 1988: 49–69; and Allison 1993: 28–30. See also Auld 1989.

24. As I noted in Chapter 2, Dtr was also reliant on Exod. 2.23 for the despair of the Ekronites in the Ark Narrative: as the Hebrews' 'outcry went up' (ותעל שועתם) to God (Exod. 2.23), so the Ekronites' 'outcry went up' (ותעל שועת) to the skies (1 Sam. 5.12).

25. This word string only appears in these two instances (cf. Judg. 13.3). The first 'to him' represents the passage from Judges while the second represents Exodus.

26. This clause only occurs in these instances.

27. Garsiel (1987: 155) noted the following links, which the Gideon narrative shares with Numbers 25. Upon their defeat, the Midianites fled as far as Beth Shittah (בית השטה) and on to Zererah (צררתה) (Judg. 7.22). Such place names are reminiscent of 'Shittim' (שטים) where the Midianites seduced Israel (Num. 25.1), Cozbi the infamous daughter of 'Zur' (צור) (Num. 25.15), and the LORD's command to Moses to 'assail' (צרור) the Midianites who 'assailed' (צרורים) Israel (Num. 25.17-18).

Gideon (Exod. 4.18; Judg. 8.20);[28] and just as Moses killed an Egyptian for beating a Hebrew, 'his brother' (אחיו), so Gideon killed Zebah and Zalmunna for killing 'my brothers' (אחי) (Exod. 2.11-14; Judg. 8.18-21).

Dtr's purpose in drawing the above parallels is consistent with his bivalent depiction of Gideon.[29] Positively, the LORD was with Gideon (Judg. 6.12, 16), Gideon was the LORD's messenger (Judg. 6.14), Gideon had found favor in the LORD's sight (Judg. 6.17), the spirit of the LORD possessed Gideon (Judg. 6.34), the LORD delivered the camp of Midian into Gideon's hand (Judg. 7.9), and Gideon rejected the invitation to rule, for he wanted only the LORD to rule Israel (Judg. 8.22-23). Negatively, Gideon was afraid to replace the altar of Baal with an altar to the LORD during the day (Judg. 6.25-27), he was afraid to attack the Midianite camp (Judg. 7.10), and, most significantly, he erected an ephod that led Israel astray (Judg. 8.24-27). The parallels also present Gideon both positively and negatively. Not unlike the depiction of Joshua as a new Moses, the parallels between Gideon and Moses are suggestive of a positive portrayal of Gideon. The positive parallels nevertheless unwind with Gideon's complaint of Judg. 6.13:

> Please, my Lord, if the LORD is with us, then why has all this befallen us? Now where are all his wondrous deeds about which our fathers told us, saying, 'Truly, the LORD brought us up from Egypt'? Now the LORD has abandoned us and delivered us into the hands of Midian!

I noted above that the LORD's statement 'for I will be with you' (כי־אהיה עמך) occurs only in the divine assurance given to Moses and Gideon (Exod. 3.12; Judg. 6.16). Whereas this parallel serves to align Gideon with Moses, Gideon's complaint concerning the absence of the LORD's presence is an inversion of the assurance to Moses – '*if* the LORD is with us' (ויש יהוה עמנו; Judg. 6.13). But the inversion goes further than what is found in Gideon's complaint, for Dtr patterned Gideon first after Moses and then after his apostate brother Aaron. The bivalent depiction of Gideon is nowhere more apparent than at the close of the Gideon narrative. In response to Israel's request that Gideon rule over them, Gideon stated, 'I will not rule over you myself, nor shall my son rule over you; the LORD alone shall rule over you' (Judg. 8.23). Yet immediately following this pious rejection Gideon requested the earrings of the Israelites – from which he made an ephod that led both Gideon and Israel astray (Judg. 8.24-27). Contiguous with this bizarre transition, the parallels with Moses cease and Gideon becomes a new, apostate Aaron. As Aaron told the Israelites to take off their rings of gold (נזמי הזהב; Exod. 32.2), so at Gideon's request the Israelites gave him their rings of gold (נזמי זהב; Judg. 8.24). Aaron thereupon made a molten calf from the rings, just as Gideon made an ephod from the rings (Exod. 32.4; Judg. 8.27). Finally, in both instances the people then worshiped the molten calf/ephod (Exod. 32.8; Judg. 8.27). The interplay of positive and negative portrayals of Gideon is thus consistent with the transition from parallels with Moses to parallels with Aaron.[30]

---

28. Elsewhere, Moses' father-in-law has the name Jethro (יתרו; Exod. 3.1; 18.1-2, 5-6, 12).
29. See Klein (1983: 67) for the ironic depiction of Gideon.
30. See also Alter 1981: 126–27.

This brings me to the many parallels that exist between Exodus–Numbers and 1 Kings 5–15. The Deuteronomistic story is an inversion of its corresponding Tetrateuchal account. Solomon was patterned after Moses only to become a new Pharaoh; Rehoboam the king of Israel similarly became a new Pharaoh; Hadad followed the Mosaic trail only to turn from it at the point of delivering oppressed Israel; Jeroboam likewise followed in the steps of Moses only up to the point of delivering Israel – at which point he, like Gideon before him, ironically became an apostate Aaron. In addition to underlining the absence of a Mosaic deliverer, Dtr's purpose in drawing such parallels was twofold. First, Dtr thereby indicted the early monarchy for having become a new Egypt that enslaved the people of God.[31] Second, by drawing the given parallels Dtr underlined the seriousness of Jeroboam's sin. Israel was to worship only in the place that the LORD would choose (Deuteronomy 12). This place becomes Solomon's temple in Jerusalem. By erecting places of worship in Bethel and Dan, Jeroboam violated this Deuteronomic command, and his sin was prototypical, for every subsequent king of Israel 'walked in the ways of Jeroboam'.[32]

That 1 Kings 5–15 amounts to the reliving of Israel's early history as a nation is first evident from the place that Dtr accorded the temple.[33] For Dtr, the tabernacle was but the temple *in utero*. This is suggested by Solomon's dedication of the temple in 1 Kings 8: the priests brought the 'tent of meeting' together with its holy vessels to the temple (1 Kgs 8.4); and they 'brought the Ark of the LORD's covenant to its place' in the holy of holies (1 Kgs 8.6). Moses, the mind behind the tabernacle, is thus the antecedent of Solomon, the constructor of the temple. Yet Solomon tragically became the antithesis of Moses. Whereas Moses brought the people out of Egypt and led them to the edge of the promised land, Solomon transmogrified the promised land into an oppressive Egypt. The relationship between Solomon and Egypt is first evident from 1 Kgs 3.1: 'Solomon allied himself by marriage with Pharaoh king of Egypt'.[34] Solomon's relationship to the law of the king in Deut. 17.14-20 also links Solomon to Egypt. As Brettler (1991: 91–92) noted, the statement 'and he shall not take many wives, lest his heart go astray' of Deut. 17.17a shares striking parallels with 1 Kgs 11.1-10:

---

31. The DtrH is replete with anti-Egypt rhetoric. The LORD had delivered Israel from that 'iron furnace' (1 Kgs 8.51) with a 'mighty hand and an outstretched arm' (Deut. 6.21; 26.8). The children were to learn this (Deut. 6.20-25). The people were to recall it at their festivals (Deut. 26.5-10). Kings were not to send the people back to Egypt (Deut. 17.16), and the final Deuteronomic curse for disobedience included returning to Egypt where the people would offer themselves as slaves (Deut. 28.68). By patterning Israel's leaders after the pharaohs of Exodus and incomplete Moses, Dtr provided a damning critique of the early monarchy: Israel had become a new Egypt.

32. In Dtr's mind the most heinous sin was the worship of the golden calves as instituted by Jeroboam, as is clear from the emphasis that it receives (1 Kgs 12.30; 14.16; 15.30, 34; 16.2, 7, 19, 26, 31; 22.53[54]; 2 Kgs 3.3; 10.29, 31; 13.2, 6, 11; 14.24; 15.9, 18, 24, 28; 17.21-22; 23.15). See Knoppers (1995).

33. At the end of this chapter, see Table 2, Retelling Mosaic Traditions in 1 Kings 5-15.

34. Some, such as Gray (1970: 116–17), have argued that 1 Kgs 3.1 is intrusive. This verse, however, which is similar to 9.24-25, is integral to the structure of 3.1–9.25 and is therefore original to the composition. See also Brettler 1991 and Long 1984: 58–59.

Its literary connection to Deut. 17.17 is clear; Deuteronomy prohibits having too many wives, using the verb רבה, 'to increase', the same root used in 11.1, נשים רבות נכריות, 'many foreign wives'. Deuteronomy, in its motive clause, warns ולא יסור לבבו, 'so his heart will not stray'; paralleled by 1 Kgs 11.2, יטו את־לבבכם [the nations…who] will sway your heart', v. 3 ויטו נשיו את־לבו 'his wives swayed his heart', v. 9 כי־נטה לבבו, 'because his heart strayed' and perhaps the mention of לבב, 'heart', twice in v. 4b.[35]

Solomon's amassing of gold and wealth in 1 Kgs 10.11-25 is similarly reminiscent of 'nor shall he amass silver and gold to excess' of Deut. 17.17b. Equally striking is Deut. 17.16, 'he shall not keep many horses or send people back to Egypt to add to his horses since the LORD has warned you, "You shall not go back that way again" '. Contrary to this command, 'Solomon assembled chariots and horses, which he stationed in the chariot towns and with the king in Jerusalem… Solomon's horses were procured from Egypt and Kue (1 Kings 10.26, 28)'.[36] In light of the parallels between Deut. 17.16-17 and Solomon, Dtr likely had the law of the king in mind in his references both to Solomon's marriage to Pharaoh's daughter and to Solomon's horses. In contrast to Moses, then, Solomon led Israel from Canaan back to Egypt and Solomon thereby inverted the Exodus story.

Consistent with the above inversion are the parallels that Dtr drew between Pharaoh of the Exodus story and Solomon. As magnificent as Solomon's building enterprises may have been, according to Dtr they were accomplished on the backs of Israelites and non-Israelites alike (1 Kgs 5.13[27]-18[32]; 9.20-22) – a portrayal that conjures up images of the pharaohs' mistreatment of Israel. Indeed, the Israelites could later say to Rehoboam that his father made their 'yoke heavy', which parallels what Pharaoh had done to their forefathers (1 Kgs 12.4; Exod. 5.6-18). More specifically, the Egyptians and Pharaoh imposed 'hard labour' (עבודה קשה) on Israel (Exod. 1.14; 6.9), even as the Israelites begged Rehoboam to lighten the 'hard labour' of his father (מעבדת אביך הקשה; 1 Kgs 12.4). Zakovitch (1991: 88) similarly noted that both Pharaoh and Solomon used slave labour to build 'store cities' (ערי מסכנות), which is again suggestive of Dtr's attempt to draw a parallel between these figures (Exod. 1.11; 1 Kgs 9.19).

What is only adumbrated with Solomon becomes developed with Hadad, for in just nine verses Dtr drew a host of parallels between Moses and Hadad (1 Kgs 11.14-22). Just as Pharaoh sought to kill all the Hebrew male infants in the time of Moses, so Joab killed every Edomite male in Hadad's day (Exod. 1.15-22; 1 Kgs 11.15-16).[37] Both Moses and Hadad escaped from their oppressors: Moses was delivered from the threat of male infanticide, and Hadad escaped the massacre of male Edomites (Exod. 1.22–2.10; 1 Kgs 11.17).[38] Whereas Moses fled from Egypt to Midian, however, Hadad fled from Midian to Egypt (Exod. 2.15; 1 Kgs 11.18). While Moses was in Midian he won the favour of Reuel the priest of Midian who

35. See also Sweeney 1995: 616–17.
36. Cf. 1 Kgs 5.1[4.21]; 5.6[4.26].
37. Because the subject of 'he struck' is unspecified, the translations differ over whether it was Joab or David who did the killing.
38. Note also Exod. 2.11-15 where Moses fled from Pharaoh after he killed the Egyptian.

then gave Moses his daughter Zipporah, who bore Moses a son, Gershom (Exod.
2.16-22). While Hadad was in Egypt he similarly won the favor of Pharaoh, who
gave his sister-in-law to Hadad as a wife, who bore Hadad a son, Genubath (1 Kgs
11.18-20). There is also a parallel between Moses and Genubath insofar as both
were weaned by someone other than their natural mothers and both were brought
up in foreign courts. Both Moses and Hadad then discovered that their oppressors
had died. As the LORD told Moses in Midian, 'Go back to Egypt, for the men who
sought to kill you are dead', so 'Hadad heard in Egypt that David had been laid to
rest with his fathers and that Joab the army commander was dead' (Exod. 4.19;
1 Kgs 11.21). Just as Moses then requested of Jethro, 'Let me go back to my kins-
men in Egypt and see how they are faring', so Hadad then requested of Pharaoh,
'Give me leave to go to my own country' (Exod. 4.18; 1 Kgs 11.21). Finally, shortly
after the Sinai event Moses and the people stayed in the wilderness of Paran (Num.
10.12), at which time they successfully urged Hobab to stay with them (Num.
10.29-32). This parallels the fact that Hadad and some Edomite men traveled to
Paran and 'took along with them men from Paran' (1 Kgs 11.18).

This brings me to the parallels between Pharaoh and Rehoboam. Whereas Moses
and Aaron asked Pharaoh to give the people reprieve from their labors and let them
go on a three-day journey for worship, after Rehoboam was asked of his people to
lighten their labors, Rehoboam instructed the people to go away for three days,
after which time he would tell them his decision (Exod. 5.1, 3; 8.23[27]; 1 Kgs
12.4-5, 9-12). In each instance the kings uttered parallel responses to the peoples'
requests for reprieve. Pharaoh commanded that the people's labors were to increase,
and Rehoboam informed the people that their labors would be sharply multiplied
(Exod. 5.6-18; 1 Kgs 12.9-14). In both accounts officials urged the king to heed the
cries of the people (Exod. 10.7; 1 Kgs 12.7). Both Pharaoh and Rehoboam, however, failed to do so (Exod. 10.8-11, 24-29; 1 Kgs 12.8). As the LORD had hardened
Pharaoh's heart to accomplish his purpose, so Rehoboam did not heed the advice
of his counselors for the LORD 'had brought it about to fulfill the promise' (Exod.
4.21; 10.1; etc.; 1 Kgs 12.15). Finally, as Israel carried off Egypt's wealth because
of Pharaoh's stubbornness, so the sins of Rehoboam and his people led to Egypt
despoiling Israel (Exod. 12.35-36; 1 Kgs 14.25-26).

The final parallels between 1 Kings 5–15 and Tetrateuchal accounts concern
the depiction of Jeroboam. In the introduction I outlined the many parallels that
Jeroboam shares with Moses. I also noted that although Jeroboam ceased following
Moses with his apostasy, Moses nevertheless reappeared on the scene in the man of
God who denounced Jeroboam.[39] As elsewhere, Dtr here gave a damning critique
of the early monarchy.

39. The proposed direction of dependence between the Moses and Jeroboam accounts is
supported by the criteria of incongruity and Deuteronomistic tendency. Concerning the criterion of
incongruity, I noted in the Introduction that Tahpenes, rather than Genubath the mother of Hadad,
weaned Hadad. Rather than following the MT's ותגמלהו (and [Tahpanes] weaned him) in 1 Kgs
11.20, a few commentators, such as Gray (1970: 282), have followed the LXX's καὶ ἐξέθρεψεν
αὐτὸν = ותגדלהו (and [Tahpanes] reared him) because Tahpanes' weaning of Hadad is incongruous (her sister was the mother). But consistent with the many parallels between Moses and Hadad,

Dtr's purpose for drawing the above sets of parallels is clearest from the flights of Hadad and Jeroboam from their oppressors. Hadad's flight was the reciprocal of Moses' flight. Whereas Moses fled to Midian from Egypt, Hadad fled to Egypt from Midian. Jeroboam's flight is similarly an inversion of the Exodus. Whereas the nation fled from Egypt to Israel, Jeroboam fled from Israel to Egypt. As with the Ark Narrative, Dtr drew such inversions to present Israel as a new Egypt. Contravening the divine prohibition to return to Egypt (Deut. 17.16; cf. 28.68), the nation's leaders made Israel itself the locale of slavery and oppression – and Egypt ironically became the land of refuge. Consonant with this inversion is the fact that, unlike their Tetrateuchal exemplar, Hadad and Jeroboam failed to deliver Israel. At the point where the implied reader expects Hadad and then Jeroboam to deliver Israel they fail – there is no new Moses to deliver oppressed Israel. If the pattern between Moses and Hadad had continued, Hadad would have been in the position to deliver Israel from pharaonic Solomon. But the parallels stop abruptly when Hadad requests to return to Edom (1 Kgs 11.22) – even as Moses had requested to return to Egypt (Exod. 4.18). The conclusion to Deuteronomy becomes all the more haunting: 'Never again did there arise in Israel a prophet like Moses' (Deut. 34.10).

What remains to be discussed is Dtr's purpose for drawing the parallels between Jeroboam and Aaron. Like Gideon before him, Jeroboam was on his way to becoming a new Moses, but he ended up as the antithesis, a new Aaron.[40] On the surface it appears that Dtr simply wanted to underline his negative portrayal of Jeroboam – and therefore the sinfulness of those kings who broke the command of centralized

it is better to regard this incongruity as Dtr's attempt to call the reader's attention to the Moses narrative (Exod. 2.9). Concerning the criterion of Deuteronomistic tendency, the fact that Dtr had a penchant for using and adapting personal names (Onan and Amnon; Bath-Sheva and Bath–Sheba; Laban and Nabal; Phinehas and Phinehas), and that he used the names of Aaron's sons elsewhere ('Nadab' and 'Abihu' become 'Abinadab' of 1 Sam. 7.1), suggests that he was also responsible for the names 'Nadab' and 'Abijah'. My conclusion that Dtr rather than his Tetrateuchal counterparts drew the given parallels has obvious ramifications for the ongoing discussion (see Knoppers 1995) concerning the relationship between the golden–calf narrative and the golden-calves narrative (Exod. 32.1-6; 1 Kgs 12.26-33). Because such parallels are but a part of a complex of parallels that commence with Solomon and extend to Jeroboam's sons, it is best to conclude that the golden-calves narrative of Kings was based on the golden-calf narrative of Exodus.

40. Out of fairness to Aaron, however, Dtr's presentation of Jeroboam is worse than the Tetrateuchal depiction of Aaron. (1) Whereas at Sinai Aaron fashioned the golden calf under duress (the people gathered against Aaron [Exod. 32.1]), Jeroboam's measures were considered and deliberate (1 Kgs 12.26-28) (Knoppers 1995: 97). (2) Whereas in Exodus 32 the people made the declaration 'these are your gods, O Israel, who brought you up from the land of Egypt' (32.4), in 1 Kings 12 Jeroboam himself made the declaration (12.28). (3) Dtr depicted Jeroboam as an anti-Moses insofar as all that he did after setting up the calves and before the encounter with the man of God was against Mosaic legislation. This is already evident in his gross infraction of the doctrine of centralized worship; but it is also clear from those statements that underline the novelty of Jeroboam's actions. Jeroboam instituted a new priesthood made up of people 'who were not of Levite descent' (1 Kgs 12.31); and in imitation of the festival in Judah he established a festival at Bethel, but the date that he set for this festival was contrary to Mosaic legislation: 'on the fifteenth day of the eighth month – *the month in which he contrived of his own mind* to establish a festival for the Israelites' (1 Kgs 12.33; cf. Lev. 23.39-41).

worship. But Dtr's purpose in drawing the parallel between Jeroboam and Aaron goes beyond the equation 'the sin of Jeroboam in 1 Kings 12 = the sin of Aaron in Exodus 32'. Jeroboam's action was the prototype of monarchic infidelity to the doctrine of centralized worship, and as such he is an anti-Moses. Another equation is therefore 'Jeroboam = the reciprocal of Moses'. The longing for a prophet like Moses is thus left unfulfilled in the DtrH. From Dtr's perspective, the promise could only remain for future fulfillment.

To this point I have asserted that the reader must interpret common features in parallel narratives together, interpret the parallel narratives in their narrative contexts, and identify methodological patterns. As I contended in this chapter, one such methodological pattern is inversion. In order to augment his concerns, Dtr was fond of upsetting the schemata that his Torah afforded him. This is particularly the case with his depiction of Moses. At best, the leaders of the nation might be distortions of Moses. Joshua was almost the mirror image of his predecessor, yet he made covenants both with Rahab and the Gibeonites. Although Elijah was a prophet like Moses, unlike his exemplar he succumbed to fear and despondency. Other leaders frustrated the Moses schema by following the Mosaic trail only to stop short of delivering the nation, as was the case with Hadad.[41] Worse than this, Dtr frustrated the Moses schema by leaders who were in some way the inverse of Moses. Solomon had become a new Pharaoh who oppressed the nation with slavery. Gideon delivered Israel like Moses only to lead the nation in apostasy like Aaron. And Jeroboam was similarly set to deliver Israel from pharaonic Rehoboam, but like Gideon he too became an apostate Aaron. For Dtr the stature of various individuals was thus proportionate to the degree to which they fulfilled or fumbled the Mosaic model.

41.   This tendency of Dtr is consistent with the cycle of reform and decline in 1 and 2 Kings. See Hoffmann 1980.

Table 1 *Moses and his Deuteronomistic Counterparts*

	Moses	Joshua	Gideon	Samuel	Hadad	Jeroboam	Elijah
Lived under oppressive regime	Exod. 2-14		Judg. 6.6			1 Kgs 12.1-14	
Suckled by mother	Exod. 2.1-9			1 Sam. 1.20-23			
Escaped genocide	Exod. 2.1-10				1 Kgs 11.15-17		
Raised in/enjoyed official office	Exod. 2.10			1 Sam. 1.24-3.19		1 Kgs 11.28	
Avenged 'brother(s)'	Exod. 2.11-14		Judg. 8.18-21				
Fled from king to a foreign land	Exod. 2.15				1 Kgs 11.17-18	1 Kgs 11.40	
Wed foreign authority's relation	Exod. 2.16-22				1 Kgs 11.19		
Authority's relation bore a son	Exod. 2.22				1 Kgs 11.20		
Encounter with angel/man	Exod. 3.1-5	Josh. 5.13-15	Judg. 6.11-24				
Received divine call	Exod. 3.1-6		Judg. 6.11-24	1 Sam. 3.1-14			
Received divine signs	Exod. 4.1-9		Judg. 6.36-40				
'Jether' a familial relation	Exod. 4.18		Judg. 8.20				
Returned at enemy's death	Exod. 4.18-19				1 Kgs 11.21-22		
Requested reprieve/relief	Exod. 5.1-3					1 Kgs 12.4	
Were denied the request	Exod. 5.1-5					1 Kgs 12.13-14	
Witnessed plagues on enemy	Exod. 5-12			1 Samuel 5-6			
Circumcision and Passover	Exod. 12.43-50	Josh. 5.2-12					
Crossed the water	Exodus 14	Joshua 3					
Victory over the enemy	Exodus 14			1 Samuel 7			
Crossed water with rod/mantle	Exod. 14.6						2 Kgs 2.8
Daily bread and meat	Exod. 16.8, 12						1 Kgs 17.6
Violent theophany	Exod. 19.16-18						1 Kgs 19.11-12
Gathered people to Sinai/Carmel	Exod. 19.17						1 Kgs 18.19
Built altar of 12 pillars/stones	Exod. 24.4						1 Kgs 18.31
'Abraham, Isaac, and Israel'	Exod. 32.13						1 Kgs 18.36
Command to Slaughter Idolaters	Exod. 32.26-28						1 Kgs 18.21, 40
Saw theophany from rock/cave	Exod. 33.21-22						1 Kgs 19.11, 13

Table 1 (continued).

	Moses	Joshua	Gideon	Samuel	Hadad	Jeroboam	Elijah
Maintenance of the covenant	Exodus 34						1 Kings 19
Fast of forty days and nights	Exod. 34.28						1 Kgs 19.8
Peoples' response to divine fire	Lev. 9.24						1 Kgs 18.38-39
Visited Paran	Num. 10.12				1 Kgs 11.18		
Was rebelled against	Numbers 11			1 Samuel 8			
Sent spies to explore land	Numbers 13	Joshua 2					

Table 2 *Retelling Mosaic Traditions in 1 Kings 5–15*

	Moses	Hadad	Jeroboam
Grandeur in the king's court	Exod. 2.10		1 Kgs 11.28
Lived under oppressive kng(s)	Exod. 2.14		1 Kgs 12.1-14
Escaped genocide	Exod. 1.15-16; 2.1-10	1 Kgs 11.15-17	
Fled from king to a foreign land	Exod. 2.15	1 Kgs 11.17-18	1 Kgs 11.40
Wed authority's daughter who bore a son	Exod. 2.16-22	1 Kgs 11.19-20	
Requested to return at death of enemy	Exod. 4.18-19	1 Kgs 11.21-22	
Requested reprieve/relief	Exod. 5.1-3		1 Kgs 12.4
Denied request for reprieve/relief	Exod. 5.1-5		1 Kgs 12.13-14
Visited Paran	Num. 10.12, 29-33	1 Kgs 11.18	

Table 2 (continued).

Aaron and Jeroboam

	Aaron	Jeroboam
Counseled to build calf/calves	Exod. 32.1	1 Kgs 12.28
Declaration of calf/calves	Exod. 32.4, 8	1 Kgs 12.28
Built/ascended altar	Exod. 32.5	1 Kgs 12.32
Celebrated festival	Exod. 32.5-6	1 Kgs 12.32-33
Priests (to be) slain	Exod. 32.26-28	1 Kgs 13.2
Worst offense in Tetrateuch/DtrH	Exod. 32.21, 30-34	1 Kgs 14.16; 15.30, 34; etc.
Sons were Nadab and Abihu/Abijah	Exod. 6.23, etc.	1 Kgs 14.1; 15.25
Sons died for cultic infractions	Lev. 10.1-2	1 Kgs 14.1-14, 17; 15.25-30
Sons had no descendants	Num. 3.4	1 Kgs 14.10-11; 15.29

Second Pharaohs

	Pharaoh(s)	Joab	Solomon	Rehoboam
Oppressed Israel	Exod. 1.8-14; 5.6-14		1 Kgs 5.27-30; 9.15-22	1 Kgs 12.13-14
Killed males	Exod. 1.15-22	1 Kgs 11.15-16		
Rejected reprieve	Exod. 5.1-5			1 Kgs 12.13-14
Increased burden	Exod. 5.6-19			1 Kgs 12.9-14
Rejected advice	Exod. 10.7-11			1 Kgs 12.7-8
Providence and sin	Exod. 4.21; etc.			1 Kgs 12.15
Plundered Egypt/Israel	Exod. 12.35-36			1 Kgs 14.25-26

Chapter 5

Judgment and Torah Schemata

In the preceding chapter I argued that Dtr frustrated the Moses schema with leaders who stopped short of delivering the nation or, worse yet, by grafting it with the Aaron schema. A similar methodological pattern for Dtr included underlining the sinfulness of characters by comparing or contrasting them with characters in his Torah, or, unlike their Torah counterparts, by denying them divine intervention.

Dtr castigated Eli the priest's reprobate sons Hophni and Phinehas, by patterning them after Aaron the priest's sons Nadab and Abihu.[1] Just as Nadab and Abihu were put to death at the same time for their cultic infraction (Lev. 10.1-3; Num. 3.4; 26.61), so cultic infractions led to the killing of Hophni and Phinehas on the same day (1 Sam. 2.12-17, 27-34; 4.17). More specifically, parallel to 'I will be honored (אכבד, *niphal*) before all the people' (Lev. 10.3) is 'for those who honor me I will honor (אכבד, *piel*)' (1 Sam. 2.30).[2] Furthermore, whereas Nadab (נדב) and Abihu (אביהוא) were the sons of Aaron, Abinadab (אבינדב) – whose name is a combination of 'Abihu' and 'Nadab' – was the son of the priest Eleazar (1 Sam. 7.1). Finally, two men bear the name Phinehas. Phinehas the son of Aaron killed Zimri and Cozbi for their cultic/sexual transgression while all Israel was weeping at 'the entrance of the tent of meeting' (פתח אהל מועד; Num. 25.6).[3] As a result, Phinehas' line was to be an 'enduring priesthood' (כהנת עולם; Num. 25.13). This contrasts with Phinehas the son of Eli whose cultic/sexual offence consisted of having sexual relations with the women at the 'entrance of the tent of meeting' (פתח אהל מועד; 1 Sam. 2.22).[4] As a result, this Phinehas was to be put to death (1 Sam. 2.25), and his line would not last forever (עד־עולם; 1 Sam. 2.30).[5] This inverted

---

1. Harvey 2001: 71–73. See also Greenstein 1990: 171.

2. The only other instance of אכבד comes in Isa. 60.13 (*piel*).

3. That their sin was sexual is evident from Num. 25.1 (the men 'committed harlotry' [זנה√] with the Moabite women), and Num. 25.8 (Phinehas evidently killed the couple, who were in the tent, with one thrust of his spear). As Lutzky (1997: 546–49) contended, the name 'Cozbi' itself carries sexual overtones. That their sin also pertained to the cult is evident from Num. 25.2 (the people sacrificed to the Moabites' god).

4. For 'entrance of the tent of meeting' Dtr was reliant both on Num. 25.6 as well as Exod. 38.8: 'the women who performed tasks at the entrance to the tent of meeting' (הצבאות אשר צבאו פתח אהל מועד). Numbers 25.6 only refers to the 'entrance of the tent of meeting', and because Dtr wished to underline the sexual nature of Phinehas' sin, he coupled Num. 25.6 with Exod. 38.8 – the only text in his Torah that refers to women at the 'entrance of the tent of meeting'.

5. Dtr relied on P texts for these parallels. With the exception of the references to Nadab and

parallel between the first Phinehas (the son of Eleazar) and the second Phinehas (the son of Eli) underline Dtr's anticipation of the certain demise of Eli's line in 1 Samuel 2–3.[6]

Similar to the above example, in order to highlight his negative depiction of Saul in 1 Samuel 14–15 Dtr patterned this story after the Eden and Flood narratives.[7] In both the Eden and Saul stories a superior prohibited people from eating on pain of death (Gen. 2.17; 1 Sam. 14.24, 28, 39): more specifically, Saul's 'he will surely die' (מות ימות; 1 Sam. 14.39) parallels the LORD God's 'you will surely die' (מות תמות; Gen. 2.17 [cf. 3.3-4]); and Saul's 'Cursed be (√ארר) the man who eats any food' (1 Sam. 14.24, 28) is reminiscent of the divine 'cursing' (√ארר) of the serpent and the ground (Gen. 3.14, 17). The command was nevertheless transgressed:

Abihu in Exod. 24.1, 9, every other reference to them has been traditionally assigned to P (Exod. 6.23; 28.1; Num. 3.2, 4; 26.61-62; Lev. 10.1; see the discussions in Childs 1974: 111–14, 499–502; and Budd 1984: 29–30, 296–97). That Dtr patterned his account after the above P texts rather than after Exod. 24.1, 9 is evident from the fact that it is only the P texts that refer to the death of Nadab and Abihu. Again, that Dtr was reliant on P is evident from the striking structural and verbal parallels between the account of P's Phinehas in Numbers 25 and Dtr's Phinehas in 1 Samuel 2 (the account in Numbers has traditionally been assigned to P [Budd 1984: 275]), as well as from the quotation of Exod. 38.8 in 1 Sam. 2.22.

6.   Two arguments may be adduced in support of the proposed direction of dependence. The first concerns the criterion of context. In Chapter 3 I argued that Dtr patterned 1 Samuel 1–8 after the corresponding Tetrateuchal accounts. The parallels between the lines of Aaron and Eli are also therefore best explained by the proposed direction of dependence, for they are embedded within those between Moses and Samuel in 1 Samuel 1–8. The second argument concerns the criterion of incongruity. Whereas 1 Sam. 1.9 and 1 Sam. 3.3 refer to 'the *temple* of the LORD' (היכל יהוה) and 1 Sam. 3.15 refers to 'the doors of the *house* of the LORD' (את־דלתות בית־יהוה), 1 Sam. 2.22 refers to 'the entrance to the *tent of meeting*' (פתח אהל מועד). 1 Samuel 2.22 thus refers to the 'tent' while 1 Sam. 1.9 and 1 Sam. 3.3, 15 refer to the 'temple' or 'house'. Similar to what exists elsewhere, this incongruity is due to Dtr's quotation of Exod. 38.8. As I noted above, parallel to 'the women who performed tasks at the entrance to the tent of meeting' (הנשים הצבאו פתח אהל מועד) of 1 Sam. 2.22 is 'the women who performed tasks at the entrance to the tent of meeting' (הצבאות אשר צבאו פתח אהל מועד) of Exod. 38.8. As elsewhere, the incongruity can therefore be explained on the basis of Dtr's citation of the given Tetrateuchal account. Partly because of the inconsistency concerning the temple/house or tent, and partly because LXX[B] and 4QSam[a] do not include the MT's 'and how they lay with the women who performed tasks at the entrance to the tent of meeting', many commentators have argued that the MT of 1 Sam. 2.22 is an interpolation. Examples include Driver (1966: 33), McCarter (1980: 81) and Klein (1983: 22); cf. Brettler (1997: 603). But this view has not considered the given incongruities in light of the other parallels between the sons of Eli and Aaron. Moreover, the LXX's omission of the MT's 1 Sam. 2.22 may be explained as the result of its pro-priesthood *Tendenz* in 1 Samuel 2. In 1 Sam. 2.16, for instance, the MT has the people tell Eli's sons to burn the fat before taking the meat whereas the LXX has the people tell them to cook the sacrifices 'as it is fitting' (ὡς καθήκει). In 1 Sam. 2.28 of the MT the LORD stated that he had given all of the offerings by fire to the house of Eli and the LXX includes the phrase 'for food' (εἰς βρῶσιν), which is a reference to the obligation of the people to the Levites (Lev. 22.7; Num. 18.9-13; Deut. 18.1-8). Whereas the MT of 1 Sam. 2.32 has Eli ask, 'Why do you do these things, *the evil things* that I hear from all these people?', out of deference for the priesthood the LXX omits 'the evil things'. Finally, whereas in 1 Sam. 2.15 of the MT 'the priest' would not accept boiled flesh but only raw, in the LXX 'the servant of the priest' would not accept boiled flesh.

7.   I adapted most of these parallels from Blenkinsopp 1964: 447–48.

Jonathan ate the honey (1 Sam. 14.27) even as Eve and Adam ate the fruit (Gen.
3.6). The 'eyes' (עינים) of the transgressor(s) were consequently opened/brightened
(Gen. 3.7; 1 Sam. 14.27), and an interrogation ensued: the LORD God questioned the
first couple (Gen. 3.8-13), and Saul sought to determine who was at fault (1 Sam.
14.37-42). The LORD God's implicating question to Eve, 'What is this you have
done?' (מה־זאת עשׂית; Gen. 3.13) parallels Saul's command to Jonathan, 'Tell me
what you have done' (הגידה לי מה עשׂיתה; 1 Sam. 14.43). Finally, the sentence of
death was not carried out: Adam was banished from the garden (Gen. 3.22-24), and
the troops saved Jonathan (1 Sam. 14.45).[8]

The parallels shared by the stories of Saul and the Flood include the following.
As 'Noah built an altar to the LORD' prior to being prohibited from eating blood, so
'Saul built an altar to the LORD' after his troops had eaten blood (Gen. 8.20; 9.4;
1 Sam. 14.32-35). In each instance the LORD decreed annihilation because of sin:
humanity together with all animals, and the Amalekites together with their animals
(Gen. 6.5-7; 1 Sam. 15.2-3). Whereas the annihilation took place under Noah, however, Saul spared the best of the Amalekites. The contrast between Noah and Saul is
equally present in the LORD's 'I regret that (נחמתי כי) I made [humanity]' and the
LORD's corresponding 'I regret that (נחמתי כי) I made Saul king' (Gen. 6.7; 1 Sam.
15.11).[9] This contrast is also implicit in Noah's finding 'favor in the eyes of the
LORD' and Saul's doing 'evil in the eyes of the LORD' (Gen. 6.8; 1 Sam. 15.19).

As elsewhere, the reader's task is to interpret the above sets of parallels in light
of their narrative context. By drawing such parallels Dtr underscored the scandalous
nature of Israel's request for a human king. Such scandal is explicit in the LORD's
statement to Saul, 'it is not *you* that they have rejected; it is *me* they have rejected
as their king' (1 Sam. 8.7).[10] Dtr furthered the dialectic between choosing divine or
human kingship with the play on the roots מאס ('to reject') and מלך ('to be king').
Mirroring the human rejection of divine kingship in 1 Samuel 8 is the divine rejection of human kingship in 1 Samuel 15 – the LORD 'rejected' Saul as 'king' (1 Sam.
15.23, 26) even as the people had 'rejected' the LORD 'from being king' (1 Sam.
8.7).[11] The play on the words שׁמע ('to obey') and קול ('voice') similarly link 1 Samuel 8 and 15.[12] The LORD commanded Samuel to 'obey the voice' of the people in
their request for a king (1 Sam. 8.7, 9); and when Samuel warned the people of the
ways of the king they refused 'to obey the voice of Samuel' (1 Sam. 8.19). Samuel
in turn accused Saul, 'Why did you not obey the voice of the LORD?' (1 Sam.
15.19; cf. 15.22). Although Saul contested this accusation in saying that he 'did
obey the voice of the LORD' (1 Sam. 15.20), he later conceded that he feared the

---

8.   The troop's 'will he die?' (ימות) with reference to Jonathan (1 Sam. 14.45) here echoes the
serpent's statement to the woman, 'you will not surely die' (לא־מות תמתון; Gen. 3.3).

9.   The clause נחמתי כי only occurs in these instances.

10.   The emphasis is on the objective pronouns 'you' and 'me' which appear before the accompanying verbs. Note also the people's declaration that they wanted a human king who would fight
their battles (1 Sam. 8.19-20), even though the LORD triumphed over Philisita in the preceding
narrative.

11.   See also Fokkelman 1993: 59–60.

12.   See also Gunn 1980: 59–61.

people and that he 'obeyed their voice' (1 Sam. 15.24[25]). This then provides another ironic link between 1 Samuel 8 and 15. The LORD told Samuel to listen to 'the voice of the people' in 1 Samuel 8, whereas in 1 Samuel 15 'the voice of the people' was Saul's undoing.[13] It is evident, then, both from explicit statements and the given word plays that Dtr was concerned with the choice between divine and human rule.

The dialectic between choosing divine or human kingship is furthered by the parallels. In three instances in 1 Samuel 14 Saul curiously takes the place of the LORD God of Genesis 2–3: both Saul and the LORD God made a prohibition; they both interrogated the transgressor(s); and they both failed to carry out the sentence of death. As for 1 Samuel 15, like his divine exemplar in the Flood narrative Saul was to annihilate the population. But unlike his exemplar, Saul failed miserably in the task set before him – such that the LORD 'regretted' that he had made Saul king even as he had 'regretted' making humanity. King Saul could not replace the divine king. Saul's failure as a king is nowhere more clear than in 1 Samuel 14–15 where he sat under a tree while Jonathan initiated the defeat of the Philistines (1 Sam. 14.1-23), where his rash vow lessened the Israelite victory and caused the men to sin (1 Sam. 14.24-32), and where he failed to carry out the LORD's command to annihilate the Amalekites and their animals (1 Sam. 15.1-26). By drawing the given parallels, Dtr underlined the absurdity of replacing divine kingship with human kingship.[14]

In accordance with the archetypical nature of the Primeval History, Dtr based various stories concerning Joshua after narratives in the Primeval History to accentuate the nature of particular offenses. Dtr used the Eden narrative, for example, as the basis for Achan's sin (Joshua 7). As the LORD commanded Adam not to eat from the tree of knowledge lest he die, so Joshua commanded the Israelites not to take the plunder of Ai for themselves lest they be destroyed (Gen. 2.17; Josh. 6.18). In both instances, however, the parties transgressed the commands. As the woman 'saw' (ותרא) that the tree was 'good' (טוב) and 'desirable' (ונחמד), and 'took' (ותקח) some of its fruit (Gen. 3.6), so Achan confessed that when he 'saw' (ואראה) a 'good' (טוב) robe and much silver among the plunder, he 'desired' (ואחמדם) and 'took' (ואקחם) them (Josh. 7.21).[15] Following the transgressions, Joshua told Achan to tell him 'what he had done' (מה עשית; Josh. 7.19) even as the LORD asked the woman 'what is this [that] you have done?' (מה־זאת עשית; Gen. 3.13). This in turn led to the confessions of the woman and Achan (Gen. 3.13; Josh. 7.20-21). Finally, the couple's banishment from the garden and eventual death is parallel to the stoning of Achan which took place outside the camp (Gen. 3.22-24; Josh. 7.24-26). By patterning the Achan story on the Eden story, Dtr emphasized the gravity of Achan's sin – a sin that led both to the humiliation of Israel and the death of Achan and his household.

---

13. Alter 1999: 90. Consistent with Dtr's use of the Eden story in 1 Samuel 14, moreover, in the recurring motif 'obey the voice' Dtr alluded to the LORD God's sentencing of Adam ('Because you *obeyed the voice* of your wife' [Gen. 3.17; cf. 3.8, 10]).

14. Damrosch (1987: 201, 210) similarly contended that Saul is an 'anti-God'.

15. This word string only occurs in these instances.

Dtr likewise patterned the Gibeonite deception in Joshua 9 after the story of Adam. As the cunning serpent deceived the woman, so the Gibeonites lied about their place of origin (Gen. 3.1-6; Josh. 9.3-14). The woman had transgressed by 'taking' (ותקח) from the fruit and, without first inquiring of the LORD, the Israelites 'took' (ויקחו) from the Gibeonites' provisions (Gen. 3.6; Josh. 9.14). After the disobedience of the first couple the LORD God called Adam, 'Where are you?', even as Joshua inquired of the Gibeonites, 'Where do you come from?' (Gen. 3.9; Josh. 9.8). Finally, the consequences of these actions were dire. The LORD God 'cursed' (√ארר) both the serpent and the ground (Gen. 3.14, 17), which the man was sentenced to work (Gen. 3.17-19, 23); and Joshua similarly 'cursed' (√ארר) the Gibeonites (Josh. 9.23), who were to become slaves of the community (Josh. 9.21).[16]

Striking parallels also exist between the story of Balaam and Samuel's rejection of Saul. Just as Balaam said, 'God is not a human being, that he should lie, or a son of man (ובן אדם) that he should change his mind (√נחם)' (Num. 23.19), Samuel said that the LORD does not 'act deceptively or change his mind (√נחם), for he is not a man (אדם) that he should change his mind (√נחם)' (1 Sam. 15.29).[17] As Balaam confessed to the messenger of the LORD 'I have sinned for (כי חטאתי) I did not know that you were standing to meet me on the way; now (ועתה) if it is evil in your eyes I will return (√שוב)' (Num. 22.34), Saul similarly confessed to Samuel, 'I have sinned for (כי חטאתי) I transgressed the LORD's commands...now (ועתה)... return (√שוב) with me' (1 Sam. 15.24-25).[18] Even though the LORD had warned Balaam not to curse Israel, Balaam nevertheless offered sacrifices in order to sway the will of the LORD (Num. 22.12; 23.1-3). Similarly, although the LORD had instructed Saul to annihilate the Amalekites and their animals, Saul nevertheless mis-

---

16. The criterion of multiple occurrence supports the proposed direction of dependence, for Dtr also based the stories of Jonathan and Achan on the account of Adam's fall. Moreover, just as the LORD God 'cursed' (√ארר) the serpent and the ground (Gen. 3.14, 17), so Saul threatened a 'curse' (√ארר) to any man who eats food (1 Sam. 14.24, 28), and so Joshua similarly 'cursed' (√ארר) the Gibeonites (Josh. 9.23). Joshua 9 and 1 Samuel 14 thus share parallels with the Eden story at precisely the same point.

17. The proposed direction of dependence is here supported by the criterion of incongruity. Commentators have long queried over the contradiction in this story: in two instances the LORD 'changed his mind' (√נחם) over having made Saul king (1 Sam. 15.11, 35), yet Samuel could state that the LORD does not 'change his mind' (√נחם) over anything (1 Sam. 15.29). McCarter's (1980: 268) conclusion (which comes close to identifying the parallel) is typical: 'the contradiction...that this statement...contains is so blatant that we must question its originality. It may be a late addition to the text (*derived from Num. 23.19?*), penned by a redactor to whom the suggestion of a divine change of mind was unacceptable' (emphasis mine). But the incongruity was intentional. Indeed, both pronouncements are parallel to Tetrateuchal accounts. As I noted above, Dtr based the LORD's statement 'I change my mind' (√נחם) of 1 Sam. 15.11 on the Flood story, even as he based Samuel's statement of divine immutability – the LORD 'does not change his mind' in 1 Sam. 15.29 – on the Balaam story. By means of the contradiction, Dtr thus called the reader's attention both to the Flood and to the Balaam schemata.

18. This word string only occurs in these two instances. Note also the grammatical resemblance between 'I have sinned for' (כי חטאתי; 1 Sam. 15.24), which Dtr based on the Balaam story, and 'I regret that' (כי נחמתי), which Dtr based on the Flood story.

takenly thought that he would please the LORD by offering sacrifices (1 Sam. 15.3, 15, 20). Samuel's interpretation of Saul's disobedience is equally reminiscent of the Balaam story. Samuel said, 'For rebellion is no less a sin than *divination* (קסם), and stubbornness is like iniquity and idolatry' (1 Sam. 15.23). Parallel to this is Balaam's statement that 'there is no enchantment against Jacob, no *divination* (קסם) against Israel' (Num. 23.23). The accounts of Balaam and Saul also share references to Amalek, the Kenites and Egypt. As Balaam prophesied that 'Amalek' would perish forever (Num. 24.20), so Saul defeated the 'Amalekites' (1 Sam. 15.6-8); as Balaam announced doom to the Kenites (Num. 24.21-22), so Saul spared the Kenites (1 Sam. 15.6); and references to Israel's deliverance from Egypt figure prominently in each account (Num. 22.5, 11; 23.22; 24.8; 1 Sam. 15.2, 6, 7). 'Agag' is similarly mentioned in both passages: Israel's king was to be greater than 'Agag' (Num. 24.7), and King Saul spared 'Agag' (1 Sam. 15.8).[19] Finally, as Balaam stated that 'the LORD their God is with them, acclaimed as a *king* among them' (Num. 23.21), so Samuel stated that 'the LORD has rejected you from being *king* over Israel' (1 Sam. 15.26).[20] Saul was a new Balaam who bowed to pressure, who did not obey the LORD, and who sought to manipulate the LORD through sacrifice.

In Chapter 2 I showed how Dtr patterned Joshua after the Tetrateuchal Moses to reinforce his positive depiction of Joshua. The stories involving Joshua nevertheless also include disconcerting characters. Dtr furthered his negative depictions of such characters by linking them with Tetrateuchal accounts involving sexual scandal. This is true, for instance, of the parallel shared by the Rahab story (Joshua 2) and the Moabite seduction of Israel (Numbers 25). The introductory verse of the Rahab story shares ominous links with the introductory verse of Moab's seduction of Israel. Joshua sent spies from 'Shittim' who later visited Rahab a 'harlot' (אשה זונה), even as the Moabite women seduced the Israelites into 'committing harlotry' (זנה√) at 'Shittim'. Rather than simply bearing geographical significance for Dtr, the place name 'Shittim' was a tag for sexual licentiousness.[21] Buttressing this interpretation is the language of the Rahab story.[22] The use of the verbs 'to lie' (שכב) and 'to come' (בא) – verbs that often connote sexual intercourse – suggest that the spies had more than the promised land in mind when they visited Rahab. In two instances the spies 'lay' at the prostitute's residence (Josh. 2.1, 8), and six times the spies are the subject of the verb 'to come' (Josh. 2.1-4). By using the place name Shittim, Dtr thus undermined the activity of the spies.[23] The difference between the

---

19. These are the only two occurrences of 'Agag'.

20. This parallel is thus consonant both with the play on the human 'rejection' (מאס√) of divine 'kingship' (מלך√) in 1 Samuel 8 and the divine 'rejection' of human 'kingship' in 1 Samuel 15.

21. Note also the play on 'Shittim' in the Gideon narrative (see Chapter 4, n. 27).

22. The ongoing significance of the Shittim episode for Dtr is implicit in Josh. 22.17-18: 'Is the sin of Peor, which brought a plague upon the community of the LORD, such a small thing to us? *We have not cleansed ourselves from it to this very day*; and now would you turn away from the LORD!'

23. This use of place names is not uncommon in literature. For example, in line 307 of his *Wasteland* T.S. Eliot cited St Augustine's *Confessions*, 'To Carthage I came'. This sentence opens Book 3 of the *Confessions* in which St Augustine recounts his sexual urges. Eliot's purpose for citing the *Confessions* at this point was to underline his own lusts.

two stories equally undermine the spies insofar as their failure to kill Rahab the prostitute is an inversion of Phinehas' execution of Cozbi in Numbers 25.[24]

The Rahab story additionally shares parallels with the account of Sodom (Genesis 19).[25] As two 'messengers' (מלאכים; Gen. 19.1, 15) arrived in Sodom in the evening, so two spies, who are later referred to as 'messengers' (מלאכים; Josh. 6.17, 25), arrived in Jericho at night (Gen. 19.1; Josh. 2.1-2). As the messengers thereupon came to Lot's house (ויבאו אל־ביתו; Gen. 19.3), so the spies came to Rahab's house (ויבאו בית־אשה; Josh. 2.1). Lot then provided lodging for the two messengers who were going to spend the night in the 'town square' (רחוב), and the two spies were then hosted by one 'Rahab' (רחב) (Gen. 19.2-3; Josh. 2.1). As the messengers 'had not yet lain down' (טרם ישכבו) when the men of Sodom came to Lot's home, so the spies 'had not yet lain down' (ישכבון טרם) when Rahab came up to them on the roof (Gen. 19.4; Josh. 2.8).[26] The men of Sodom then said to Lot, 'Where are the men who came to you (האנשים אשר־באו אליך) tonight? Bring them out to us (הוציאם אלינו)' (Gen. 19.5). Rahab was likewise then commanded by the king of Jericho, 'Bring out the men who came to you' (הוציאי האנשים הבאים אליך; Josh. 2.3). In both instances such demands were denied. The messengers struck the men of Sodom with blindness, and Rahab sent the king's men off in the wrong direction (Gen. 19.11; Josh. 2.4-5). Finally, although both Sodom and Jericho were subsequently destroyed (Gen. 19.23-25; Josh. 6.24), the hosts together with their families were nevertheless spared (Gen. 19.15-22; Josh. 6.17, 25). More specifically, just as the messengers seized Lot and his family and 'brought him out and left him outside the city' (ויצאהו וינחהו מחוץ לעיר; Gen. 19.16), so the spies 'brought out [Rahab's] whole family and left them outside the camp of Israel' (כל־משפחותיה הוציאו ויניחום מחוץ למחנה ישראל; Josh. 6.23).[27]

---

24. In this regard Frymer-Kensky (1997: 66) rightly argued, '[h]ad this same Phinehas been at Jericho, Rahab would have been killed rather than spared'. The proposed direction of dependence between Numbers 25 and Joshua 2 is supported by the criterion of multiple occurrence. As I argued above, Dtr based 1 Samuel 2–4 in part on the Moabite seduction story.

25. See also Hawk 1991: 64–65.

26. This word string only occurs in these two instances.

27. The criterion of multiple occurrence supports the proposed direction of dependence. I argued in Chapter 1 that Dtr based Deut. 2.25 on Exod. 15.14. In Chapter 2 I similarly noted that the reaction of the nations to the crossing of the Sea and the Jordan are similar (Exod. 15.15-16; Josh. 5.1). Rahab's speech is also parallel to Exod. 15.14-16.

Exod. 15.14–16	*Josh. 2.9–10*
(14) the peoples have heard (שמעו)...	(9) dread of you (אימתכם)
(15) the dwellers (ישבי) in Canaan	has fallen upon us (נפלה עלינו)
are quaking (נמגו)...	and all the inhabitants (ישבי) of the land
(16) dread (אימתה)...	are quaking (נמגו) before you
fell upon them (תפל עליהם)	(10) for we have heard (שמענו)...

The fact that Dtr based Deut. 2.25 on Exod. 15.14 and Josh. 5.1 on Exod. 15.15-16, suggests that Dtr also based Josh. 2.9-10 on Exod. 15.14-16. The proposed direction of dependence is also supported by the criterion of context. This parallel is embedded within several parallels shared between Moses and Joshua. Because the Joshua accounts were demonstrably based on the corresponding

Dtr drew the above parallels between Genesis 19 and Joshua 2 to underline the spies' infraction of the Deuteronomic law of *herem*. Whereas the messengers spared Lot and his family, in contravention of the law of *herem* the spies spared Rahab and her family. Moses had ordered the Israelites to annihilate the inhabitants of the land, they were not to make a covenant with them or show them mercy, and they were not to intermarry with them lest the Israelites be led astray by their gods (Deut. 7.1-3). The Israelites transgressed such directives in the Rahab story. Rather than annihilating Rahab and her family, the spies spared Rahab's father, mother, brothers, sisters and all who belonged to them (Josh. 2.13). The spies showed such 'grace and mercy' (חסד ואמת; Josh. 2.12, 14) – typical covenant language – because they had 'sworn' (√שבע; Josh. 2.17, 20) to do so. This was tantamount to intermarrying with Rahab's clan, for there is the haunting conclusion that Rahab 'lives among the Israelites to this day' (Josh. 6.25; 9.27).[28] Alongside Israel's failure to keep the law of *herem* is the literary function of the parallels between the stories of Sodom and Rahab. Whereas the messengers annihilated the wicked of Sodom, in the Rahab story the spies spared the wicked. The Tetrateuchal schema thus broke down at the point where the spies spared Rahab – the spies' failure to kill Rahab the Canaanite (or have her killed) is an inversion of the messengers' annihilation of the wicked in Sodom.[29]

Tetrateuchal accounts, it is most reasonable to draw the same conclusion in this instance. Finally, there is the criterion of incongruity. The redundant nature of Josh. 2.3 is suggestive of its dependence on Gen. 19.5. The two texts read as follows.

Gen. 19.5   איה האנשים אשר־באו אליך הלילה הוציאם אלינו
            Where are the men who came to you tonight? Bring them out to us.

Josh. 2.3   הוציאי האנשים הבאים אליך אשר־באו לביתך
            Bring out the men who came to you, who came to your house.

That Josh. 2.3 is dependent on Gen. 19.5 is probable from its redundancy concerning the arrival of the men to Rahab/Rahab's house. This redundancy likely marks Dtr's attempt to pattern his source (which also read that 'the men came') after Genesis 19. Butler (1983: 26) similarly argued that the MT is here a conflation of traditions.

28.   Dtr's negative evaluation of showing mercy to non-Israelites is equally present in his inversion of the Rahab story in the Achan story: whereas in the Rahab story the *herem* (Rahab and her family) was saved, in the Achan story Achan became *herem* and was destroyed with his family (see also Frymer-Kensky 1997: 63). The inverted *herem* was a favorite motif of Dtr: the tribes of Israel were almost successful in annihilating one of their own tribes (Judges 21); and although Saul failed to annihilate the Amalekites he was successful in annihilating Nob with its priests, men and women, children and infants, oxen, donkeys and sheep (1 Samuel 15; 1 Sam. 22.14-19).

29.   Dtr's bivalent depiction of Rahab is in line with the above inversions. Although Rahab's ethnicity, livelihood and name were abominable to Israel, Dtr presented this Canaanite prostitute as nevertheless being exemplary (for the sexual overtones of the name 'Rahab' see Barstad 1989: 43–49). As I noted above, Rahab freely recounted the Exodus story and quoted Moses' Song of the Sea. Rahab's familiarity with Israel's sacred story is also evident from her confession, 'for the LORD your God alone is God in heaven above and on earth below' (Josh. 2.11), which parallels Moses' admonition, 'for the LORD alone is God in heaven above and on earth below' (Deut. 4.39) (Hawk 1991: 66). Even the actions of Rahab situate her with the Exodus community: just as the Israelites applied blood to their doorframes and remained indoors to avoid the wrath of the

The nation's infidelity followed by divine retribution was for Dtr an inflexible rubric. Curses followed disobedience, and rebellion necessarily brought chastisement. As one encounters in Judges, such punishment is sometimes passive in nature – rather than 'raising up' oppressors the LORD simply absconded from the action to let Israel fall. This is implicit in the nation's confession following Jair's rule:

> Then the Israelites cried out to the LORD, 'We stand guilty before you, for we have forsaken our God and served the Baalim'. But the LORD said to the Israelites... 'You have forsaken me and have served other gods. No, I will not deliver you again. Go cry to the gods you have chosen; let them deliver you in your time of distress' (Judg. 10.10-14).

Consistent with the absence of divine intervention following sin are those instances in which Dtr's characters failed to complete Tetrateuchal schemata of deliverance. I noted this in the preceding chapter concerning those who faltered on Moses' path. In each instance there was no new Moses and hence no divine intervention. Two other accounts that provided Dtr with schemata of deliverance were the Sodom story (Genesis 18–19) and the Akedah (Genesis 22). In this section I contend that Dtr based the murder of the Levite's concubine and Jepthah's sacrifice of his daughter on the Sodom story and the Akedah. Unlike these Tetrateuchal accounts in which both Lot and Isaac were rescued from dire circumstances, however, divine intervention in Dtr's stories is absent. The divine sentence is implicit in the frustrated schema.

Perhaps the most extensive parallel between the Tetrateuch and the DtrH is that between the divine punishment of Sodom and the murder of the Levite's concubine (Genesis 18–19; Judges 19–21).[30] The linguistic parallels between these passages are striking, and most of them are unique to these parallel narratives. As Abraham requested the messengers to receive his hospitality, so the Bethlehemite urged the Levite to remain as his guest (Gen. 18.1-5; Judg. 19.1-9). More specifically, as Abraham 'saw' (וירא) the messengers and ran 'to meet them' (לקראתם), so the Bethlehemite 'saw [the Levite]' (ויראהו) and was glad 'to meet him' (לקראתו) (Gen. 18.2; Judg. 19.3). As Abraham then said to the messengers 'let me fetch a morsel of bread (פת-לחם)...afterward you may go on (אחר תעברו)', so the Bethlehemite then said to the Levite, 'Eat a morsel of bread (פת-לחם) and afterward you may go (ואחר תלכו)' (Gen. 18.5; Judg. 19.5). Shortly thereafter, Lot, who was a resident alien in Sodom (Gen. 19.9), urged the messengers to 'spend the night' (לינו) at his home and wash their feet (ורחצו רגליכם), even though they expressed the desire to stay 'in the town square' (ברחוב) (Gen. 19.1-3). Similarly, the resident alien of Gibeah successfully coaxed the Levite not to 'stay the night in the town square' (אל-תלן ברחוב), and the Levite and his companions thereupon 'washed their feet' (וירחצו רגליהם) (Judg. 19.20-21). Both Lot and the resident alien of Gibeah then

---

destroying messenger, so Rahab tied a cord in her window and remained indoors to avoid the Israelite destruction of Jericho (Exod. 12.21-23; Josh. 2.17-20) (Zakovitch 1990: 92–93).

30. For another analysis of the parallels between Genesis 19 and Judges 19 see O'Connell 1996: 250–52.

provided a feast for the visitor(s) (Gen. 19.3; Judg. 19.21). The episodes with the townsmen also play out in the same way. 'The men of the city' (אנשי העיר) 'gathered about/to the house' (נסבו על\את־הבית) (Gen. 19.4; Judg. 19.22), and they demanded that the host 'bring out' (יצא, *hiphil*) the men/man 'who came to' (אשר בא[ו] אל) the host in order that they might 'have sex with' (ידע) them/him (Gen. 19.5; Judg. 19.22).[31] Both hosts then 'went out to them' (ויצא אליהם) to dissuade them (Gen. 19.6; Judg. 19.23). In each story the host stated, 'Please my brothers, do not commit wrong' (אל־נא אחי תרעו [Gen. 19.7]; אל־אחי אל־תרעו נא [Judg. 19.23]). The host's proposed solution to the dilemma is the same in each account: he introduced his proposal with the particle הנה ('behold') and thereupon offered two female relations (Lot's daughters/the host's daughter and the Levite's concubine) in place of the visitor(s). The host said that he would 'bring out' (אוציאה־נא) the women/woman and the townsmen could do whatever they wished to them (ועשו להן\להם טוב בעיניכם).[32] The townsmen, however, were not to harm the visitor(s) – requests that the townsmen refused (Gen. 19.8-9; Judg. 19.24-25). The visitor(s) then acted to bring resolution to the conflict: the messengers struck the townsmen with blindness and the Levite pushed his concubine out to the rapacious horde (Gen. 19.10-11; Judg. 19.25). On the following morning the visitor(s) left the city (Gen. 19.15-22; Judg. 19.27-28);[33] and as the LORD destroyed Sodom for its sin so Israel destroyed Gibeah for the rape of the concubine (Gen. 19.12-29; Judges 20). Finally, as (Lasine 1984: 40) noted, in both cases there are 'bizarre attempts at repopulation' of the given people. Concerned about their lack of progeny, Lot's daughters deceptively inebriated Lot so they might lie with him (Gen. 19.30-38). The Israelites were similarly concerned that a tribe of Israel was close to extinction so they deceptively had the surviving Benjaminites seize the girls of Shiloh for themselves (Judges 21).[34]

31.   Dtr also used the relative clause אשר באו in patterning the story of Rahab (Josh. 2.3) after Genesis 19. As with Dtr's use of whole Tetrateuchal narratives, his varying use of the same relative clause suggests that Torah paradigms were for him applicable to different contexts (cf. Hays' [1989: 33] discussion of Paul's use of the Old Testament).

32.   Two verbal links which, unlike all the above parallels, do not occur in the same place in the narratives, include 'Please turn aside' (סורו נא) of Gen. 19.2 and 'Come pray, let us turn aside' (לחה־נא ונסורה) of Judg. 19.7; and 'he implored them' (ויפצר־בם) of Gen. 19.3 and 'he implored him' (ויפצר־בו) of Judg. 19.11 (Greenstein 1990: 169–70). This is again suggestive of the fact that the lexical features of Torah schemata were fluid in Dtr's mind.

33.   The departure of the messengers is implicit in Gen. 19.22.

34.   Some have argued for the primacy of Judges 19 over Genesis 19. Westermann (1985: 300) contended that 'if one can speak of priority here, and this is questionable, then it falls to Judg. 19'. His primary reason for this conclusion is that Judg. 19.15-25 is integral to Judges 19–20. Niditch (1982: 376) similarly argued that Judg. 19.10-30 requires the preceding episode to explain how the Levite had found himself in Gibeah and that the rape at Gibeah was the motivation for the civil war that followed in ch. 20. But the close relationship between Judg. 19.15-25 and its context is only typical of Dtr's tendency to integrate the Tetrateuchal paradigms into his history. Moreover, this argument wrongly presupposes that Gen. 19.1-11 is not as closely related to its context as the episode in Judges 19 is to its context (see Lettelier 1995 and Van Seters 1975: 215–16). The criterion of multiple occurrence supports the posited direction of dependence. Dtr based Joshua 2 in part on

Dtr drew the parallels between Judges 19–21 and Genesis 18–19 to emphasize the corrupt state of pre-monarchic Israel. Out of the ashes of wicked Sodom, pre-monarchic Israel was born. But Dtr did not simply equate Lot's Sodom with pre-monarchic Israel. Three differences between the stories suggest that for Dtr pre-monarchic Israel was even more corrupt than Sodom. The first difference concerns the depiction of the hosts. Lasine (1984: 39) rightly noted that whereas Lot in his overblown hospitality offered his two virgin daughters, the Levite's host turned Lot's hospitality into inhospitality by offering, in addition to his own virgin daughter, the Levite's concubine. Similarly, unlike the Genesis account, in Judges the host explicitly told the townsmen to 'violate' (ענה√) the women (Judg. 19.24), a term that is often used for sexual atrocities.[35] In both instances the host is thus portrayed more negatively in Judges than in Genesis. A second difference between the stories concerns the portrayal of the visitor(s). Although in each account the visitors brought resolution

Genesis 19. Indeed, Joshua 2 and Judges 19 share parallels with the same terms and phrases of Genesis 19. This is true of Josh. 2.3 and Judg. 19.22, which are both parallel to Gen. 19.5.

Gen. 19.5	*Josh. 2.3*	*Judg. 19.22*
איה האנשים אשר־באו אליך הלילה הוציאם אלינו ונדעה אתם	הוציאי האנשים הבאים אליך אשר־באו לביתך	הוצא את־האיש אשר־בא אל־ביתך ונדענו
Where are the men who came to you tonight? Bring them out to us, so that we might know them.	Bring out the men who came to you, who came to your house.	Bring out the man who came to your house, so that we might know him.

Josh. 6.23 and Judg. 19.25 similarly share parallels with Gen. 19.16.

Gen. 19.16	*Josh. 6.23*	*Judg. 19.25*
ויחזקו האנשים בידו וביד־אשתו וביד שתי בנתיו בחמלת יהוה עליו ויצאהו וינחהו מחוץ לעיר	ויבאו הנערים המרגלים ויציאו את־רחב ואת־אביה ואת־אמה ואת־אחיה ואת־כל־אשר־לה ואת כל־משפחותיה היציאו ויניחום מחוץ למחנה ישראל	ויחזק האיש בפילגשו ויצא אליהם החוץ
So the men seized his hand, and the hands of his wife and his two daughters – in the LORD's mercy on him – and brought him out and left him outside the city.	So the young spies went in and brought out Rahab, her father and her mother, and her brothers, and all that belonged to her – they brought out her whole family and left them outside the camp of Israel.	So the man seized his concubine and brought her out to them.

Note also the use of the root רחב in Genesis 19, Joshua 2, and Judges 19: in Gen. 19.2-3 the messengers arrived in the 'town square' (רחוב); in Josh. 2.1 the two Hebrew spies were hosted by one 'Rahab' (רחב); and in Judg. 19.15 the Levite was urged not to stay the night 'in the town square' (ברחוב).

   35. Gen. 34.2; Deut. 21.14; 22.24, 29; Judg. 20.5; 2 Sam. 13.12, 14, 22, 32; Lam. 5.11.

to the conflict, the means of resolution differ vastly. In Genesis the people rejected Lot's proposal and sought to make him the object of their depravity, but the messengers rescued him by striking the people with blindness (Gen. 19.9-11). This is in contrast to the story in Judges where the host's proposal was also rejected, but the Levite satisfied the people's lust by giving them his concubine (Judg. 19.25). Even the particular actions of the visitors in each account stand opposite to each other. In Genesis the visitors brought deliverance, while in Judges the visitors brought death: to rescue Lot and his family, the messengers 'seized' (ויחזקו) their hands and 'sent him' (ויצאהו) out of the city, whereas the Levite 'seized' (ויחזק) his concubine and 'sent' (ויצא) her to her rape and ultimate death (Gen. 19.16; Judg. 19.25). The difference between the visitors is equally clear from their final actions. Whereas in their effort to rescue Lot and his family the messengers said 'rise (קום), take (קח) your wife' (Gen. 19.15), the Levite only commanded his concubine to 'rise' (קומי) after she had died, at which point 'he took her' (ויקחה) (Judg. 19.28). The third and most striking difference between the stories concerns divine intervention. Whereas the messengers intervened to rescue Lot and his family, divine intervention for the concubine is noticeably absent.[36] This lacuna is a silent indictment of pre-monarchic Israel. Because Israel was unrighteous, as exemplified in this sordid tale, it did not merit the favor of God.[37]

As with Genesis 18–19, Dtr used the story of the Akedah (Gen. 22.1-19) to underline the absence of divine intervention. The parallels between the Akedah and the outrage in Gibeah include the following.[38] As Abraham took along with him one ass, two servants and a familial relation, so the Levite took two asses, one servant and a familial relation (Gen. 22.3; Judg. 19.10-11).[39] Abraham and Isaac journeyed together (שניהם יחדו) to Moriah even as the Levite and his father-in-law travelled together (שניהם יחדו) (Gen. 22.6, 8; Judg. 19.6).[40] As Abraham 'arose…in the morning…and went' (וישכם…בבקר…וילך; Gen. 22.3), so the Levite 'arose…in the morning…to go' (וישכם…בבקר…ללכת; Judg. 19.8). Abraham and the Levite similarly journeyed in the region of Jerusalem – Abraham was to take Isaac to the land of Moriah, and after departing from his father-in-law the Levite journeyed to Jebus (Gen. 22.2; Judg. 19.10). As 'Abraham lifted his eyes and saw' (וישא אברהם את־עיניו וירא; Gen. 22.4) the place in the distance, the host 'lifted his eyes and saw' (וישא את־עיניו וירא; Judg. 19.17) the Levite in the town square of Gibeah. Finally, both Abraham and the Levite raised their knives against the relation (Gen. 22.10; Judg. 19.29). The clause 'and he took the knife' (ויקח את־המאכלת) occurs just prior to

---

36. Common to the three differences is their inversive nature. Klein (1988: 172) rightly argued that '[t]he situation in Genesis is used for parody; it is copied and inverted. The ironic inversions depict the inverted moral condition of Israel, the utter perversity to which the Israelites have sunk'. See also Matthews 1992 and Lasine 1984.

37. Jüngling's (1981: 291) argument that the theory of literary dependence does not explain the differences between the accounts thus fails.

38. I adapted the following from Unterman 1980.

39. These are the only instances in which there is an enumeration of asses (חמר) and servants (נער) accompanying a man on a journey.

40. This phrase occurs only in these two narratives.

divine intervention in Genesis 22, and in Judges 19 it occurs immediately before the dismemberment of the concubine.[41] Finally, just as at the close of the Akedah Abraham named the site of the near-sacrifice 'the LORD will see' even 'as it is said' (Gen. 22.14), so at the close of the Gibeah story the narrator tells the reader that 'all who saw [the corpse] said' (Judg. 19.30). As with other instances, the absence of divine intervention in Judges 19 is striking when it is contrasted with the Akedah. This contrast is highlighted by the parallel 'and he took the knife'. Whereas in Genesis this clause refers to the divine provision of a ram to Abraham, in Judges it is used by those who were appalled at the sight of the dismembered concubine. Similar to the parallels between Genesis 18–19 and Judges 19–21, then, whereas Isaac was spared by the LORD, the concubine was dismembered. The absence of divine intervention is a poignant reminder of pre-monarchic Israel's alienation from God.

The Akedah similarly served as Dtr's schema in the story of Jephthah's sacrifice of his daughter (Judg. 11.29-40). These are the only narratives that concern a Hebrew's (near-) sacrifice of his child to the LORD. More specifically, the LORD commanded Abraham to 'offer [Isaac] (והעלהו)...as a burnt offering' (לעלה והעליתיהו), and Jephthah declared 'whatever comes out of my home...I shall offer (והעליתהו) as a burnt offering (עולה)' (Gen. 22.2; Judg. 11.31). In the Akedah Isaac is referred to as Abraham's 'only son' (יחיד), even as Jephthah's daughter is referred to as his 'only child' (יחידה) (Gen. 22.2; Judg. 11.34), and in both accounts the victim addressed the father as 'My father' (אבי) (Gen. 22.7; Judg. 11.36).

There are two notable differences between the literary functions of Abraham's near-sacrifice of Isaac and Jephthah's sacrifice of his daughter. First, in the Genesis account the divinely sanctioned near-sacrifice of Isaac is arguably the climax of the Abraham cycle. Unlike the previous threats to the divine promise of progeny, the threat against the long-awaited Isaac comes from the LORD himself. The subsequent divine intervention, together with the reiteration of the promise of progeny, is therefore climactic. This is in contrast to Jephthah's sacrifice of his daughter. Though by means of the spirit of the LORD Jephthah soundly defeated the Ammonites, the needless sacrifice of his daughter that follows was tragic. The second notable difference between the stories is that whereas the LORD gave the command to sacrifice Isaac and then intervened to deliver him, Jephthah himself made a rash vow and the LORD did not intervene.[42] These two differences are similar to those between Genesis 18–19 and Judges 19–21, and Genesis 22 and Judges 19. The outcome in Judges 11 is tragic whereas the outcome in Genesis 22 is climactic; and unlike Genesis 22 there was no divine intervention in Judges 11. Because of the nation's unrighteousness, the LORD would not deliver Israel again.

The absence of divine intervention as the consequence of sin is nevertheless softened by anticipations of future deliverance. Given that Dtr viewed the past through the lens of his Torah, it should occasion no surprise that his anticipations for the

---

41. This clause appears only in these two instances, as does the singular מאכלת.

42. That Jephthah's vow was unnecessary is evident from the fact that 'the spirit of the LORD' had come upon him (Judg. 11.29), a motif that always ensures success in the book of Judges (see Webb 1987: 60–65; and O'Connell 1996: 183). For further discussion of the differences between the two accounts see Trible 1981: 63–64 and Marcus 1986: 38–39.

future were similarly governed by Torah schemata. More specifically, the close of the DtrH begs the question of future deliverance. Disenchanted with Gedaliah's accession to power, Judahite troops executed him (2 Kgs 25.22-25). As a consequence, 'all the people, young and old, and the officers of the troops set out and went to Egypt because they were afraid of the Chaldeans' (2 Kgs 25.26). This is the great tragedy of the DtrH: Israel became a nation with the Exodus from Egypt, and by Dtr's time the nation had collapsed and the people found themselves once again in Egypt.[43] Knowing that the Exodus story could be repeated, even as it had in the past, Dtr and his readers could only hope for a new Exodus – this time from Babylon.[44] Accompanying this Exodus there would naturally be a new Moses. The manumission of Jehoiachin and the quasi-regnal status that he enjoyed before Evil-merodach of Babylon might also have given Dtr's first readers hope for a restored Davidic monarchy.[45] This supposition is in accord with Dtr's use of Balaam's blessings of Israel (Numbers 24) in the eschatologically nuanced Last Words of David (2 Sam. 23.1-7). Balaam introduced himself with, 'the oracle of Balaam son of Beor, and the oracle of the man whose eye is opened' (Num. 24.3, 15). Nearly verbatim to this, David introduced himself with, 'the oracle of David son of Jesse, and the oracle of the man who was raised up' (2 Sam. 23.1). More specifically, Balaam's prediction that 'a star shall come forth from *Jacob*, a scepter from Israel', which would defeat Moab, Seth, Edom and Ir (Num. 24.17-19) finds fulfillment in the house of David.[46] The pericopes, moreover, share a common eschatological tone in their emphasis on the judgment of the nations and the fructifying nature of Israel: just as Israel was to devour hostile nations (Num. 24.8), so David stated that foreigners cringe before him (2 Sam. 22.45); and while Balaam likened the dominion of Israel to lush valleys and forests (Num. 24.5-7), David stated that his house gives light and verdancy to the earth (2 Sam. 23.3-5). Like all Torah accounts, and like a classical text, the iterative power of the Exodus, Moses, and Balaam schemata spanned the generations.

43. This tragedy was already anticipated by the final Deuteronomic sentence for covenant infidelity, 'The LORD will send you back to Egypt in galleys, by a route which I told you you will not see again' (Deut. 28.68; cf. 17.16). Skweres (1979: 193–94) rightly argued that the referent of Deut. 28.68 is Exod. 14.13.

Deut. 28.68	אמרתי לך לא־תסיף עוד לראתה
	I said to you, 'You shall not again see [Egypt]'.
Exod. 14.13	לא תסיפו לראתם עוד עד־עולם
	You shall never see [the Egyptians] again.

44. Trompf (1979: 223–24) similarly stated that '[t]he Deuteronomist almost certainly assumed that patterns of events similar to those he recorded would happen in the future, if the same kinds of transgressions and deeds were effected. By reviewing their chequered past, then, the Israelites had much to learn for the future consolidation of their nation and faith'. On the hope proffered by the close of the DtrH, see Wolff 1978, Levenson 1983, and McCarthy 1974.

45. See Begg 1986.

46. 'The anointed of the God of *Jacob*' of 2 Sam. 23.1 may be an allusion to the star that rises from 'Jacob' of Num. 24.17. Later interpretation similarly regarded the 'star' figure as messianic. For example, whereas the MT reads that 'a sceptre (שבט)' was to rise out of Israel, the Targum reads 'the Messiah (משיחא)' would do so (cf. War Scroll 11.6).

CONCLUSION

I will now discuss some of the implications that the existence and nature of the parallel narratives have for various historical-critical concerns. To begin with, there is the question of the historical veracity of the parallel narratives in the Former Prophets. Some have stressed the importance of detecting the history of thought rather than historical verisimilitude in the biblical record. After outlining the problems associated with identifying historicity in the Bible, Zakovitch (1983: 60) could write: 'The learning of actual history from biblical narrative except in the most general and vague terms is an unachievable task, even irresponsible. The ideological history of the nation of Israel is the task worthy of effort'. In a similar vein, Thompson (1994: 86) could refer to the DtrH as the 'mother of all fictions'. To be sure, there can be no question that in his use of Tetrateuchal traditions Dtr was very creative. This is far from saying, however, that such creation was *ex nihilo*. Objective and unbiased historiography is a 'fiction', and like every historian Dtr assembled and reworked the sources that he received through his historiographical presuppositions. As tendentious as Dtr's historiography was, however, relegating the task of the historian to tracing the history of Hebrew thought and using the unqualified word 'fiction' is equally telltale of tendentious historiography. A more modest approach is to look for varying degrees of plausibility rather than entertain either/or dichotomies.[1] I argued in Chapter 3, for instance, that Dtr patterned the account of David and Nabal (1 Samuel 25) after that of Jacob and Laban (Genesis 29–31). A 'nonhistorical' feature of Dtr's account is immediately present in the name Nabal. In addition to the fact that 'Nabal' is an inversion of 'Laban', it is most unlikely that someone would name their child 'fool'. But it does not follow from this that the whole narrative is fictitious. After extracting the obvious literary features from 1 Samuel 25, Levenson (1978: 25–26) persuasively argued that in historical terms, 'David's marriage to Abigail was the pivotal move to his ascent to kingship at Hebron' and that 'the man whose name has been altered to Nabal must have been a very powerful figure'.[2] As with every other investigation, in this instance one can only speak in terms of degrees of plausibility. Levenson's methodology of distinguishing between what is obviously literary and what is historical is on the mark, and his conclusions regarding various historical features of 1 Samuel 25 are plausible.

---

1.   Brettler (1995: 142–43) used the helpful analogy of the historian as a detective and jurist who looks not for certitude but a preponderance of evidence. See also Halpern's (1988: 207–80) extensive discussion.

2.   See also Levenson and Halpern (1980).

With respect to Dtr's use of sources, I once had the impression that Dtr sat among many works concerning his nation's history. At times Dtr copied extensive sections almost verbatim from a scroll. At other times Dtr had an array of scrolls before him, parts of which he collated before including them in his own history. Only rarely did Dtr interject his own work. Perhaps Dtr did so because his sources lacked pertinent information, because they were in some way offensive, or because it was necessary to bridge his sources with seams. But judging from Dtr's use of Tetrateuchal sources both in Deuteronomy 1–3 and in the Former Prophets, this understanding of Dtr's use of sources is fundamentally flawed. As Dtr freely adapted and manipulated Tetrateuchal schemata, so he ingeniously reworked his sources. If, for instance, accounts of Samuel's birth and childhood (1 Sam. 1.1–4.1a) and an ark narrative (1 Sam. 4.1b–7.1) existed prior to the sixth century, then they were totally reworked by Dtr as they are heavily reliant on Tetrateuchal accounts pertaining to the life of Moses. Again, although 1 Samuel 14 and 15 may have had independent origins, the fact that they are both based on stories in the Primeval History shows that in their present form they are the product of Dtr. Similarly, if the History of David's Rise (1 Sam. 16.14–2 Sam. 5.10) was at one time an independent source, the fact that Dtr based much of 1 Samuel 18–19 on Genesis 29–31, and 1 Samuel 24–26 on Genesis 27–33 shows that this source also underwent a Deuteronomistic reworking. Finally, if the so-called Succession Narrative (2 Samuel 9–20; 1 Kings 1–2) ever had an independent existence, at a minimum one must conclude that Dtr reworked the story of Absalom in 2 Samuel 13–14. It includes parallels with the fratricide of Cain (Genesis 4), the Sodom story (Genesis 19), the rape of Dinah (Genesis 34), the story of Tamar (Genesis 38), and the near-seduction of Joseph (Genesis 39). The same is true of 1 Kings. Dtr may have been reliant on 'the annals of Solomon' (1 Kgs. 11.41) and 'the annals of the kings of Israel' (1 Kgs. 14.19) for 1 Kings 5–15, but it is clear from his creative use of Exodus that he was directly responsible for much in these chapters. Again, many have argued that traces of Dtr's work in the Elijah cycle are slight. Cross (1973: 191–92) could assert that '[1 Kings 18 and 19] are marked strongly by traits of oral composition, and in their present form are little shaped by the Deuteronomistic Historian'. Similarly, although Gray (1970: 376–77 n. e) presented the more notable parallels between Moses and Elijah, even calling Elijah a 'new Moses', he assumed that these parallels were not drawn by Dtr: '[t]he tradition proclaimed its own message without undue Deuteronomistic comment'. Once again, the similar ways in which Tetrateuchal accounts are used in the Former Prophets undermines such conclusions as these.

My final comments concerning redaction criticism broach the subject of Deuteronomistic language. For too long scholarship has been swayed by the assumption that Dtr's work is best identified by the presence of Deuteronomistic language. The problem with this assumption is its reductionistic character. In addition to being a theologian, Dtr composed narratives that are neither expressly theological nor laden with the rhetoric and style that is so common in Deuteronomy and the Deuteronomistic speeches. In this work I have used words that I have seldom used before, and I may never use such words again. This is, I should think, universal to the writing experience. Although one may therefore make positive assertions about the

Deuteronomistic lexicon, it is at best Procrustean to conclude that this or that passage is not Deuteronomistic because it does not include Deuteronomistic language. I am not thereby seeking to undermine the criterion of Deuteronomistic language. I only wish to rescue it from perilous heights.

This brings me to some of the implications that my findings have for Tetrateuchal studies. To begin with, Dtr knew Tetrateuchal accounts very well: Dtr used the same stories in vastly different narrative settings; he used precisely the same Tetrateuchal lexical features from story to story; he adjusted Tetrateuchal paradigms to complement his narrative concerns; and he creatively used names of Tetrateuchal people and places. But Dtr was dealing with a unified Tetrateuch, not disparate Tetrateuchal stories. The fact that Dtr patterned stories after narratives in every section of the Tetrateuch suggests that by his time some form of the Tetrateuch existed.[3]

As for Genesis, Dtr based three of his stories on accounts in the Primeval History: the stories of Achan's sin, the Gibeonite deception and Jonathan's transgression of his father's prohibition on the Eden story; the fratricide of Amnon on the fratricide of Abel; and the LORD's rejection of Saul on the Flood narrative. Dtr similarly based ten of his stories on the Abraham cycle: Dtr based Joshua's conquest of Canaanite kings and David's conquest of Ziklag on Abram's defeat of Mesopotamian kings; he based Gideon's encounter with the messenger of the LORD, Elisha's promise to the barren woman, the Gibeah episode, the annunciation to Manoah's wife, and Rahab's hospitality toward the spies on the Sodom story; he based the sacrifice of Jephthah's daughter and the dismemberment of the Levite's concubine on the Akedah; and he based David's purchase of the threshing floor on Abraham's purchase of a burial plot. As for the remainder of Genesis, Dtr based David's experiences with Saul and Nabal on the stories of Jacob and Laban; Mamoah's encounter with 'the angel of the LORD' on Jacob's tussle with a 'man'; the Danite conquest of Laish on Jacob's flight from Laban; and on the Israelites' destruction of Shechem; the rape of Tamar on the rape of Dinah; the rape of Tamar on the sexual exploitation of Tamar; and the story of young David, and the rape of Tamar on stories concerning Joseph.

This brings me to the book of Exodus. With regard to the introduction of Moses, Dtr patterned the early life and call of Samuel on the early life and call of Moses, various early kings of Israel on the pharaohs, two of Solomon's adversaries on Moses, and the appearance of the captain of the LORD's host to Joshua on the appearance of the messenger of the LORD. As for the plagues narrative, it served as Dtr's basis for the ark narrative, and Joshua's Passover and circumcision. Dtr cited the account of the Exodus itself seven times in Deuteronomy 1–3, once in Rahab's speech, and several times in the ark narrative. Dtr similarly patterned Joshua's crossings of the Jordan and Samuel's defeat of the Philistines on the Exodus story. With regard to the wilderness traditions in Exodus, Dtr patterned the divine provision of water and food for Elijah on the LORD's provision for the wilderness generation; and he used the account of the appointment of officials as a basis for the synoptic

---

3. See the appendix for a list of the parallel narratives shared by the Tetrateuch and the DtrH.

account in Deuteronomy 1. As for the Sinai tradition of Exodus, Dtr drew upon it for his depictions of Jeroboam and Elijah.

All that remains are the wilderness traditions of Leviticus and Numbers. Dtr drew upon the inauguration of the Aaronic priesthood in his recounting of the people's response to the fire from the LORD in the story of Elijah. Dtr similarly used the stories of Aaron's sons Nadab and Abihu in his outline of Eli's sons Hophni and Phinehas and in his depiction of Nadab and Abijah the sons of Jeroboam. Dtr used the story of the rebellion against the LORD in the synoptic account of Deuteronomy 1 as well as in Isael's rejection of the LORD in 1 Samuel 8. Dtr used the expedition of the spies for his synoptic account in Deuteronomy 1, the story of Joshua's spies, and the migration of the Danites. Dtr used the Transjordan ventures in Deuteronomy 2–3. Dtr based the account of Samuel's rejection of Saul after the Balaam story, and he similarly patterned the last words of David on Balaam's oracles. Finally, Dtr patterned the accession of Elijah after the appointment of Joshua.

Not including Deuteronomy 1–3, Dtr patterned approximately four dozen of his narratives after accounts from each section of the Tetrateuch. This suggests that by Dtr's time some form of the Tetrateuch existed.[4]

With regard to source criticism of the Tetrateuch, in addition to relying on the J story, Dtr also used P texts. Limiting myself to direct citations, Dtr used the following P texts. In his account of the spies in Deut. 1.19-46 Dtr cited three P texts from the corresponding account in Numbers 13–14 (Num. 13.26 and Deut. 1.25; Num. 14.9 and Deut. 1.29; Num. 14.31 and Deut. 1.39), as well as Num. 20.1 (= Deut. 1.46) which has also traditionally been assigned to P. In 1 Samuel 2–7 Dtr cited five P texts: 1 Sam. 2.12 is verbally parallel to Exod. 5.2 (both Eli's sons and Pharaoh 'did not know the LORD'); 1 Sam. 2.22 is verbally parallel to Exod. 38.8 (both accounts refer to 'the women who performed tasks at the entrance to the tent of meeting'); 1 Sam. 2.30 is verbally parallel to Lev. 10.3 ('I will honor/be honored'); 5.12 is verbally parallel to Exod. 2.23 ('and the outcry went up'); and 1 Sam. 6.2 is verbally parallel to Exod. 7.11 ('Pharaoh summoned [two groups of officials]'; 'The Philistines summoned [two groups of officials]). In 1 Kgs. 17.6 Dtr cited Exod. 16.8 (daily provision of bread and meat). Finally, Dtr based 1 Kgs. 18.38-39 on Lev. 9.24 (fire from the LORD consumed the offerings). Throughout this work I asserted that when various accounts in the Former Prophets share parallels with both P and

---

4.   In their analysis of various parallel narratives shared by the Tetrateuch and the Former Prophets, various scholars have pointed to this. Biddle (2002: 620) concluded that the author of 1 Samuel 25 intended this story 'to be read against the background' of the Genesis narrative. Alter (1999: 267) asserted that 'the author of the David story was familiar at least with the J strand of the Joseph story in a textual version very like the one that has come down to us' (see also Alter 1992: 164). Fields (1997: 23–24) likewise argued that '[w]hatever happens from creation to the end of Moses' life is paradigmatic, conceptually prescriptive, setting precedent and creating prototypes for all times'. Damrosch (1987: 155, 180) similarly contended that stories in 1 and 2 Samuel were assessed and understood in light of 'Yahwistic stories of the foundations of society' and that 'the early materials of the David story already seem to presuppose something rather like the Yahwistic form of Genesis 2–11, of at least a version of patriarchal narratives, and of the Exodus story'. According to Damrosch (1987: 188), contemporary history was thus understood in light of 'the emblematic early history of the people'.

non-P layers of given Tetrateuchal accounts Dtr was responsible for drawing the parallels. One may apply this conclusion to the entire Tetrateuch. There has been a growing consensus to argue that although P may consist in part of an independent source or sources, it presupposes knowledge of and interacts with non-P accounts. Because Dtr based several narratives in part after P accounts, it follows that he was dealing not simply with disparate accounts but a unified Tetrateuch.[5]

Tied to the conclusions that a Tetrateuch existed by Dtr's time and that it afforded a repository of schemata is the contention that it – possibly together with synoptic corpora – enjoyed authoritative status.[6] A universal phenomenon of religious traditions is their proclivity to define the world through the lens of their scriptures. Although Dtr's Torah was not 'scripture' in the modern sense, the preceding analysis demonstrates that it was the lens through which he envisioned history.[7]

5.   The relationship between this Tetrateuch and the DtrH may best be explained by combining von Rad's theory of a Hexateuch with Noth's theory of a DtrH. In my opinion, Dtr's Torah consisted of Genesis–Numbers and various sections in Joshua that pertain to the land which, prior to Noth, were assigned to P. Dtr edited this corpus and appended his history to it, thus producing Genesis–Kings (that Genesis–Kings was at one point a single work has been advocated among others by Freedman 1962; 1987; 1994: 128–52; Petersen 1980; Peckham 1985, 1993; Schmitt 1997; Akenson 1998: 19–90; and Minette de Tillesse 1999). This view is consistent with the Hexateuchal theory of von Rad, the Tetrateuchal theory of Noth, and it does justice both to the presence of Deuteronom(ist)ic redaction in Genesis–Numbers as well as the presence of P in Joshua. (Partly because P was thought to be later than D, Noth [1981: 66–67] was compelled to contend that Joshua 13–22 was a post-Deuteronomistic addition. But see Petersen [1980], who persuasively contended that Dtr interpolated P material in Joshua 13–22.)

6.   The existence of several competing 'Pentateuchs' in the postexilic period is likely (Shaver 1986).

7.   For discussions on scripture as paradigm see Green 1989: 106–13 and Lindbeck 1984: 113–24).

Appendix

PARALLEL NARRATIVES SHARED BY THE TETRATEUCH AND THE DTRH[1]

Deuter. Texts	Deuteronomistic Stories	=	Tetrateuchal Texts	Tetrateuchal Stories	Page Numbers
Joshua 2	Two spies sent by Joshua		Numbers 13	12 spies sent by Moses	39
Joshua 2, 6	The destruction of Jericho		Genesis 19	The destruction of Sodom	88–89
Joshua 3–4	Crossing of the Jordan River		Exodus 12–15	Crossing of Sea of Reeds	39–40
Joshua 5	Circumcision under Joshua		Exodus 12	Circumcision under Moses	40–41
Joshua 5	Appearance of 'man' prior to defeat of Jericho		Exodus 3	Appearance of the messenger of the LORD prior to defeat of Egypt	41
Joshua 7	Achan's sin		Genesis 3	Adam's sin	85
Joshua 9	Gibeonites' deception		Genesis 3	Serpent's deception	86
Joshua 10	Joshua's defeat of royal coalition		Genesis 14	Abram's defeat of royal coalition	36–37
Judges 6	Commissioning of Gideon		Exodus 2–4	Commissioning of Moses	72–73
Judges 6	Gideon's reception of the messenger of the LORD		Genesis 18	Abraham's reception of three 'men'	38
Judges 11	Jephthah's sacrifice of his daughter		Genesis 22	Abraham's near-sacrifice of his son Isaac	94
Judges 13	Annunciation of a son to Manoah's wife		Genesis 18	Annunciation of a son to Sarah	38–39
Judges 13	Manoah's encounter with the 'angel of the LORD'		Genesis 32	Jacob's tussle with a 'man'	39
Judges 18	The Danite's illegitimate destruction of Laish		Genesis 34	The Israelite's illegitimate destruction of Shechem	67
Judges 18	Danites left Canaan for Laish		Genesis 31–33	Jacob left Padan Aram for Cannan	68
Judges 18	12 Danite spies and conquering of Laish		Numbers 13	12 Israelite spies and reconnoitering the land	66–68
Judges 19–21	The rape of the concubine, the defeat of the Bejaminites, and the stealing of women		Genesis 18–19	The near-rape of Lot's daughters, the destruction of Sodom, and the seduction of Lot by his daughters	90–93
Judges 19	Hospitality of Levite's father-in-law		Genesis 18	Hospitality of Abraham	37–38
Judges 19	The dismemberment of the concubine		Genesis 22	The near-sacrifice of Isaac	93–94
1 Samuel 1–3	Early years of Samuel		Exodus 2–3	Early years of Moses	45–46
1 Samuel 2–4	Sin of Samuel's sons Hophni and Phinehas		Numbers 25; Leviticus 10	Righteousness of Aaron's son Phinehas	82–83
1 Samuel 4–6	Plagues against Philistines		Exodus 5–12	Plagues against Egyptians	46–48

Deuter. Texts	Deuteonomistic Stories	=	Tetrateuchal Texts	Tetrateuchal Stories	Page Numbers
1 Samuel 7	Defeat of Philistines		Exodus 14	Drowning of Egyptians	48
1 Samuel 8	Israel's request for a king		Numbers 11	Israel's complaint over manna	48–49
1 Samuel 14–15	Governance of King Saul		Genesis 2–3	Governance of the LORD God in Eden	83–84
1 Samuel 14–15	Governance of King Saul		Genesis 8–9	Governance of the LORD God with the Flood	84
1 Samuel 15	Divine rejection of Saul		Numbers 23–24	Divine rejection of Balak's counsel	86–87
1 Samuel 16–17	Young David		Genesis 37	Young Joseph	58–59
1 Samuel 18–19	David's quest for Michal the younger sister		Genesis 29, 31	Jacob's quest for Rachel the younger sister	59
1 Samuel 24, 26	David duped his 'father' Saul		Genesis 27	Jacob duped his father Isaac	63
1 Samuel 25	David and the wealthy shepherd *Nabal*		Genesis 29–31	Jacob and the wealthy shepherd *Laban*	63–65
1 Samuel 25	Actions of David and Abigail		Genesis 32–33	Actions of Jacob and Esau	64–65
1 Samuel 30	David rescuing his people and defeating Amalekites		Genesis 14	Abram rescuing his people and defeating kings	37
2 Samuel 13	Absalom's rape of Tamar		Genesis 19	Sodom story	56
2 Samuel 13	Absalom raped Tamar		Genesis 34	Shechem raped Dinah	56
2 Samuel 13	Absalom raped his sister Tamar		Genesis 38	Judah had sex with his daughter-in-law Tamar	56–57
2 Samuel 13	Absalom's rape of Tamar		Genesis 39	Near seduction of Joseph by Potiphar's wife	57
2 Samuel 14	Absalom murdered Amnon		Genesis 4	Cain murdered Abel	57–58
2 Samuel 23	David's prophecy of the pre-eminence of his dynasty		Numbers 24	Balaam's prophecy of Israel's preeminence	95
2 Samuel 24	David's purchase of threshing floor		Genesis 23	Abraham's purchase of burial plot	60
1 Kings 5–10	Solomon's reign		Exodus 1, 5–6	Moses and the Pharaohs	74–75
1 Kings 11	Solomon's adversary Hadad		Exodus 1–4	Moses' adversaries the Pharaohs	75–76
1 Kings 12	Rehoboam and multiplied labour		Exodus 4–5, 10	Pharaoh and multiplied labor	76
1 Kings 11–15	Jeroboam, the golden calves, and the divided kingdom		Exodus 32	Moses, Aaron, and the golden calf	1–2
1 Kings 13	Man of God prophesied against Jeroboam		Numbers 12	Miriam and Aaron repudiated for countering Moses the prophet	2–3
1 Kings 17–19	Stories involving Elijah		Exodus 16, 19, 32–34; Leviticus 9	Various stories involving Moses	69–71
2 Kings 4	Childless Shunemite and the promise of a son		Genesis 18	Barren Sarah and the promise of a son	39

1.   This table neither includes Dtr's use of Tetrateuchal accounts in Deuteronomy 1–3 nor the many lone allusions to Tetrateuchal accounts throughout the DtrH.

BIBLIOGRAPHY

Aberbach, Moses and Leivy Smolar
    1967   'Aaron, Jeroboam, and the Golden Calves', *JBL* 86: 129–40.

Akenson, Donald Harmen
    1998   *Surpassing Wonder: The Invention of the Bible and the Talmuds* (Montreal and Kingston: McGill-Queens University Press).

Allan, George
    1986   *The Importances of the Past: A Meditation on the Authority of Tradition* (Albany, NY: State University of New York Press).
    1993   'Traditions and Transitions', in *Philosophical Imagination and Cultural Memory. Appropriating Historical Traditions* (Durham and London: Duke University Press): 21–39.

Allison, Dale C.
    1993   *The New Moses* (Minneapolis: Fortress Press).

Alter, Robert
    1981   *The Art of Biblical Narrative* (New York: Basic Books).
    1983   'How Convention Helps Us Read: The Case of the Bible's Annunciation Type-Scene', *Prooftexts* 3: 115–30.
    1990   'Samson without Folklore', in Susan Niditch (ed.), *Text and Tradition. The Hebrew Bible and Folklore* (Atlanta, GA: Scholars Press): 147–56.
    1992   *The World of Biblical Literature* (San Francisco: Basic Books).
    1999   *The David Story* (New York: W.W. Norton).

Auld, A. Graeme
    1979   'Joshua: The Hebrew and Greek Texts', in *Studies in the Historical Books of the Old Testament* (VTSup, 30; Leiden: E.J. Brill).
    1989   'Gideon: Hacking at the Heart of the Old Testament', *VT* 39: 257–67.
    2000   'Samuel and Genesis: Questions of Van Seters's "Yahwist"', in Steven L. McKenzie *et al.* (eds.), *Rethinking the Foundations: Historiography in the Ancient World and in the Bible. Essays in Honour of John Van Seters* (New York: De Gruyter): 23–32.

Ausloos, H.
    1997   '*Les Extremes se Touchent...* Proto-Deuteronomic and Simili-Deuteronomistic Elements in Genesis-Numbers', in M. Vervenne and J. Lust (eds.), *Deuteronomy and Deuteronomic Literature* (BETL, CXXXIII; Belgium: Leuven University Press): 341–66.

Barstad, H.M.
    1989   'The Old Testament Personal Name *rahab*: An Onomastic Note', *SEÅ* 54: 43–49.

Bartlett, John R.
    1978   'The Conquest of Sihon's Kingdom: A Literary Re-examination', *JBL* 97: 347–51.

Bauer, Uwe F.W.
    1998   *'Warum nur gehör SEIN Geheiss!' Eine synchrone Exegese der Anti-Erzäh-*
                lung von Richter 17–18 (BEATAJ, 45; Bern/Frankfurt A.M.: Peter Lang).
Begg, Christopher
    1980   'The Literary Criticism of Deut. 4, 1-40: Contributions to a Continuing
                Discussion', *ETL* 56: 10–55.
    1986   'The Significance of Jehoiachin's Release: A New Proposal', *JSOT* 36:
                49–56.
Berger, Peter L.
    1963   *Invitation to Sociology: A Humanistic Perspective* (Garden City, NY: Anchor
                Books).
Biddle, Mark E.
    2002   'Ancestral Motifs in 1 Samuel 25: Intertextuality and Characterization', *JBL*
                121: 617–38.
Blenkinsopp, Joseph
    1964   'Jonathan's Sacrilege. 1 Sam. 14, 1-46: A Study in Literary History', *CBQ*
                26: 423–49.
    1966   'Theme and Motif in the Succession History (2 Sam. XI 2ff) and the Yah-
                wist Corpus' (VTSup, 13; Leiden: E.J. Brill): 25–42.
    1992   *The Pentateuch: An Introduction to the First Five Books of the Bible* (The
                Anchor Bible Reference Library; New York: Doubleday).
Bloch, Renée
    1978   'Midrash', in W.S. Green (ed.), *Approaches to Ancient Judaism*, 1 (Missoula,
                MT: Scholars Press).
Boling, Robert G. and G. Ernest Wright
    1975   *Judges: A New Translation with Introduction and Commentary* (AB, 6A;
                Garden City, NY: Doubleday).
    1982   *Joshua: A New Translation with Introduction and Commentary* (AB, 6; Gar-
                den City, NY: Doubleday).
Boorer, Suzanne
    1992   *The Promise of the Land as Oath: A Key to the Formation of the Pentateuch*
                (BZAW, 205; Berlin and New York: W. de Gruyter).
Bourke, Joseph
    1954   'Samuel and the Ark: A Study in Contrasts', *Dominican Studies* 7: 73–103.
Brettler, Marc Zvi
    1991   'The Structure of 1 Kings 1–11', *JSOT* 49: 87–97.
    1995   *The Creation of History in Ancient Israel* (London and New York: Rout-
                ledge).
    1997   'The Composition of 1 Samuel 1–2', *JBL* 116: 601–12.
Brueggemann, Walter
    1968   'David and his Theologian', *CBQ* 30: 156–81.
Budd, Philip J.
    1984   *Numbers* (WBC, 5; Waco, TX: Word Books).
Butler, Trent C.
    1983   *Joshua* (WBC, 7; Waco, TX: Word Books).
Campbell, Anthony F.
    1975   *The Ark Narrative (1 Sam. 4-6; 2 Sam. 6). A Form-Critical and Traditio-*
                Historical Study (Missoula, MT: Scholars Press).

1994   'Martin Noth and the Deuteronomistic History', in Steven L. McKenzie and
            M. Patrick Graham (eds.), *The History of Israel's Traditions: The Heritage
            of Martin Noth* (JSOTSup, 182; Sheffield: Sheffield Academic Press):
            31–62.

Carlson, R.A.
1964   *David, the Chosen King. A Traditio-Historical Approach to the Second Book
            of Samuel* (Stockholm: Almqvist and Wiksell).

Carr, David
2001   'Method in Determination of Direction of Dependence: An Empirical Test
            of Criteria Applied to Exod. 34, 11-26 and its Parallels', in *Gottes Volk am
            Sinai. Untersuchungen zu Ex 32-34 und Dtn 9-10. Herausgegeben von
            Matthias Köckert und Erhard Blum* (Veröfflentlichungen der Wissenschaft-
            lichen Gesellschaft für Theologie, 18; Chr. Kaiser/Gütersloher Verlaghaus):
            107–40.

Carroll, R.P.
1969   'The Elijah-Elisha Sagas: Some Remarks on Prophetic Succession in Ancient
            Israel', *VT* 19: 401–15.

Childs, Brevard S.
1962   *Memory and Tradition in Israel* (SBT, 37; London: SCM Press).
1974   *The Book of Exodus: A Critical, Theological Commentary* (OTL; Philadel-
            phia: Westminster Press).
1980   'On Reading the Elijah Narratives', *Int* 34: 128–37.

Coxon, P.W.
1981   'A Note on Bathsheba in 2 Samuel 12.1-6', *Bib* 62: 247–50.

Crites, Stephen
1997   'The Narrative Quality of Experience', in Lewis P. Hinchman and Sandra K.
            Hinchman (eds.): 26-50. Originally published as 'The Narrative Quality of
            Experience', *Journal of the American Academy of Religion* 49 (1971) 117–34.

Cross, F.M.
1973   *Canaanite Myth and Hebrew Epic: Essays in the History of the Religion of
            Israel* (Cambridge, MA: Harvard University Press).

Culley, Robert C.
1976   *Studies in the Structure of Hebrew Narrative* (Missoula, MT: Scholars Press).

Damrosch, David
1987   *The Narrative Covenant: Transformation of Genre in the Growth of Biblical
            Literature* (New York: Harper and Row).

Daube, David
1963   *The Exodus Pattern in the Bible* (London: Faber and Faber).

DeVries, Simon J.
1985   *1 Kings* (WBC, 12; Waco, TX: Word Books).

Dijkstra, Meindert
2003   'The Law of Moses: The Memory of Mosaic Religion in and after the
            Exile', in Albertz Rainer, and Bob Becking (eds.), *Yahwism after the Exile:
            Perspectives on Israelite Religion in the Persian Era: Papers Read at the
            First Meeting of the European Association for Biblical Studies, Utrecht, 6–9
            August 2000* (Assen: Van Gorcum): 70–98.

Doron, Pinchas
1978   'Motive Clauses in the Laws of Deuteronomy: Their Forms, Functions, and
            Contents', *HAR* 2: 61–77.

Driver, S.R.
1916   *Deuteronomy* (ICC; New York: Charles Scribner's Sons).
1966   *Notes on the Hebrew Text and the Topography of the Books of Samuel* (Ox-
            ford: Clarendon Press, 2nd edn).
Durham, John I.
1987   *Exodus* (WBC, 3; Waco, TX: Word Books).
Eckart, Otto
1998   *'Das Deuteronomium krönt die Arbeit der Propheten'. Gesetz und Prophetie
            im Deuteronomium. Ich bewirke da Heil und erschaffe da Unheil (Jesaja
            45,7). Studien zur Botschaft der Propheten: Festschrift für Lothar Rupert
            zum 65. Geburtstag* (FB, 88; Würzburg: Echter Verlag).
Eslinger, Lyle
1989   *Into the Hands of the Living God* (JSOTSup, 84; Sheffield: Almond Press).
Fields, Weston W.
1997   *Sodom and Gomorrah: History and Motif in Biblical Narrative* (JSOTSup,
            231; Sheffield: Sheffield Academic Press).
Fishbane, Michael
1980   'Revelation and Tradition: Aspects of Inner-Biblical Exegesis', *JBL* 99:
            343–61.
1985   *Biblical Interpretation in Ancient Israel* (Oxford: Clarendon Press).
Fohrer, George
1957   *Elia* (Zürich: Zwingli Verlag).
Fokkelman, J.P.
1986   *Narrative Art in the Books of Samuel*. II. *The Crossing of the Fates (1 Sam.
            13-31 and 2 Sam. 1)* (Assen: Van Gorcum).
1993   *Narrative Art and Poetry in the Books of Samuel. A Full Interpretation Based
            on Stylistic and Structural Analyses*. IV. *Vow and Desire (1 Sam. 1-12)*
            (Assen: Van Gorcum).
Freedman, D.N.
1962   'Pentateuch', *IDB*: 711–27.
1987   'The Earliest Bible', in Michael P. O'Connor and D.N. Freedman (eds.),
            Backgrounds for the Bible (Winona Lake, IN: Eisenbrauns): 29–37.
1994   with Jeffrey C. Geoghegan, 'Martin Noth: Retrospect and Prospect', in
            Steven L. McKenzie and M. Patrick Graham (eds.): 128–52.
1997   'Dinah and Shechem, Tamar and Amnon', in John R. Huddlestun (ed.),
            *Divine Commitment and Human Obligation. Selected Writings of David Noel
            Freedman*. I. *History and Religion* (Grand Rapids, MI: Eerdmans): 485–95.
Frymer-Kensky, Tikva
1990   'The Sage in the Pentateuch: Soundings', in John Gammie and Leo G.
            Perdue (eds.), *The Sage in Israel and the Ancient Near East* (Winona Lake,
            IN: Eisenbrauns): 275–87.
1997   'Reading Rahab', in Mordechai Cogan *et al.* (eds.), *Tehillah le-Moshe: Bib-
            lical and Judaic Studies in Honor of Moshe Greenberg* (Winona Lake, IN:
            Eisenbrauns): 57–67.
Gadamer, Hans Georg
2000   *Truth and Method* (New York: Continuum, 2nd rev. edn).
Garsiel, Moshe
1985   *The First Book of Samuel: A Literary Study of Comparative Structures,
            Analogies and Parallels* (Israel: Revivim Publishing House).

1987 *Biblical Names: A Literary Study of Midrashic Derivations and Puns* (trans. Phyllis Hackett; Ramat Gan: Bar-Ilan University).

1993 'The Story of David and Bathsheba: A Different Approach', *CBQ* 55: 244–62.

Gordon, Robert P.
1980 'David's Rise and Saul's Demise: Narrative Analogy in 1 Samuel 24-26', *TB* 31: 37–64.

Gradwohl, Roland
1963 'Das 'Fremde Feuer' von Nadab und Abihu', *ZAW* 75: 288–96.

Gray, John
1970 *I and II Kings* (OTL; Philadelphia: Westminster).

Green, Garrett
1989 *Imagining God: Theology and the Religious Imagination* (San Francisco: Harper & Row).

Greenstein, Ed
1990 'The Formation of the Biblical Narrative Corpus', *AJS Review* 15: 151–78.

Grohman,.E D.
1962 'Nebo, Mount', *IDB*: 529.

Gunn, David M.
1980 *The Fate of King Saul: An Interpretation of a Biblical Story* (JSOTSup, 14; Sheffield: Sheffield Academic Press).

1990 'Threading the Labyrinth': A Response to Albert B. Lord', in Susan Niditch (ed.), *Text and Tradition: The Hebrew Bible and Folklore* (Atlanta, GA: Scholars Press): 19–24.

Halpern, Baruch
1988 *The First Historians: The Hebrew Bible and History* (San Francisco, CA: Harper and Row).

Harris, William
1989 *Ancient Literacy* (Cambridge, MA: Harvard University Press).

Harvey, John E.
2001 *Tendenz* and Textual Criticism in 1 Samuel 2–10', *JSOT* 96: 71–81.

Hauerwas, Stanley and L. Gregory Jones (eds.)
1989 *Why Narrative? Readings in Narrative Theology* (Grand Rapids, MI: Eerdmans).

Hawk, L. Daniel
1991 *Every Promise Fulfilled: Contesting Plots in Joshua* (Louisville, KT: Westminster/John Knox Press).

Hays, Richard B.
1989 *Echoes of Scripture in the Letters of Paul* (New Haven and London: Yale University Press).

Hertzberg, Hans Wilhelm
1964 *I & II Samuel* (OTL; Philadelphia: Westminster Press).

Hinchman, Lewis P. and Sandra K. Hinchman (eds.)
1997 *Memory, Identity, Community: The Idea of Narrative in the Human Sciences* (Albany, NY: State University of New York).

Hoffmann, H.-D.
1980 *Reform und Reformen: Untersuchungen zu einem Grund-thema der deuteronomistischen Geschichtsschreibung* (Zürich: Theologischer Verlag).

Hulst, R.
1965 'Der Jordan in den alttestamentlichen Überlieferungen', *OTS* 14: 162–88.

Hyatt, J. Philip
　1970　　　'Were There an Ancient Historical Credo in Israel and an Independent Sinai Tradition?', in Harry Thomas Frank and William L. Reed (eds.), *Translating and Understanding the Old Testament: Essays in Honor of Herbert Gordon May* (Nashville and New York: Abingdon Press): 152–70.
Jermias, J.
　1967　　　'Μωυσῆς', *TDNT*, IV: 848-73.
Jüngling, H.W.
　1981　　　*Richter 19 – Ein Plädoyer für das Königtum: Stilistische Analyse der Tendenzerzählung Ri 19, 1-30a; 21.25* (AnBib, 84; Rome: Pontifical Biblical Institute).
Klein, Lillian R.
　1988　　　*The Triumph of Irony in the Book of Judges* (JSOTSup, 68; Sheffield: Almond Press).
Klein, Ralph W.
　1983　　　*1 Samuel* (WBC, 10; Waco, TX: Word Books).
Knoppers, Gary N.
　1995　　　'Aaron's Calf and Jeroboam's Calves', in Astrid B. Beck *et al.* (eds.), *Fortunate the Eyes that See: Essays in Honor of David Noel Freedman in Celebration of His Seventieth Birthday* (Grand Rapids, MI: Eerdmans): 92–104.
　1996　　　'The Deuteronomist and the Deuteronomic Law of the King: A Reexamination of a Relationship', *ZAW* 108: 329–46.
Koch, Klaus
　1969　　　*The Growth of the Biblical Tradition: The Form Critical Method* (New York: Charles Scribner's Sons).
Lasine, Stuart
　1984　　　'Guest and Host in Judges 19: Lot's Hospitality in an Inverted World', *JSOT* 29: 37–59.
Lemche, Niels Peter
　1978　　　'David's Rise', *JSOT* 10: 2–25.
Lettelier, Robert Ignatius
　1995　　　*Day in Mamre, Night in Sodom: Abraham and Lot in Genesis 18 and 19* (Biblical Interpretation, 10; New York: E.J. Brill).
Levenson, Jon D.
　1978　　　'1 Samuel 25 as Literature and History', *CBQ* 40: 11–28.
　1983　　　'The Last Four Verses in Kings', *JBL* 103: 353–61.
Levenson, Jon D. and Baruch Halpern
　1980　　　'The Political Impact of David's Marriages', *JBL* 99: 507–18.
Levinson, Bernard M.
　1991　　　*The Hermeneutics of Innovation: The Impact of Centralization upon the Structure, Sequence, and Reformulation of Legal Material in Deuteronomy* (unpublished PhD dissertation, Brandeis University).
　1997　　　*Deuteronomy and the Hermeneutics of Legal Innovation* (Oxford: Oxford University Press).
Lindars, Barnabas
　1995　　　*Judges 1–5: A New Translation and Commentary* (ed. A.D.H. Mayes; Edinburgh: T. & T. Clark).
Lindbeck, George A.
　1984　　　*The Nature of Doctrine* (Philadelphia: Westminster Press).

Loewenstamm, S.E.
1992 'The Formula בעת ההיא in the Introductory Speeches in Deuteronomy', in *From Babylon to Canaan: Studies in the Bible and its Oriental Background* (Jerusalem: Magnes Press): 42–50.

Lohfink, Norbert
1960 'Darstellungskunst und Theologie in Dtn. 1,6–3,29', *Bib* 41: 105–34.
1990 *Die Väter Israels im Deuteronomium: mit einer Stellungnahme von Thomas Römer* (OBO, 111; Göttingen: Vandenhoeck & Ruprecht).
1997 'Geschichtstypologisch orientierte Textstrukturen in den Büchern D-euteronomium und Josua', in M. Vervenne and J. Lust (eds.), *Deuteronomy and Deuteronomic Literature* (BETL, CXXXIII; Belgium: Leuven University Press): 133–60.
1998 'Geschichtstypologie in Deuteronomium 1–3', in Klaus-Dietrich Schunck und Matthias Augustin (eds.), *Lasset uns Brücken bauen... Collected Communications of the 15th Congress of the International Organization for the Study of the Old Testament, Cambridge 1995* (BEATAJ, 42; Frankfurt: Lang): 87–92.

Long, Burke
1984 *1 Kings, with an Introduction to Historical Literature* (FOTL, 9; Grand Rapids, MI: Eerdmans).

Lutzky, Harriet C.
1997 'The Name 'Cozbi' (Numbers 25.15, 18)', *VT* 47: 546–49.

Lyke, Larry L.
1997 *King David with the Wise Woman of Tekoa: The Resonance of Tradition in Parabolic Narrative* (JSOTSup, 255; Sheffield: Sheffield Academic Press).

MacIntyre, Alasdair
1989 'Epistemological Crises, Narrative, and Philosophy of Science', in Stanley Hauerwas and L. Gregory Jones (eds.), 1989: 138–57.

Marcus, David
1986 *Jephthah and His Vow* (Lubbock: Texas Tech).

Martinez, F. Garcia, A. Hilhorst, J.T.A.G.M. VanRutten and A.S. van der Woude (eds.)
1994 *Studies in Deuteronomy in Honour of C.J. Labuschagne on the Occasion of his 65th Birthday* (Leiden: E.J. Brill).

Matthews, Victor H.
1992 'Hospitality and Hostility in Genesis 19 and Judges 19', *BTB* 22: 3–11.

Mayes, A.D.H.
1979 *Deuteronomy* (NCBC; London: Marshall, Morgan & Scott).

McCarter, P. Kyle, Jr
1980 *1 Samuel* (AB, 8; Garden City, NY: Doubleday).
1990 'The Sage in the Deuteronomistic History', in John Gammie and Leo G. Perdue (eds.), *The Sage in Israel and the Ancient Near East* (Winona Lake, IN: Eisenbrauns): 289–93.

McCarthy, D.J.
1974 'The Wrath of Yahweh and the Structural Unity of the Deuteronomistic History', in James L. Crenshaw and John T. Willis (eds.), *Essays in Old Testament Ethics* (New York: Ktav): 99–110.

McConnell, Frank (ed.)
1986 *The Bible and the Narrative Tradition* (Oxford: Oxford University Press).

McDonough, Sean M.
  1999   ' "And David was old and advanced in years": 2 Samuel 24.18-25, 1 Kings
              1.1, and Genesis 23–24', *VT* 49: 128–31.
McKenzie, John L.
  1967   'The Historical Prologue of Deuteronomy', in *Fourth World Congress of
              Jewish Studies* (Jerusalem: World Union of Jewish Studies): 95–101.
McKenzie, Steven L.
  1994a   with M. Patrick Graham, *The History of Israel's Traditions. The Heritage of
              Martin Noth* (JSOTSup, 182; Sheffield: Sheffield Academic Press).
  1994b   'The Books of Kings in the Deuteronomistic History', in Steven L. McKenzie
              and M. Patrick Graham (eds.): 281–307.
Milgrom, Jacob
  1976   'Profane Slaughter and a Formulaic Key to the Composition of Deuteron-
              omy', *HUCA* 47: 1–17.
Miller, Patrick D., Jr, and J.J.M. Roberts
  1977   *The Hand of the Lord: A Reassessment of the 'Ark Narrative' of 1 Samuel*
              (Baltimore, MD: The Johns Hopkins University Press).
Minchin, Elizabeth
  1992   'Scripts and Themes: Cognitive Research and the Homeric Epic', *Classical
              Antiquity* 11: 229–41.
Minette de Tillesse, Caetano (Gaëtan)
  1999   'La Crise du Pentateuque', *ZAW* 111: 1–9.
Moran, W.L.
  1963   'The End of the Holy War and the Anti-Exodus', *Bib* 44: 333–42.
Niditch, Susan
  1982   'The "Sodomite" Theme in Judges 19–20: Family, Community, and Social
              Disintegration', *CBQ* 44: 365–78.
Nohrnberg, James
  1995   *Like Unto Moses: The Constituting of an Interruption* (Bloomington and
              Indianapolis: Indiana University Press).
Noth, Martin
  1968   *Numbers* (OTL; Philadelphia: Westminster Press).
  1981   *The Deuteronomistic History* (Sheffield: JSOT Press).
O'Connell, Robert H.
  1996   *The Rhetoric of the Book of Judges* (VTSup, LXIII; Leiden: E.J. Brill).
Peckham, Brian
  1985   *The Composition of the Deuteronomistic History* (HSM, 35; Atlanta, GA:
              Scholars Press).
  1993   *History and Prophecy: The Development of Late Judean Literary Traditions*
              (New York: Doubleday).
  1999   'History and Time', in Robert Chazan, William Hallo, Lawrence Schiffman
              (eds.), *Ki Baruch Hu: Ancient Near Eastern, Biblical, and Judaic Studies in
              Honor of Baruch A. Levine* (Winona Lake, IN: Eisenbrauns): 295–314.
Perlitt, Lothar.
  1985   'Deuteronomium 1-3 im Streit der exegetischen Methoden', in N. Lohfink
              (ed.), *Das Deuteronomium: Entstehung, Gestalt und Botschaft* (BETL, 68;
              Leuven: Leuven University Press).
  1988   'Priesterschrift im Deuteronomium?', *ZAW* 100: 65–88.

Petersen, John E.
1980   'Priestly Materials in Joshua 13–22: A Return to the Hexateuch?', *HAR* 4: 131–46.

Pleins, J. David
1995   'Murderous Fathers, Manipulative Mothers, and Rivalrous Siblings: Rethinking the Architecture of Genesis–Kings', in Astrid B. Beck *et al.* (eds.), *Fortunate the Eyes that See: Essays in Honor of David Noel Freedman in Celebration of His Seventieth Birthday* (Grand Rapids, MI: Eerdmans): 121–36.

Plöger, J.G.
1967   *Literarkritische, formgeschichtliche und stilkritische Untersuchungen zum Deuteronomium* (Bonn: Peter Hanstein).

Polanyi, Michael
1962   *Personal Knowledge: Towards a Post-Critical Philosophy* (Chicago: The University of Chicago Press).

Rendsburg, Gary A.
1986   'David and his Circle in Genesis XXXVIII', *VT* 36: 438–46.

Roberts, J.J.M.
1971   'The Hand of Yahweh', *VT* 21: 244–52.

Rofé, Alexander
1993   'The Piety of the Torah Disciples at the Winding-Up of the Hebrew Bible: Josh. 1.8; Ps. 1.2; Isa. 59.21', in Helmut Merklein *et al.* (eds.), *Bibel in Jüdischer und Christlicher Tradition. Festschrift für Johann Maier vum 60. Geburstag* (Frankfurt am Main: Hain): 78–85.

Römer, Thomas
1990   *Israels Väter: Untersuchungen zur Väterthematik im Deuteronomium und in der deuteronomistischen Tradition* (OBO, 99; Göttingen: Vandenhoeck & Ruprecht).
1997   'Transformations in Deuteronomistic and Biblical Historiography', *ZAW* 109: 1–11.

Rosenberg, Joel
1986   *King and Kin: Political Allegory in the Hebrew Bible* (Bloomington and Indianapolis: Indiana University Press).

Scharbert, J.
1992   *Numeri* (NEB, 27; Würzberg: Echter Verlag).

Schearing, Linda S. and Steven L. McKenzie (eds.)
1999   *Those Elusive Deuteronomists: The Phenomenon of Pan-Deuteronomism* (JSOTSup, 268; Sheffield: Sheffield Academic Press).

Schmitt, H.-C.
1997   'Das spätdeuternomistische Geschichtswerk Genesis i–2 Kings xxv und seine theologische Intention', *Congress Volume* (Leiden: E.J. Brill): 261–79.

Seebass, H.
1978   'Num. XI, XII und die Hypothese des Jahwisten', *VT* 28: 214–23.

Shaver, J.R.
1986   *Torah and the Chronicler's History Work: An Inquiry into the Chronicler's References to Laws, Festivals, and Cultic Institutions in Relationship to Pentateuchal Legislation* (BJS, 196; Atlanta: Scholars).

Skweres, Dieter Eduard
    1979   *Die Rückverweise im Buch Deuteronomium* (AnBib, 79; Rome: Biblical Institute).
Smalley, Jocelyn Penny
    1997   *Wax Tablets of the Mind: Cognitive Studies of Memory and Literacy in Classical Antiquity* (London: Routledge).
Smelik, Klaas D.
    1992   *Converting the Past: Studies in Ancient Israelite and Moabite Historiography* (OTS, XXVIII; New York: E.J. Brill).
Sommer, Benjamin D.
    1999   'Reflecting on Moses: The Redaction of Numbers 11', *JBL* 118: 601–24.
Sonsino, Rifat
    1980   *Motive Clauses in Hebrew Law: Biblical Forms and Near Eastern Parallels* (SBLDS, 45; Chico, CA: Scholars Press).
Stanley, Christopher D.
    1992   *Paul and the Language of Scripture* (Cambridge: Cambridge University Press).
Stoellger, Philipp
    1993   'Deuteronomium 34 ohne Priesterschrift', *ZAW* 105: 26–51.
Sweeney, Marvin A.
    1995   'The Critique of Solomon in the Josianic Edition of the Deuteronomistic History', *JBL* 114: 607–22.
Talstra, E.
    1993   *Solomon's Prayer: Synchrony and Diachrony in the Composition of 1 Kings 8, 14-61* (Kampen, The Netherlands: KOK Pharos).
Tannen, Deborah
    1979   'What's in a Frame? Surface Evidence for Underlying Expectations', in Roy O. Freedle (ed.), *New Directions in Discourse Processing* (Norwood, NJ: Ablex): 137–81.
Thompson, Thomas L.
    1994   'Martin Noth and the History of Israel', in Steven L. McKenzie and M. Patrick Graham (eds.): 80–90.
Tigay, Jeffrey H.
    1975   'An Empirical Basis for the Documentary Hypothesis', *JBL* 94: 329–42.
Tov, Emmanuel
    1992   *Textual Criticism of the Hebrew Bible* (Minneapolis, MN: Fortress Press).
Trible, Phyllis
    1981   'A Meditation in Mourning: The Sacrifice of the Daughter of Jephthah', *USQR* 36: 59–73.
Trompf, G.W.
    1979   'Notions of Historical Recurrence in Classical Historiography', in J.A. Emerton (ed.), *Studies in the Historical Books of the Old Testament* (VTSup, XXX; Leiden: E.J. Brill): 212–29.
Unterman, Jeremiah
    1980   'The Literary Influence of "The Binding of Isaac" (Genesis 22) on "The Outrage at Gibeah" (Judges 19)', *HAR* 4: 161–66.
Van Seters, John
    1972a   'Confessional Reformulation in the Exilic Period', *VT* 22: 448–59.

1972b 'The Conquest of Sihon's Kingdom: A Literary Examination', *JBL* 91: 182–97.

1975 *Abraham in History and Tradition* (New Haven and London: Yale University Press).

1980 'Once Again – the Conquest of Sihon's Kingdom', *JBL* 99: 117–24.

1983 *In Search of History: Historiography in the Ancient World and the Origins of Biblical History* (New Haven: Yale University Press).

1986 'The Plagues of Egypt: Ancient Tradition or Literary Invention?', *ZAW* 98: 31–39.

1992 *The Life of Moses: The Yahwist as Historian in Exodus-Numbers* (Louisville: Westminster/John Knox).

Vervenne, Marc

1994 'The Question of 'Deuteronomic' Elements in Genesis to Numbers', in Garcia Martinez *et al.* (eds.): 243–68.

von Rad, Gerhard

1953 'The Deuteronomistic Theology of History in the Books of Kings', in *Studies in Deuteronomy* (London: SCM Press): 74-91.

1962 *Old Testament Theology*, I (trans. D.M.G. Stalker; San Francisco, CA: Harper and Row).

1965 *Old Testament Theology*, II (trans. D.M.G. Stalker; Edinburgh and London: Oliver and Boyd).

1966 *Deuteronomy* (OTL; Philadelphia: Westminster).

1991 *Holy War in Ancient Israel* (Grand Rapids, MI: Eerdmans).

Walters, Stanley D.

1988 'Hannah and Anna: The Greek and Hebrew Texts of 1 Samuel 1', *JBL* 107: 385–412.

Waltke, Bruce K. and M. O'Connor

1990 *An Introduction to Biblical Hebrew Syntax* (Winona Lake, IN: Eisenbrauns).

Webb, Barry G.

1987 *The Book of Judges: An Integrated Reading* (JSOTSup, 46; Sheffield: JSOT Press).

Weinfeld, Moshe

1972 *Deuteronomy and the Deuteronomic School* (Oxford: Clarendon Press).

1991 *Deuteronomy 1–11* (AB, 5; New York: Doubleday).

Wenham, Gordon J.

1971 'The Deuteronomic Theology of the Book of Joshua', *JBL* 90: 140–48.

Westermann, Claus

1985 *Genesis 12–36: A Commentary* (Minneapolis, MN: Augsburg).

Willis, John T.

1971 'An Anti-Elide Narrative Tradition form a Prophetic Circle at the Ramah Sanctuary', *JBL* 90: 288–308.

Wilson, Robert R.

1980 *Prophecy and Society in Ancient Israel* (Philadelphia: Fortress Press).

Wolff, Hans Walter

1978 'The Kerygma of the Deuteronomistic Historical Work', in Walter Brueggemann and Hans Walter Wolff (eds.), *The Vitality of Old Testament Traditions* (Atlanta: John Knox): 83–100.

Wyatt, Nicolas
    1979   'The Old Testament Historiography of the Exilic Period', *ST* 33: 45–67.
Zakovitch, Yair
    1983   'Story Versus History', *Proceedings of the Eighth World Congress of Jew-
                  ish Studies: Panel Sessions: Bible Studies and Hebrew Language* (Jerusa-
                  lem: World Union of Jewish Studies): 47–60.
    1985   'Assimilation in Biblical Narratives', in Jeffrey Tigay (ed.), *Empirical
                  Models for Biblical Criticism* (Philadelphia: University of Pennsylvania
                  Press): 174–96.
    1990   'Humor and Theology or the Successful Failure of Israelite Intelligence: A
                  Literary-Folkloric Approach to Joshua 2', in Susan Niditch (ed.), *Text and
                  Tradition: The Hebrew Bible and Folklore* (Atlanta, GA: Scholars Press):
                  75–98.
    1991   *'And You Shall Tell Your Son...' The Concept of the Exodus in the Bible*
                  (Jerusalem: Magnes Press).

INDEX OF REFERENCES

BIBLE

Retelling the Torah